MELISSA A. KUCINSKI

A PRACTICAL HANDBOOK FOR THE CHILD'S ATTORNEY

EFFECTIVELY REPRESENTING CHILDREN IN CUSTODY CASES

Defending Liberty
Pursuing Justice

SECTION OF
FAMILY LAW

Cover design by Tahiti Spears/ABA Design.

Printed in the United States of America.

22 21 20 19 18   5 4 3 2 1

ISBN: 978-1-64105-184-2

e-ISBN: 978-1-64105-185-9

Library of Congress Cataloging-in-Publication Data

Names: Kucinski, Melissa A., author.
Title: Handbook for the child's attorney : effectively representing children in custody / Melissa A. Kucinski.
Description: Chicago : American Bar Association, 2018. | Includes index.
Identifiers: LCCN 2018022511| ISBN 9781641051842 (alk. paper) | ISBN 9781641051859 (ebook)
Subjects: LCSH: Children–Legal status, laws, etc.–United States. | Custody of children–United States. | Trial practice–United States. | Parent and child (Law)–United States.
Classification: LCC KF547 .K83 2018 | DDC 346.7301/73–dc23 LC record available at https://lccn.loc.gov/2018022511

Discounts are available for books ordered in bulk. Special consideration is given to state bars, CLE programs, and other bar-related organizations. Inquire at Book Publishing, ABA Publishing, American Bar Association, 321 N. Clark Street, Chicago, Illinois 60654-7598.

www.shopABA.org

CONTENTS

"I'm Winston Wolf. I solve problems." I had been representing a nine-year-old boy for a few months when his father called me the "Wolf." Unfamiliar with this pop culture reference, I feared the worst. Lawyers are often called sharks. Some may be called rats. I, however, was the Wolf. My client's father assured me that being the Wolf was a positive thing for his family. The family was in the thick of a relocation case. The father had been accused of inappropriately touching my child client. There were accusations of domestic violence. The child was in therapy. Both parents were frustrated with the legal system. Both parents' lawyers were lost, not knowing where the truth lay. Their positions were as far apart as they could be. There were complicated cross-jurisdictional legal issues. The child would not communicate with either parent. What could this family do? That is where I came in. A large part of my family law practice is child representation. I'm the Wolf. I enter the case, help educate the child, take stress and pressure off the lawyers, investigate the situation, and pursue positions for the child's best interests. I solve problems.

When I was asked to write this book, I hesitated. Although I have been consistently representing children in their parents' custody disputes for most of my career, I always have the genuine fear I am doing something wrong. There is no set formula for this type of work. It requires significant flexibility. Every case is different from the last. I am not a therapist—who am I to tell you how to speak to a child? I am not a psychologist—you should probably not listen to me when I opine on child behavior. I am not an educator, swim coach, violin instructor, or crossing guard. In fact, I am not even a parent. I cringe when one of my child client's parents asks me whether I have children of my own, as if that is the benchmark for being a competent child's attorney. I am not a social worker. I am most certainly not a judge.

Why should you read this book, filled with my practices for representing a child client? I hope I am careful, meticulous, thorough, thoughtful, and communicative. I have been told I "do my homework" so well that no one can "argue with" me over the position I ultimately take on behalf of my child client. I do not jump to conclusions. The truth is these cases are never easy. They will drain you. You will need to rearrange your schedule to meet with your child clients when you wish to be home eating dinner with your family. You will be going to your child client's basketball game instead of your own child's football game. You will take on the genuine need to protect these children. You will get mad at them. You will be frustrated with them, almost as if you were their parent. However, your role will be absolutely unique. You will have limitations, set by court orders and the law. You will think about these children as you drive to the office, as you wash your hair in the shower, and as you lie awake in bed at night.

I share my experiences and my war stories to give you some confidence in working with these extraordinary young individuals who are experiencing one of the most difficult times of their lives. I hope that some of you who read this book will reach out to me and share your stories, so I can continue to learn and grow in my work with these children. Above all, I hope this book will help you to be the problem solver that all children's attorneys must be.

ACKNOWLEDGMENTS

I want to wish the sincerest thanks to my child clients. Your strength and poise in the most difficult of circumstances amazes me on a daily basis. I am by far one of the most privileged people because I get to work with you. I wish the very best to all of you. I am grateful for the life lessons you have taught me, as well as the rich and full memories I will carry with me from having met you.

I also want to thank Professor Linda Elrod. Her passion for child advocacy has inspired me throughout my career and led me to this unique role as a child's attorney.

I want to thank my colleagues, including Elizabeth Landau, Christy Zlatkus, Inna Loring, Phil Stahl, Rebecca Stahl, and David Jackson, for their support, their research, their comments, and their calming influence while I was writing this manuscript. I also want to thank Ann Haralambie. Ann wrote *The Child's Attorney* in 1993 for the ABA, which served as direct inspiration for this book. Ann is, by far, the expert on child representation.

Finally, I want to thank Michael Coffee, from whom I learn on a daily basis. His fearless desire to correct my imprecision makes me a better lawyer. His love and dedication to his children inspires me to be a better child's attorney.

ABOUT THE AUTHOR

Melissa Kucinski is an attorney and mediator in Washington, D.C., and Maryland. She served as a consultant to the Hague Conference on Private International Law in 2013 and has written a dozen articles published in more than one language on international children's issues, the mediation of complex cross-border custody, and child abduction cases. Melissa has presented at national and international conferences on international children's issues and mediation. Melissa was part of a U.S. Delegation sent to Tokyo, Japan, in 2014 to train Japanese mediators to handle international parental child abduction cases under the 1980 Hague Convention on Parental Child Abduction.

Melissa has been a long-standing member of the U.S. Secretary of State's Advisory Committee on Private International Law. She served as a private sector advisor to the U.S. Delegation to The Hague's Sixth Special Commission meeting in 2011 to review the practical operation of two international children's treaties, and she attended the Seventh Special Commission meeting in 2017 with International Social Service (ISS). She currently chairs ISS's efforts to create a global network of international family mediators. Melissa has served in a variety of capacities within the American Bar Association, including past chair of an International Family Mediation Task Force, where she spearheaded the effort to design and host a weeklong advanced international family mediation training.

Melissa has taught the International Family Law course at the George Washington University School of Law since 2010. She is a fellow of the International Academy of Family Lawyers. Melissa is a member of the Uniform Law Commission's Joint Editorial Board on Uniform Family Laws, and has been an observer or advisor on numerous study and drafting committees since 2012.

INTRODUCTION

1

Children are the central focus in any custody case. However, parents, lawyers, and even judges frequently lose sight of this. Opinions are evolving about how to keep the child as the case's focus. One such opinion believes that a child's voice should play a key role in any custodial arrangement. This opens up a wide range of questions and concerns, such as why we should listen to a child, what potential concerns exist when listening to them, and how we should solicit their opinions.

Why should we listen to a child? Children are the people most affected by any custodial arrangement. They also have the most pertinent and relevant information as to what is in their best interests. Children can learn better coping skills when dealing with their parents' separation if their voices are appropriately incorporated into the resolution process.

What potential concerns exist when listening to a child? Children who are included in the decision-making process may feel an increased level of stress if the process by which they are included is not child-focused in and of itself. Children need to be assured they are not the final decision-makers, and their preferences are not what will dictate the final outcome. If a child is involved in the process in a way that is not child-focused and appropriately tailored to the child's age, maturity, and developmental stage, that child may experience increased emotional distress. Furthermore, given the complex nuances inherent to child development, if the child's voice is not solicited—and interpreted—appropriately, the child's words may not yield helpful information. A child's words do not always express their genuine thoughts or feelings. A child does not always know what is best for him or her. A child may express positions or make statements geared toward what the child feels his or her parent wants to hear. It takes a highly trained individual and a structured process to elicit clear, articulate, and genuine statements from a child, and then further interpret those statements, weigh them against other data, and understand them (including the child's motivation).[1]

How do we solicit a child's opinion? A variety of methods may be used to hear a child's voice. These methods fall along a continuum, such as through court-appointed counsel, giving testimony in open court, being interviewed by a judge in chambers, speaking to a custody evaluator, being deposed, executing an affidavit, or participating in confidential settlement negotiations (including in collaborative law, through a child specialist, or in mediation).[2] The most important thing for a child's attorney to understand is that the person who interviews a child needs to be properly trained to communicate with a child *and* to interpret what that child says. The interviewer should have other information at his or her disposal to help interpret the child's words. Several factors will affect the accuracy of a child's words. The child may be reluctant to share candid information with an unfamiliar adult. A child may have poor linguistic skills because of age, maturity, education, socioeconomic status, or because English is not their first language. A child may have poor memory retention of events and may tend to forget information more readily than does an adult.[3] A child may attempt to fill in gaps for information they lack, rather than disappoint an authority figure by having nothing to say. A child may feel a need to give answers, even when they do not have answers. Two children, of different ages, may recollect the same event very differently. Parents, adults, friends, television, or a variety of other external factors may contaminate a child's memory. If a parent is routinely telling a child the other parent does bad things, it may not matter if those things have actually happened; the child may create false memories of those events happening. A child may try to provide information adults want to hear (or the child believes the adult wants to hear).

---

1. Richard A. Warshak, *Payoffs and Pitfalls of Listening to Children*, 52 FAM. REL. 373 (2003).

2. *Id.* at 375.

3. Kathryn Kuehnle, Lyn R. Greenberg, & Michael C. Gottlieb, *Incorporating the Principles of Scientifically Based Child Interviews into Family Law Cases*, 1 J CHILD. CUSTODY 97 (2004).

The appointment of a child's attorney is an excellent means by which a child's voice may be heard while protecting the child. A child's attorney can engage professionals, take the necessary time and care, and perform the requisite outside investigation to put the child's words into context and appropriately interpret them. Beyond what a mental health professional can do, the child's attorney can work alongside others, educate the child, and protect the child's interests in legal processes that will affect the child. Beyond what judges can do, a child's attorney can build the necessary rapport, gather the necessary information, and take sufficient time to pull together a full picture of what may be happening in this child's life. A child's attorney may be the best ally to gather the child's words and preferences in the safest, clearest, and most comprehensive way.

A child's attorney may hold a variety of titles—best interest attorney, guardian *ad litem*, child advocate, child's attorney, etc. These terms may mean different things depending on the jurisdiction where the attorney practices. When I refer to a child's attorney in this book, I will briefly explain the attorney's role to distinguish between the various titles throughout the text; the general title "child's attorney" (or child's counsel, child's lawyer, or child's representative) is used to more broadly reference the many roles a lawyer can take when working with a child as legal counsel.

Given the range of roles, titles, and the variety of guidelines and standards (which all vary by state and country), I have focused this handbook primarily on the American Bar Association (ABA) Standards of Practice for Lawyers Representing Children in Custody Cases. I recognize that child's attorneys in some jurisdictions still testify, write reports, or have limitations such that they cannot represent a child's "best interests." Therefore, I will distinguish these different roles in the text, while remaining true to the ABA Standards.[4]

This introductory chapter focuses primarily on the basic principles that are foundational to representing children, provides a review of the differences between the ABA Standards and the 2006 standards promulgated by the American Academy of Matrimonial Lawyers, provides examples of the many roles of a child's attorney by providing case studies from a handful of U.S. states, and begins a discussion about the competency required to take on this sometimes-overwhelming role of a child's attorney.

---

4. The ABA Standards can be found in their entirety in Appendix 4.

Finally, although lawyers may represent children in a variety of cases, such as adoptions, guardianships, and abuse or neglect matters, this book focuses only on custody cases. Throughout the book, I refer to a child's "parents" and your interaction with those parents; however, I recognize that modern families may have other caretakers, actors, or intervenors in a custody case who are parties to the action or tied to the child in a manner that is akin to a parent. My intent is not to limit the litigants in a custody case to a biological mother and father.

§1.01 STANDARDS AND MODEL ACTS

a. ABA Standards of Practice for Lawyers Representing Children in Custody Cases

In August 2003, the ABA approved the Standards of Practice for Lawyers Representing Children in Custody Cases. The ABA Standards attempt to clarify the role of a child's attorney—something that had become muddled by appointments of parenting coordinators, referees, facilitators, evaluators, and expert (or lay) witnesses. The ABA Standards chose to distinguish between two separate roles for a lawyer who represents a child. The first is deemed a *child's attorney* (or, alternatively, a child's advocate), who represents a child in the same manner—and with the same professional duties—as a lawyer representing an adult client. The second is a *best interest attorney*, who represents a child's interests without being bound by the child's directives. The ABA Standards were drafted as a mechanism to provide more predictability, uniformity, quality assurance, and professionalism; they require certain clarity of a lawyer's role and his or her performance when representing a child. The ABA Standards avoid the use of the title "Guardian *Ad Litem*" (GAL), which was the name routinely used for a child's attorney. The title was believed to have become too synonymous with expert or lay opinions because a GAL was often required to testify or provide a report—tasks that purposely excluded in the ABA Standards. This handbook is premised on the two distinct types of lawyers outlined by the ABA Standards. The ABA Standards apply regardless of whether the attorney is retained by the child or is court appointed.

The key to representing a child in a contested custody matter is to know your own limitations—emotionally, professionally, and legally. Do not work with a child if it will cause you—or the child—emotional distress. Do not work with a child if the work requires expertise beyond that of a lawyer, unless you can competently represent the child with the guidance of outside professionals. Do not work with a child outside of the scope of your legal limitations, whether set by the law, ethics, or a court order. For example, the ABA Standards anticipate that you, as a child's attorney, are responsible for monitoring the implementation of the court's custody orders and addressing a parent's noncompliance with those orders; however, this may actually be outside the scope of your court-ordered appointment. Representing a child is, in many ways, significantly different from representing one of the child's parents, even though your ethical obligations may be identical. You will be working with an individual who is the most vulnerable, requires the most protection, may be the least communicative, may have the most information but no mechanism by which to share it in a comprehensive and understandable manner, and may need the most education in the least "legal" of ways.

b. American Academy of Matrimonial Lawyers Representing Children: Standards for Attorneys for Children in Custody or Visitation Proceedings

In 2011, the American Academy of Matrimonial Lawyers (AAML) revisited its 1994 standards for representing children in custody and visitation cases to give more clarity to parties and the courts. The AAML Standards acknowledge that, in U.S. family courts, parents often cannot afford their own counsel; therefore, paying for a child's attorney may be beyond the reach of a particular family, requiring alternatives to hearing a child's voice by judicial or professional interviews. The AAML Standards further acknowledge the value of a child's attorney as an advocate for the child's wishes and someone who tries to shield the child from acrimonious litigation, but tempers those observations with the reality that an attorney who works with a child is placing that child squarely in the middle of litigation. The AAML Standards differ from the ABA's Standards in a material way: The AAML Standards have only one role for a child's attorney—that is, as an attorney representing the child in the role of traditional counsel.

The AAML Standards favor limited assignment of a child's attorney to cases; when assigned to a case, the attorney must be specially trained and designated for the role of a child's attorney in the lawyer's jurisdiction. The AAML Standards mandate the child's attorney to assess each child client's capacity to direct his or her own representation, and to decline the appointment as counsel if the child lacks capacity. The child's attorney, if appointed, must then represent the child's goals and seek to attain those goals for the child. If a parent is manipulating the child toward a certain outcome, the child's attorney must fully and frankly counsel the child. The child's attorney may seek withdrawal under local ethics rules if the child client is insisting on taking action with which the lawyer has a fundamental disagreement. The lawyer must not represent the child's "best interests," except to the extent that those interests align identically to the child's stated wishes. The lawyer does not make any recommendation on the outcome.

c. Uniform Law Commission Model Representation of Children in Abuse, Neglect, and Custody Proceedings Act

In 2007, the Uniform Law Commission (ULC) concluded a model act to improve the representation of children in proceedings directly affecting their custody by defining the roles and responsibilities of the child's attorney. The Model Act addresses the role of a child's attorney in more than just custody proceedings. The Model Act gives the court discretion to appoint an attorney for a child in a custody proceeding. Much like the ABA Standards, it defines two separate types of lawyers for children: a child's attorney and a best interest attorney. The Model Act also defines a best interest advocate who is distinct from an attorney. The Model Act gives guidelines to judges on when it may be appropriate to appoint an attorney or advocate for a child, as well as the factors a judge should consider when deciding whether to appoint someone. The Model Act gives guidance to a court in drafting an order appointing an attorney, its contents (including a mandate that the attorney have access to the child and confidential information related to the child), and its duration. The Model Act includes a list of duties for an attorney who represents a child client, such as meeting with the child, consulting with others, investigating facts, and encouraging settlement, among other tasks. The Model Act also limits who may sue the attorney for malpractice to only the child client. Finally, the Model Act provides for the attorney to be paid for his or her services to the child.

No state has adopted this Model Act.

§1.02 U.S. State Laws, Policies, and Procedures

a. Overview

Each state determines how to set standards for a child's attorney. Some states have that role defined in statute, others in guidelines or court rules, and still others through administrative orders. Even if you find language within your jurisdiction's laws permitting appointment of a child's attorney, you still must assess whether your jurisdiction has clearly defined rules that give your role structure and definition. In this book's Appendixes, you will find charts that provide information about the diversity of how jurisdictions clarify the role of a child's attorney.[5] Because this area of practice continues to redefine itself on a routine basis, it is difficult to compile a full summary of the current status of each state. The ABA Family Law Section's scholarly journal, the *Family Law Quarterly*, publishes yearly summaries of the law in all states, which provide guidance and updates.[6] You do not need to know the law in all states—you simply need to know what *your* state is doing. As an illustration, I share several case studies below, each from a different state, to provide perspective on the disparities in state practice and law when it comes to a child's attorney.

b. Case Study: Maryland (*by Melissa Kucinski*)

In Maryland Rule of Civil Procedure 9-205.1, a court may appoint an attorney for a child in a custody or access case. The rule provides factors a judge should consider in determining whether an appointment is prudent and necessary. It also mandates that certain minimum information must be included in a court order appointing a child's attorney. Maryland has its own Guidelines for Practice for Court-Appointed Lawyers Representing Children in Cases Involving Child Custody and Access, appended to the Maryland Rules of Civil Procedure.

Maryland recognizes three distinct roles for attorneys who represent children. The first, defined as a Child's Best Interest Attorney, clearly protects the child's best interests and is not bound by the child's directives or objectives. The second, a Child's Advocate, is a pure advocate for the child's expressed desires and acts as independent legal counsel, owing the same duties an attorney would to an adult client. The third role (almost a subset) of a child's attorney is the Child's Privilege Attorney, which was originally defined by case law in *Nagle v. Hooks*, 296 Md. 123 (1983). This lawyer is appointed by the court to decide whether to assert or waive, on behalf of the child, any privilege an adult would be entitled to waive—most typically a

---

5. Appendix 1 contains charts from the Uniform Law Commission's model act drafting committee in 2006.

6. *See* the *Family Law Quarterly* annual publication, "Family Law in the Fifty States Case Digests," at https://www.americanbar.org/groups/family_law/resources/family_law_in_the_50_states.html (last accessed 10/29/17). Chart 2 on Custody Criteria includes a yearly summary on the states' provisions for attorneys for children.

mental health privilege, where, in many jurisdictions, it would be the parents who would be required to consent to waiving the child's privilege so the court could gather otherwise private information. This third type of attorney is subsumed into the first two—the best interest attorney and the child advocate attorney who both have the duty and role of a child privilege attorney, but also have the more expansive role.

The Maryland Guidelines provide guidance on how to determine whether a child has "considered judgment" (in some jurisdictions, called capacity or maturity) by focusing the attorney on the child's decision-making process rather than on the child's decision, and deterring the attorney from making a decision about considered judgment solely on any child's cognitive or emotional capabilities. The Maryland Guidelines also mandate a minimum of six hours of training, including the topics of child development, child abuse, substance abuse, and what resources are available to the attorney and child. The Guidelines set minimum requirements to be appointed as a child's attorney, in addition to the training. They also require courts to establish compensation structures and assurances the attorney receives compensation in a timely fashion (including the use of retainers and entering money judgments when not paid).

The Maryland Guidelines in many ways mirror the ABA Standards. They give the court guidance as to when to appoint a child's attorney and lawyers guidance on their tasks in representing a child (depending on the type of appointment). The Guidelines do impose a prohibition on testifying and filing any report with the court.

c. Case Study: Washington (*by Linda Mason Wilgis*)

Under Washington state law, a court may appoint an attorney to represent a child's interests on parenting plan issues in dissolutions of marriage, domestic partnerships, and legal separations. This authorization is discretionary, not mandatory. Revised Code of Washington (RCW) 26.09.110 provides: "The court shall enter an order for costs, fees, and disbursements in favor of the child's attorney. The order shall be made against either or both parents, except that, if both parties are indigent, the costs, fees, and disbursements shall be borne by the county."

A child does not have a guarantee of attorney representation, but the child's wishes about how much time they spend with each parent are considered by the court if the child has the mental capacity to express these wishes. The child's wishes are one of several factors the court considers in developing a residential schedule.[7] The requirement that a child have the autonomous capacity to rationally articulate what he or she wants is tied to the fundamental principle that "a normal client-lawyer relationship is based on the assumption the client, when properly advised and assisted, is capable of making decisions about important matters."[8]

Although Washington state law requires the court to consider the wishes of certain children, it does not state this must be through counsel. The Washington Court of Appeals held the trial court was not required to specifically appoint an attorney, but should appoint an attorney *or otherwise order an investigation* of relevant facts to address a situation where the parties failed to adequately develop relevant factors to make an objective decision to serve the best interest of the child.[9] Similarly, the court of appeals found that the trial court should have appointed an attorney or a GAL to assist the court in reaching an objective decision on custody.[10] The trial court judge had allowed an unrepresented, fourteen-year-old child to testify in chambers that she wanted to live with her mother. The mother had a significant history of mental illness. The court of appeals recognized the lower court's "difficulty in reconciling [the child's] strongly stated preference for her mother with the court's finding of mental illness" and concluded that the input of a GAL or attorney would have been beneficial in determining custody.

The law is scant on detail in that it does not specify an age by which a child is considered by the court to be sufficiently mature to express preferences, nor does it provide other indicia of maturity; however, its flexibility does provide attorneys a foothold by which to request that the court appoint the child an attorney in family law cases. Children age twelve years or older must consent to the release of their medical records and counseling records that may be relevant to an investigation in family law cases.[11] Additionally, in the dependency realm (cases in which the child has been alleged to have

---

7. WASH. REV. CODE § 26.09.187 directs the court to consider "the wishes of a child who is sufficiently mature to express reasoned and independent preferences as to his or her residential schedule" WASH. REV. CODE § 26.09.187(3)(vi). Other child-centered factors specified by WASH. REV. CODE § 26.09.187(3) include: (i) The relative strength, nature, and stability of the child's relationship with each parent; (iv) the "emotional needs and developmental level of the child;" and (v) "the child's relationship with siblings and with other significant adults, as well as the child's involvement with his or her physical surroundings, school, or other significant activities."

8. Comment [1] to Washington Rules of Professional Conduct (RPC) 1.14. *Client with Diminished Capacity.*

9. *In re* Waggener's Marriage, 13 Wash. App. 911, 917; 538 P.2d 845 (1975).

10. *In re* Marriage of Nordby, 41 Wash. App. 531, 705 P.2d 277 (1985).

11. WASH. REV. CODE § 26.09.220(2).

been abused or neglected and the state has intervened to protect the child), children age twelve years or older must be notified of their right to request an attorney.[12] Thus, although there is not a bright-line rule to guide attorneys on when the court will grant a request for attorney representation in a family law custody case, age twelve years is recognized as a significant age of demarcation as to consent in other legal contexts in Washington. This suggests that attorneys in a family law context will have greater likelihood of having their motion granted if their potential client is age twelve years or older.

In the majority of dissolution cases in the state of Washington, children are not appointed attorneys. The culture of practice, an outgrowth of the court having the *discretion rather than mandate* to appoint an attorney, is such that most cases proceed without counsel even requesting they be appointed to represent a child. In contrast, it is common practice in several counties across the state for the court to appoint a GAL or a Parenting Evaluator to investigate and make findings and recommendations to the court. The primary mandate of a GAL is to represent the "best interests of a child."[13] However, this statute also states that, "If a child expresses a preference regarding the parenting plan, the guardian ad litem shall report the preferences to the court, together with the facts relative to whether any preferences are expressed voluntarily and the degree of the children's understanding."[14] These experts are called to testify at trial in contested cases, so this becomes the main avenue in Washington cases to convey the preferences of a child as to a residential schedule.

d. Case Study: Kansas (*by Ashlyn Yarnell*)

In Kansas, GALs are governed by Supreme Court Rule 110A,[15] which outlines the educational requirements, responsibilities, and general guidelines for involvement in both domestic and child in need of care proceedings. The general understanding is that Kansas GALs act as a "Best Interest Attorney" as defined by the ABA Standards, which define a best interest attorney as a lawyer who provides independent legal services for the purpose of protecting a child's best interest, without being bound by the child's directives or objectives.

---

12. WASH. REV. CODE § 13.34.100(7).
13. WASH. REV. CODE § 26.12.175(1)(b).
14. *Id.*
15. *See* Rule 110A (http://www.kscourts.org/rules/District_Rules/Rule%20110A.pdf).

The only reference or guidance in the Kansas Rules to ethical restrictions is to the Kansas Rule of Professional Conduct 3.7(a),[16] which states that "a lawyer shall not act as an advocate at a trial in which the lawyer is likely to be a necessary witness except where: 1) the testimony relates to an uncontested issue; 2) the testimony relates to the nature and value of legal services rendered in the case; or 3) the disqualification of the lawyer would work substantial hardship on the client." Thus, in essence, GALs should be treated as all other attorneys on the matter. They should not receive any sort of power from the court to testify or offer written reports to the court without agreement of the involved parties, waiving the ethical restriction of their involvement on the case.

GALs do not share confidentiality with the children whose interests they represent. The GAL may request an advocate[17] in Child in Need of Care proceedings by a showing of good cause to the court or if the child's wishes conflict with their recommendations to the point that an additional attorney needs to advocate for a particular position. The appointment of an advocate, however, is permissive by the court. No such provision exists by statute to appoint an advocate under the domestic code.

GALs are required to conduct an independent and ongoing investigation and to have ongoing contact with the child client. They must also explain the proceedings and their role to the child client in a way that is appropriate for that child. GALs in Kansas, above all, serve as attorneys and as parties to the action, filing pleadings, participating in all hearings, advocating for their recommendations, and supervising their subsequent implementation.

e. Case Study: Minnesota (*by Valerie Arnold and Micaela Wattenbarger*)

In Minnesota, a child generally does not have an independent right to counsel as part of a child custody or parenting time proceeding in family court. However, where the court has reason to believe that the child in question "is a victim of domestic child abuse or neglect," the appointment of a GAL to represent the child's best interests, incident to the child custody or parenting time proceeding, is mandatory.[18] In addition, the court has the discretion to appoint GALs to represent the minor child's best interests if the

---

16. *See* KAN. R. PROF. C. 3.7 (http://www.kscourts.org/rules/Rule-Info.asp?r1=Rules+Relating+to+Discipline+of+Attorneys&r2=28).

17. Pursuant to KAN. STAT. ANN. § 38-2205(a).

18. MINN. STAT. § 518.165, subd. 1 and 2.

court has concerns about the child's welfare, even if the court does not suspect child abuse.[19]

In juvenile court proceedings, the court "shall appoint a [GAL] to protect the interests of the minor when it appears, at any stage of the proceedings, that the minor is without a parent or guardian, or that the minor's parent is a minor or incompetent, or that the parent or guardian is indifferent or hostile to the minor's interests, and in every proceeding alleging a child's need for protection or services… In any other case the court may appoint a guardian ad litem to protect the interests of the minor when the court feels that such an appointment is desirable."[20]

The GAL program in Minnesota consists of specially trained community volunteers and state employees. A GAL may or may not be a licensed attorney. The role of a GAL in either a custody and parenting time proceeding or a juvenile court proceeding is to (1) conduct an independent investigation to determine the facts relevant to the situation of the child and the family; (2) advocate for the child's best interests; (3) maintain the confidentiality of information related to the case, with the exception of sharing information as permitted by law; (4) monitor the child's best interests throughout the judicial proceeding; and (5) present written reports on the child's best interests that include conclusions and recommendations and the facts upon which they are based.[21] Regardless of the GAL's credentials, a GAL does *not* function as the child's attorney and does not provide direct services to the child.[22] Nevertheless, the GAL may be afforded standing as a party to the child custody or parenting time proceeding and may be represented by counsel.[23]

In juvenile court proceedings in Minnesota, in addition to utilizing the services of a GAL when a child is found to be in need of protection and/or services, a child "has the right to effective assistance of counsel."[24] Except in cases where the sole basis for the petition is habitual truancy, the court is to appoint counsel to represent the child at public expense if a child aged ten years or older desires counsel but is unable to employ counsel.[25] The social services agency involved in the child protection proceeding must (within ten days after filing the petition or at the emergency removal hearing if the

19. *Id.*
20. MINN. STAT. § 260C.163, subd. 5(a).
21. MINN. STAT. § 518.165, subd. 2a; Minn. Stat. 260C.163, subd. 5(b).
22. *Id.*
23. MINN. GEN. R. PRAC. §§ 302.02(b) and 357.01.
24. MINN. STAT. § 260C.163, subd. 3(a).
25. *Id.* at subd. 3(b).

child is present) inform the child of the child's right to be represented by appointed counsel upon request and shall notify the court as to whether the child desired counsel.[26] An attorney representing a child has the same professional obligations in that representation as he or she would have in representation of an adult. In juvenile delinquency cases, the attorney appointed for the child is to initially meet with the child privately, outside of the presence of the child's parent(s) or guardian.[27] The attorney "shall act solely as counsel for the child."[28]

f. Case Study: Germany (*by Jutta Carrington-Conerly*)

Since changes in German Family Law and new regulations became effective on September 1, 2009, courts can and shall appoint an attorney for a minor child in custody, visitation, child neglect, limitation of access to a child, child abduction cases, and all other child and parent matters to represent the child's interests independently from either one of his or her parents.[29]

If a child is between fourteen and eighteen years of age, he or she can request a representative of his or her choice, as long as the individual meets the necessary criteria to represent the child adequately. As a general rule, the appointment of a specialist (usually a lawyer or psychologist, or in rare cases, a specially trained social worker) is required by law in these cases and in cases where the court may be required to remove the child from a parent or legal guardian for the child's own protection (i.e., mental or physical abuse).

A judge should appoint a child's attorney as early as possible in any court proceeding and, in its order, explain the role of the child's attorney in detail. Through the court appointment, the attorney becomes a participant in the proceedings. The parties are prohibited from filing motions or appealing any custody decision. The GAL has his or her own right to appeal a decision in the best interests of the child despite the fact that the GAL is not the legal representative of the child. The GAL will determine the interests of the child in the disputed legal matter and inform the court about the results of the GAL's review of the case, as well as any interviews done with the child to learn more about the situation from the child's point of view. Once the court

---

26. *Id.* at subd. 3(d).
27. MINN. R. JUV. DEL. P. § 3.01.
28. *Id.*
29. The exact description of the duties can be found in § 158 FamFG (Act on the Procedure in Family Matters and in Matters of Non-Contentious Jurisdiction).

makes a decision and the GAL does not appeal that decision on behalf of the child, the appointment, if not previously rescinded because of a settlement or other closure, shall expire with the decision becoming final.

The GAL is reimbursed with a one-time flat fee paid by the government as compensation for the performance of his or her duties and depending on whether the GAL had direct communication with the child. Because the GAL is typically a professional in the field of family law or psychology, judges tend to adhere to their advice. Therefore, the role of a GAL is of great importance and influence in any child-related legal matter in Germany.

§1.03 TYPES OF LAWYERS FOR CHILDREN

Who decides the role, designation, and mandate of the attorney working with a child? The court? The attorney? The short answer is that, if your jurisdiction has distinct and multiple roles for a child's attorney, then the court (at least initially) will likely determine what role you take when it appoints you. This initial determination, however, may not limit you, as the attorney, from petitioning the court to change your role or appoint a second attorney on behalf of the child as you become familiar with the child's position, maturity, and judgment. If you believe at some point in your representation that your child client requires a different type of attorney (e.g., a best interest attorney if you feel the child does not have sufficient judgment to form a position as to his or her best interests), you need to follow your ethical guidelines in determining the next step. You cannot prejudice your child client's position, nor disclose confidential information, which may make this next step more difficult for you. Throughout the process, you must continue advising your child client and communicating with him or her about the case. There may be circumstances, however, when you may ultimately need to withdraw from their representation.

The ABA Standards prohibit a child's attorneys from testifying, filing a report, or making recommendations. A child's attorney may explain what the child client wants, proffer what the lawyer anticipates the evidence will prove, and provide evidence to support a position or argument. The lawyer acts independently and must exercise independent judgment. Their loyalty is to the child client, no matter who pays for the lawyer's services. The lawyer, regardless of his or her role (as a child's advocate or a best interest attorney), needs to consistently assess and reassess the child's viewpoint. The child's viewpoint may vary over time, change as circumstances change (particularly in protracted and lengthy litigation), or result from fear, intimidation, or manipulation. Thus, a more in-depth analysis by the lawyer would be required, including work with other professionals to facilitate communication with the child and fully understand the child's views.

a. Lawyers Who Represent a Child's Best Interests

Even though the ABA and the ULC both provide for two distinct roles for a child's attorney, the AAML instead limited a child's attorney to the traditional legal representation afforded a parent, where the client dictates his or her own objectives. Given the AAML's decision to limit the role of a child's attorney to that of a pure advocate, one must ask whether a lawyer should be making an independent assessment about what is best for his or her client and then advocating for that position. We do not—and cannot—take on that role when representing a parent. Why is a child different, particularly when there are many professionals that can provide a bona fide analysis and reach a conclusion on the child's best interests, such as custody evaluators, psychologists, and even therapists?

One might argue that a mental health professional is a much more appropriate advocate for a child's "best interests" because this professional has a rigorous structure in place that provides guidelines on how to reach such a conclusion and has had training in making such an assessment. How is a lawyer truly able to know what is best for the child client? Perhaps this is an appropriate segue to our discussion on why a child may need a lawyer in the first place. Lawyers do much more than advocate. They educate, advise, and counsel. They also shield and act as a buffer between the court process and the client. A lawyer, whether representing a child's interests or position, has a role to discover admissible evidence geared squarely at helping a court reach a conclusion, presenting it clearly, and ensuring the client understands the process and the outcomes. Not all children have considered judgment/capacity/maturity (or any other word you wish to substitute here). Should those children not have the benefit of legal guidance simply because a lawyer cannot ethically advocate for their stated wishes? The role of a best interest attorney may require counsel to rely very heavily on those other professionals, including mental health professionals, when ultimately taking a position on behalf of the child.

b. Lawyers Who Advocate for the Child's Position

If you are hired or court appointed to represent a child's stated position, this role does not obviate the need to perform an independent investigation of the child client's circumstances. Your investigation serves to help you, as the child's attorney, understand the child's communication, represent his or her position, present the best evidence to attain the client's goal, and, most importantly, know whether the child is able to actually take a position. Some children are not mature enough to take a position. Some may take a position, but lack the judgment necessary to understand and appreciate the impact of that position, even with your guidance. Your investigation also furnishes you with information sufficient to counsel your client. If your client elects to take a position that makes little sense to you, after your investigation, you can help educate the child about the practical outcome if the child's goals were reached.

If you are representing a child's position, you are playing a traditional lawyer role. You must ensure that you meet all ethical standards, regardless of the child's behavior, position, disclosures, or actions contrary to his or her own interests. This may be difficult if you disagree with your child client. You will need to carefully weigh your ability to work with a client who is difficult to counsel. You may have opportunities during the representation to ask the court to vacate your appointment or to amend your role to that of an advocate for the child's interests, not position. Regardless, you will need to maintain your client's confidentiality and be able to explain to the child why you are asking to change the dynamic and your role.

c. Lawyers Who Address a Child's Privilege

A child holds the same privileges that an adult holds, and this will most prominently be seen if the child is in therapy with a mental health professional. As a child's attorney, you clearly need access to the information that a mental health provider has about your client. Do your jurisdiction's laws and/or your order of appointment permit you access to otherwise privileged information about your child client? Assuming the person from whom you are requesting privileged information is permitted to share their information with you, what can *you* share with this person? You may also have a privilege with your child client. When you are talking to the person who is treating your client, you may be tempted to share information with this treatment provider, particularly if it relates to the child's health and well-being. Tread carefully. Ensure you are not crossing any ethical boundaries. Furthermore, any conversation you intend to have with this person should be discussed with the child client first. Although you may not need the child's permission or authorization to speak with the treatment provider, your client should understand what steps you are taking in their representation. This is particularly important so that you do not destroy any confidence the child has in you or in their treatment provider.

If you gather privileged information from your child client's provider, when can you use this information in your representation of your child client? Depending on your jurisdiction's rules, simply speaking with the individual does not mean that the child's privilege has been waived with that person. Each state has different rules as to who may waive a child's privilege. In some jurisdictions, it may be the child (if the child is of a certain age). In others, it may be the parents (and, clearly, this will require the parent or parents with legal custody to waive privilege, which may ultimately yield information that is contrary to their position in court). In still others, you, as the child's attorney, may have the sole authority to waive the child's privilege. If I have the authority to waive a child's privilege, I start from the premise that the privilege exists for a very important reason—to protect a relationship between the child and their treatment provider. If this treatment provider were to share private information with others (including a judge, lawyers, or even the parents), how would that affect the child's ongoing treatment? Will the child need ongoing therapy? Does the child understand that their communication with their treatment provider is private? Are you able to obtain admissible evidence about the child from other sources than the treatment provider? How important is the treatment provider's information to a final custody determination? Often, treatment providers obtain most of their information from the child client's parents and may have very few unique details, observations, or assessments. It may also be that the child has no privilege with the treatment provider because the provider was evaluating the child and not treating the child. The child may have seen the treatment provider so few times that the provider has no real assessment of the child's situation.

What will happen once the child's privilege is waived? Depending on where the treatment provider is situated, that provider may now be asked to provide records or oral testimony, either in deposition or in court. The treatment provider may be subject to the Health Insurance Portability and Accountability Act (HIPAA). Under HIPAA, health care providers may share protected health information if obligated to do so by a court order (limited to only what is covered by the court order). A subpoena by a court clerk or a lawyer will need to follow additional notification requirements before the HIPAA provider is obligated to release information.[30]

As you can imagine, mental health professionals and other doctors are going to be very hesitant to speak with you. Not only are you a lawyer (and when people get calls from lawyers, it raises red flags), but also they do not want to violate their ethical obligations to their patient. Be courteous and understanding of these concerns. Ensure your order of appointment or other court order clearly gives them permission (or a mandate) to communicate with you. Share that order with the providers well in advance of scheduling a meeting, so that they can consult with their lawyers before speaking with you.

d. Lawyers Who Are Experts

As seen from the ABA Standards, the AAML Standards, and the ULC Model Act, the expectation in today's legal climate is that a child's attorney is truly a lawyer in all senses of the word. The child's attorney will not testify, provide a report, or give an opinion. Jurisdictions have adapted and clarified the role of a child's attorney, in most instances, because of the influx of new processes and professionals available to families (e.g., custody evaluators, parenting coordinators). The clarifications have also emerged as a way to protect lawyers. A lawyer that adheres to a very clear set of guidelines, practice rules, and ethics is less likely to lose a lawsuit when sued for malpractice. Nonetheless, some jurisdictions still permit child's counsel to draft a report or testify; when doing so, that lawyer has to ensure that he or she is following the jurisdiction's guidelines. Will hearsay rules apply? Must the information provided by the child's attorney be admissible evidence upon which the lawyer would rely if it were offered in trial? If you are testifying or writing a report, will you be qualified as an expert? Will you be required to use a specific methodology when conducting your investigation? Must your testimony or report cite to standards, publications, or other quantifiable research? Is your work product subject to discovery or subpoena? If your jurisdiction's rules, guidelines, and the court order appointing you as the child's attorney are unclear, you need to be certain what they are before putting your name, reputation and expertise before the court. Must you rely on other professionals when opining, such as mental health professionals?

---

30. *See* https://www.hhs.gov/hipaa/for-individuals/guidance-materials-for-consumers/index .html (last accessed 7/14/17).

Is your role one where you may request psychological or psychiatric evaluations? Is your report required to provide verbatim testimony or proffers of those you interviewed?

If you are going to take on a role that places you squarely in the position of giving the court an opinion, you clearly need to document everything you do. Will the child's words to you be protected by a privilege? Will you be required to disclose other protected information? How do you describe your role to the child?

e. Lawyers Who Are Hired Privately by the Child/One Parent

In some situations, a child may need his or her own attorney, but the court has refused, failed, or has no legal authority to appoint an attorney for the child. In situations where the child may testify, be interviewed, is asked to sign an affidavit, or has the right to intervene, the child must understand his or her rights but should not be counseled by his or her parents. This child may be in a position to hire private counsel who is not specifically court appointed.

A lawyer who is not court appointed may have more difficulty securing information from third parties. A privately retained lawyer may need to file motions with the court (if permitted to do so) to request permission for access to information, particularly if the child client is unable to provide the information or consent to its release.

Another potential issue is whether the attorney is paid, and by whom. Typically, when the court appoints a child's attorney, it provides for payment, including an hourly rate or flat fee, and any retainer obligation. The order may also dictate the terms under which the lawyer may collect, whether he or she may obtain a judgment, and whether the attorney is obligated to begin work before collecting a retainer. If a lawyer is not court appointed, the lawyer may require a retainer agreement, which is a complicated legal document for a child to understand and an overwhelming burden for the child to afford. A child's parent may become involved in retaining the lawyer, which gives the impression that the lawyer is not necessarily representing the child's interests so much as representing the person who pays the bills.

When a lawyer is privately retained, what guidelines should the lawyer abide by? While the ABA Standards specify that the guidelines apply to lawyers who are court appointed *or* privately retained, certain states dictate that their guidelines (and also therefore requirements regarding training and experience) are only mandatory for court-appointed lawyers.

If the privately retained attorney determines that a child has no capacity or is immature and cannot direct his or her own representation, then the lawyer must—like all lawyers—abide by the Rules of Professional Conduct and Rules of Court to terminate the relationship with the child client and withdraw from the case as counsel for an intervening party (who may or may not have standing). When you are privately retained, to have permission to stand in court and represent your client, you need to request permission for your child client to intervene (if this is even the role for which you are retained). This may be a difficult concept to sell to a judge who would rather the child not be involved at all. If the child is merely a witness, the lawyer may only work with the child client on a limited basis to prepare the child to testify and attend any hearing to make appropriate objections on behalf of the child.

f. Case Study

You represent a sixteen-year-old child. She goes to the courthouse, unhappy with the existing access schedule outlined in her parents' custody order. She has been refusing to spend time with her father. The child completes a form at the courthouse asking to change the access schedule to eliminate the time with her father. Assuming the matter proceeds (and there are not grounds on which to reject the child's court filing) or (at the very least) the child's filing provokes the parents to seek to modify their access order, what happens to the child now? She is clearly invested enough in the outcome that she wants to be directly involved. If her court pleading remains in the file, she is now put in the middle of litigation.

The child comes home from school one day and tells her mother that her friend Carol's mother was represented by you in a custody case and that the child wants to meet with you. At a loss for what to do, the mother takes her daughter to meet you. How do you proceed? You need to set guidelines for this type of situation. Do you treat this like an initial consultation with the child and maintain that the child has a confidential relationship with you? Do you meet with the parent, either separately or simultaneously with the child? Do you get paid? Do you even ask for money? How are you retained? Would discussing finances with the child only further entrench her in the middle of a difficult situation? Assuming you can actually resolve getting paid, then what?

If you have questions for your child client, what do you do? Would you ask the child client permission to begin calling others? What happens if the others refuse to talk to you? How do you evidence that you are representing the child? At what point do you approach the parents and request releases to speak to medical providers and others on behalf of the child? What happens if one or both of the parents refuse to sign the release? Do you go to the court and request that you be appointed as the child's "court-appointed" attorney? Do you have authority to do that, particularly if your client's petition was dismissed or the court rejected her ability to intervene? What happens if the parents disagree with your involvement? Do you merely serve as a lawyer to help educate the child? What happens if the other lawyers will not communicate with you and keep you abreast of what is happening, so that you do not know what to tell your child?

This type of role is fraught with difficulty. If you agree to accept a child as privately retained counsel, you need to understand the complexity that is involved, review the rules of conduct in your jurisdiction, and be prepared that you may have a significantly limited role that is not accepted by all parties or their counsel.

§1.04 TRAINING AND COMPETENCY

While a child's attorney must be familiar with laws, rules, guidelines, and ethical principles, one of the most important concepts that a competent child's attorney must study is child development. In preparing to represent children as clients, a child's attorney must build a network of other professionals with whom to consult so that they understand the child's communication and are adequately communicating back to the child in a manner understandable by a child of that age and maturity. Some jurisdictions may mandate training and continuing education for a child's attorney to accept cases.

a. Elements in Training Programs

The ABA Standards list substantive topics that should be covered in specialized training for child's attorneys. These topics include relevant laws and regulations; legal standards; the guidelines in that jurisdiction; the court process and key personnel (including court and private services typically used in these cases, such as custody evaluations or mediation); child development and needs; communicating with children; how to prepare and present a child's viewpoint; child testimony; alternatives to direct child involvement; how to recognize, evaluate, and understand child abuse or neglect; family dynamics, particularly with the presence of domestic violence and substance abuse; resources, including local resources; services available to children and families, including welfare, mental health, educational, special needs, placement, evaluation, and treatment services; and advanced laws such as child custody jurisdiction laws, relocation laws, and abduction laws.

Besides training, should a child's attorney be trained in any other legal disciplines? Should the lawyer be a practicing custody attorney or family lawyer? Can or should a lawyer who does not practice in the family law field undertake representation of a child client?[31] Regardless of your background and whether you meet your jurisdiction's standards, you must be comfortable with the complex and dynamic relationship you will have with a child client.

b. Experience

It goes without saying that even if you have significant training, you need to feel comfortable communicating with children of all ages, learning abilities, needs, cultures, and circumstances. Although you can improve these communication skills through study and practice, some will simply be innate. Being a parent does not mean you can adequately communicate in an appropriate, healthy, and understandable way with a child who is in a distressed state. You may want to consider working as co-counsel for a child, if your jurisdiction so permits this type of appointment, so that you can have a mentor to learn the skills necessary to work with children as their attorneys. You may also want to engage in local, national, or international networks of child's attorneys to be able to discuss more complicated issues and how to address them when they arise in your cases. Finally, be sure to befriend competent child psychologists, therapists, and mental health professionals in your jurisdiction. Not only will they be helpful when you need a referral for the court or the parents, but they are an excellent resource of information when you need guidance on a variety of questions, such as, "How do I ask a child if they are gay?," "How do I tell my five-year old client that their mom and dad are in court?," or "What is my child client really saying when he tells me that he does not want to eat at his mother's house?"

c. Model Rule 1.1—Competence

A child's attorney has an ethical duty to provide competent representation to their child client. Model Rule 1.1 of the ABA Model Rules of Professional Conduct states that "competent representation requires the legal knowledge,

---

31. *Representing Children in Dependency and Family Court: Beyond the Law*, by Rebecca M. Stahl and Philip M. Stahl, publishing in 2018.

skill, thoroughness and preparation reasonably necessary for the representation." When you represent a child, this competency will require you to have knowledge about your child client and his or her abilities and needs, the skill to speak with and properly advise your child client in an understandable and relatable manner, the thoroughness to gather information that your child client may not have or be able to share, and the preparation to advance your child client's best interests. You need to be competent in the law, but also in so much more. It is rare that a law school would offer a class that prepares you for the undertaking of representing a child client. Whether or not your jurisdiction has minimum requirements to accept court appointment as a child's attorney, you should be prepared to go beyond those minimum requirements. You need to continually educate yourself. Each child will have different needs and abilities, different ways of communicating, different circumstances and problems, and different networks and allies. You need to be an investigator, a confidant, an armchair psychologist, a skilled communicator, and a confident advocate.

d. Need for Pro Bono Help in Courts

It may be impossible for a family who desperately needs a lawyer for their child to secure one, simply because of cost. Even if the family can afford a child's attorney, the likelihood is that this lawyer is the third one in the case, increasing costs for the entire family. Given that your role is unique and requires a lot of independent investigation to verify details, facts, and to understand the child's viewpoint (as opposed to simply having the client tell you his or her position and the facts needed to make your case), it can be costly. You may need to travel to your child client, to his or her school, activities, or elsewhere. Your work will not be restricted to your office and the courthouse. If you represent a child client, your workweek will be predominantly out of the office. This may leave the most vulnerable of family members without a necessary advocate. For lawyers who represent children, you will become accustomed to accepting cases at lower hourly rates, capped fees, or pro bono. Courts may hold special funds to pay counsel their fees. Other courts may have rosters of pro bono child's attorneys.

ETHICAL AND MALPRACTICE ISSUES

2

§2.01 INTRODUCTION

If you are a strong advocate for your child client, it is likely that at least one of the child's parents, if not both, will be unhappy with you. In fact, "unhappy" may be an understatement. I have observed angry parents file false grievances against the child's attorney, write angry reviews online, try to turn the child against his or her own lawyer, and even appear at the attorney's home to start an argument. As you can imagine, in family law cases, emotions could provoke parents to act in even more aggressive ways, including attempting to harm the other parent, the child, or the child's attorney.

In my two jurisdictions, typically a child's attorney is appointed in only the most acrimonious of cases, including cases where the issues are so complex that a judge needs the help afforded by independent counsel for the child. Therefore, you will typically be dealing with a family that has been through the court system more than once; someone with a mental illness or substance abuse issue; allegations of domestic violence, abuse, or neglect; or a case with a significant volume of information that neither parent, their lawyers, nor the court can access or digest. The court may see significant contention in a case and, in a moment of pure concern for the child, appoint a child's attorney. The expectation is that the lawyer may be able to provide sufficient insight to the parents and, more importantly, the judge, thus guiding the court to a fair and reasonable result.

Given the age, capacity, and communication style of a child, the lawyer will need to dig deep for information; he or she may insist on speaking with individuals and obtaining information that one or both parents find unflattering, at best. Finally, particularly if it is the attorney's job to advocate for a best interest position (as opposed to the child's wishes), the attorney may be in a difficult situation where at least one parent is very angry at the position taken on behalf of the child. Although some parents may take this anger out on you by refusing to pay your fees (even if court ordered to do so), others may do so by filing attorney grievances against you or suing you for malpractice. Perhaps even worse, the parent may take this anger and frustration out on the child. If you are unfortunate enough to be in a case where at least one person is mentally unstable, you may also receive threats; thus, be sure to take precautions, such as removing your home address from publication or keeping your office door locked during the workday.

In the end, particularly because many courts value a child's attorney's position (and give it weight, whether the court should or not), the court may enter a final custody order that mirrors or reflects much of what the child's attorney posited. When you represent the parent, it is easier to pass blame (to the judge, the other parent, opposing counsel, the rules of evidence, etc.) when your client does not receive their chosen result. This is not the case for the child's attorney, particularly if the attorney advocates for a best interest position and the judge's final order reflects a similar analysis and result. Be certain to call your malpractice carrier before any child representation and ensure it is included on your policy. This section of this book aims to high-light some of the more troublesome areas for child's attorneys.

§2.02 ASSESSING A CHILD CLIENT'S CAPACITY AND JUDGMENT

a. Model Rule 1.2—Scope of Representation and Allocation of Authority Between Client and Lawyer

Model Rule 1.2[1] of the ABA Model Rules of Professional Conduct mandate that an attorney abide by a client's decisions concerning the objectives of

---

1. Model Rule 1.2 states the following:

(a) Subject to paragraphs (c) and (d), a lawyer shall abide by a client's decisions concerning the objectives of representation and, as required by Rule 1.4, shall consult with the client as to the means by which they are to be pursued. A lawyer may take such action on behalf of the client as is impliedly authorized to carry out the representation. A lawyer shall abide by a client's decision whether to settle a matter. In a criminal case, the lawyer shall abide by the client's decision, after consultation with the lawyer, as to a plea to be entered, whether to waive jury trial and whether the client will testify.

the attorney's representation of that client and consult with the client as to the means of pursuing those objectives. This rule, in and of itself, presents a challenge for a lawyer representing child clients, who have legal incapacity by virtue of their age and may be unable to fully understand, assess, and instruct a lawyer as to their objectives by virtue of their immaturity. A child may not understand his or her own goal in this dispute. Some children may clearly state that their goal is to have their parents reunite—something that is highly unlikely and not within the lawyer's purview to pursue. A lawyer who represents a child client must be extremely adept at communicating with his or her client and must be very clear with the client about the practical reality of the situation (while recognizing that it may be difficult and extremely stressful for a child to hear this information). The lawyer must also be keenly observant and diligent in his or her independent investigation, so that the lawyer fully understands what the child communicates (verbally and non-verbally) and understands the client, including what the client has not said or is incapable of verbalizing. An attorney should not assume that a child lacks maturity, is disabled, is impaired, or is incapable of expressing an opinion simply because of the child's age. A lawyer must look at all circumstances surrounding the child's communication and recognize that a child's expressions may simply be contextual, intermittent, related to a specific incident or interaction with a specific person, or ameliorated by education or reliable information. A child may be able to contribute to his or her representation at certain times but not others, as well as in certain situations but not others.

Is a child who cannot verbally communicate automatically immature or incapacitated? What if the child is mature, but his or her communication is indirect, not clear, or indecisive at times? What if the child is very clear and very adamant in his or her position, but the lawyer is concerned that the position was generated by circumstances and not from the child's genuine goals (e.g., a parent's coercion, a friend's parents' divorce, a lesson plan in school, a book the child is reading)?

(b) A lawyer's representation of a client, including representation by appointment, does not constitute an endorsement of the client's political, economic, social or moral views or activities.

(c) A lawyer may limit the scope of the representation if the limitation is reasonable under the circumstances and the client gives informed consent.

(d) A lawyer shall not counsel a client to engage, or assist a client, in conduct that the lawyer knows is criminal or fraudulent, but a lawyer may discuss the legal consequences of any proposed course of conduct with a client and may counsel or assist a client to make a good faith effort to determine the validity, scope, meaning or application of the law.

b. Capacity of Children

(i) *Model Rule 1.14—Client with Diminished Capacity*

Model Rule 1.14[2] of the ABA Model Rules of Professional Conduct mandates that a lawyer maintain a normal relationship with their child client,
as far as reasonably possible, and reveal otherwise protected information about the client if it is reasonably necessary to protect the client's
interests.

(ii) *How Does an Attorney Assess a Child's Capacity/Judgment/Maturity?*

The sixth edition of *Black's Law Dictionary* defines capacity as "legal quali-
fication (i.e., legal age), competency, power or fitness. Mental ability to
understand the nature and effects of one's acts."

Clearly, by virtue of a child's age, the child has a legal incapacity to
do certain things, such as enter into a contract. The child, however, may be
mature, understand the details of the court case that is ensuing, and have a
rational, educated opinion as to what outcome is preferable to him or her.
The best way to assess a child's maturity is to have a solid understanding
of the child's background. I have worked with far too many professionals
that take a child's statements to be fact. At times, I cannot lay blame on that
professional. He or she may only have the child's words but no context,
ability to speak with others, or access to documents, records, or collateral
information. A child's attorney is often empowered (and, at times, mandated
by his or her appointment order) to conduct an independent investigation,
speak with collaterals, review documents, speak with the child, and propose

---

2. Model Rule 1.14 states the following:

(a) When a client's capacity to make adequately considered decisions in connection with
a representation is diminished, whether because of minority, mental impairment or for some
other reason, the lawyer shall, as far as reasonably possible, maintain a normal client-lawyer
relationship with the client.

(b) When the lawyer reasonably believes that the client has diminished capacity, is at risk
of substantial physical, financial or other harm unless action is taken and cannot adequately
act in the client's own interest, the lawyer may take reasonably necessary protective action,
including consulting with individuals or entities that have the ability to take action to protect
the client and, in appropriate cases, seeking the appointment of a guardian ad litem, conserva-
tor or guardian.

(c) Information relating to the representation of a client with diminished capacity is protected
by Rule 1.6. When taking protective action pursuant to paragraph (b), the lawyer is impliedly
authorized under Rule 1.6(a) to reveal information about the client, but only to the extent reasonably necessary to protect the client's interests.

methods of gathering additional information (e.g., therapy, evaluations). The child's attorney can, in most cases, be the most educated and knowledgeable individual in a trial, which also means he or she may be considered the most persuasive by a judge; that attorney may have access to information, witnesses, exhibits, and other evidence that the parents' lawyers never knew existed. Through this investigation, the attorney can weigh a child's words, assess whether the child can or should direct the litigation, or decide that the lawyer must take additional steps to protect the child client (e.g., by filing a motion to have the attorney's role shifted from one of advocate to one of best interest attorney).

(iii) *What If a Child Has No Capacity, Judgment, or Maturity?*

A child does not have legal capacity. You may run into a mincing of words when you represent a child. Words such as *capacity*, *disability*, *maturity*, and *judgment* may be thrown about when speaking about a child's ability to understand and engage in the process, state preferences, and direct objectives in the litigation.

In Maryland, for example, an attorney (regardless of their designation as an advocate or a best interest attorney) needs to assess whether a child client has "considered judgment." The Maryland Guidelines[3] give the attorney some direction in making this assessment. The attorney needs to focus on the child's decision-making process (not simply the child's decision), whether the child can understand the risks and benefits of his or her position, and whether the child can reasonably communicate his or her wishes. The Maryland Guidelines specifically mandate that the attorney seek guidance from professionals, family members, school officials, and other concerned persons. The attorney can determine whether an evaluation is needed and may request one when the attorney feels it is appropriate. The Maryland Guidelines further encourage attorneys to be sensitive to culture, race, ethnicity, and economic status, as an acknowledgment that these factor into whether a specific child may have considered judgment and whether an attorney who is of a different background may be attuned to the child's considered judgment. Another interesting caveat delineated in the Maryland

---

3. *See* the Maryland Guidelines at http://www.montgomerycountymd.gov/cct/Resources/Files/Maryland_Guidelines_Child_Counsel.pdf (last accessed 1/31/18).

Guidelines is the statement that a child may be capable of having considered judgment despite significant cognitive or emotional disabilities.[4]

If a lawyer determines that a child has no "capacity" (i.e., is incapable of directing the objectives of the court case), the lawyer may need to consider whether the role for which he or she was appointed is the one that best serves that child client's needs. The lawyer may need to do additional investigation to ensure that he or she has sufficient information to help the child in whatever negotiations or litigation ensues.

(iv) *Is It the Attorney, Court, Parent, or Another Who Makes This Determination?*

If a child is testifying in court or playing a direct role in the litigation, then a court will need to determine if a child is mature and able to exercise his or her judgment in expressing an opinion; based on that assessment, the court gives the child's statements the weight the court feels is appropriate. If a child is undergoing a psychological or mental health evaluation, then the evaluator is best situated to evaluate the child's communications and their underlying meanings. However, when an attorney is representing a child, that attorney has an obligation to account for all information, including any mental health evaluation and statements made to a court, in determining whether the child's expressed wishes are a mature statement that should be considered at face value. Your role to assess your client's maturity or judgment, as the child's attorney, does not end as soon as you are appointed. It continues on a daily basis as you gather additional information and may be a fluid determination.

(v) *How Does the Attorney's Role Differ for a Child Who Has Capacity Than That for a Child Who Does Not?*

If the child has capacity to direct the litigation's objectives or take a position, you as counsel should be an advocate for that child in every traditional sense of being an attorney, just as if you were the attorney for either of the child's parents. If you feel the child has capacity and is still making a poor decision as to his or her best interests, you need to take on an educational role. Ensure that your child client is fully comprehending the situation, the outcome, and the future path that his or her life will take. If you cannot work with a child given the position he or she takes (i.e., it conflicts with your assessment),

---

4. *See* https://www.montgomerycountymd.gov/circuitcourt/Resources/Files/FamilyDivision/ Maryland_GuideLine_for_Child_Counsel.pdf (last accessed 5/1/17).

then you need to consider withdrawing from representation in a manner that is least detrimental to your client's goals and needs. If the child has no capacity, then the onus is entirely on you to form a position on his or her behalf and be an advocate for that child's interests. If your appointment does not permit this "best interest" role, then you need to seek a reappointment, a redesignation of your role, a second attorney, or a withdrawal.

(vi) *When Should This Assessment Occur?*

Your assessment of your child client's decision-making abilities should occur every single day, with every single piece of information you receive, every single question you ask of the child or any collateral, every document you read, and every detail you uncover. Your conclusion as to your child's maturity is fluid and can change with any new piece of information.

§2.03 ADVOCACY REQUIREMENTS

a. Filing Pleadings

As with everything in this handbook, be certain to check your jurisdiction's rules, practices, and your order of appointment to determine the scope of what you are permitted to do and what you cannot do as a child's attorney. If you are a child's attorney, the ABA's Standards envision that you have the right and obligation to pursue certain court filings to protect your client's interests in the case in which you are appointed. The question becomes: When does this obligation end? Do you have an ongoing obligation after the court issues its final custody order to file a motion to alter or amend that final order if you feel it does not meet your child client's best interests? If you truly feel the court abrogated its duties, can you (or should you) file an appeal? When does your appointment end? What happens if there is a companion court case filed, such as a protection order case? Do you have an obligation to the child client in that case, where you were not appointed? Can you file appropriate pleadings in that case to protect your child's interests? Should you file a motion to intervene (and are you legally permitted to do so)? How zealous should you get in filing pleadings on behalf of your child client? Must you respond to every pleading filed by either parent? One must also remember that if the parents are paying your fees, you are a third attorney that is draining this family's resources. Unless a pleading requires a response, a response is particularly helpful to the court, an error exists in the pleading that is filed, or a responsive pleading would expedite a resolution for the child, I typically abstain from filing a response simply to minimize the costs for the family.

b. Pursuing Evidence

A typical order of appointment permits a child's attorney to participate in discovery and prohibits him or her from giving a written report or testifying, making it unlikely that the attorney can respond to discovery on behalf of a child client without breaching one of the core principles in the ABA Standards and any order of appointment. A child's attorney has a genuine obligation to pursue evidence on behalf of his or her child client. Any position the attorney takes at trial must be based on admissible evidence. The child's attorney is independent of the parents and their lawyers; although they may take a position on behalf of the child client, they should truly want the court to have all relevant evidence to ensure that the judge can make a well-reasoned decision on behalf of the child client. The ABA Standards are clear that a child's attorney cannot testify or provide a written report, so the attorney needs to present evidence. Thus, the child's attorney may need to issue subpoenas, take depositions, and issue discovery.

Even though the child's attorney, through their order of appointment, typically has unfettered access to school records, medical files, and third-party collaterals, he or she needs to be cognizant of the rules of evidence, obtain business records certifications, send subpoenas to witnesses, and not assume the parents and their lawyers will call all crucial witnesses. In a case where there are one or two self-represented litigant parents, the child's attorney may be the only source of information for the court. If discovery deadlines have already passed before the child's attorney is appointed, the self-represented litigants are not responding to discovery requests, or third parties are not cooperating, the child's attorney needs to take on the burden of gathering admissible evidence so the court can do its job. If your order of appointment is clear as to what the parties in a case must provide to you, then you may seek to enforce that order of appointment to compel production of certain information, much like you would seek to enforce it if you were not paid pursuant to its terms.

c. Communicating with Your Child Client

You will need to communicate with your child client, advise him or her, gather the child's viewpoint, weigh it against other information, and consult professionals to ensure your communication with the child is appropriate and that you understand what the child communicates to you.

Model Rule 1.4[5] of the ABA Model Rules of Professional Conduct mandates that a lawyer reasonably consult with his or her client about the means to accomplish the client's objectives, keep the client reasonably informed about the status of the case, and promptly comply with reasonable requests for information. You must ensure that your child client understands your role and its limitations. You are not only counselor, but also educator. You need to reality-test situations with your child client, ensure that the child visualizes potential outcomes, and ensure that the child understands the role of the judge and court and what can and cannot happen. You need to advise your child client about the investigation you are obligated to undertake, and you must also meet your ethical obligations to share the information you gather in your investigation with your child client.

It is extremely important to gather information from your child client and to impart the *important* information to him or her. You will have a balancing act when determining what is important. What information do you need to ethically share with your child client? If you share too much, will it distress the child? Will it run up the legal bills? You may find that the most important information you receive comes from a collateral, not from the child client. You should use other professionals (e.g., mental health professionals) as sources of information and guides on how best to work with your child client. You want to avoid communication with your child client that could be easily misunderstood or misinterpreted, or causes stress to the child. You need to educate yourself about how a child communicates and how you need to change your communication style to ensure your child client understands you. You need to find mechanisms by which to communicate

---

5. Model Rule 1.4 states the following:

(a) A lawyer shall:

(1) promptly inform the client of any decision or circumstance with respect to which the client's informed consent, as defined in Rule 1.0(e), is required by these Rules;

(2) reasonably consult with the client about the means by which the client's objectives are to be accomplished;

(3) keep the client reasonably informed about the status of the matter;

(4) promptly comply with reasonable requests for information; and

(5) consult with the client about any relevant limitation on the lawyer's conduct when the lawyer knows that the client expects assistance not permitted by the Rules of Professional Conduct or other law.

(b) A lawyer shall explain a matter to the extent reasonably necessary to permit the client to make informed decisions regarding the representation.

with your child client, whether it is in person or electronically, while recognizing the child's needs for privacy and comfort. As the child's attorney, you must approve of any final settlement, if one is reached; thus, you must ensure that the child understands the settlement, the child has a voice in the outcome, and, if you are representing the child's expressed wishes, the child approves of the settlement.

When you represent a child, you should understand that there is a distinction between a child who is unable to express a position (e.g., a preverbal child, a child with certain medical conditions that preclude him or her from communicating) and a child who fails or refuses to express a position. Even more complex is when a child expresses a position, but the lawyer has reason to doubt the child's words or believes that some outside force (e.g., a parent, a sibling, a friend) influenced this position. This creates difficulty for a lawyer who is appointed to represent the child's position. An otherwise mature child may nonetheless be influenced and either refuse to express a position (in which case, the lawyer may simply represent the child's legal interests) or express a position that the lawyer truly feels is contrary to the child's interests.

What should you do if you are appointed to represent a child's wishes, but you truly believe the child's position is not good for him or her? You may need instruction from the court, including seeking reappointment as a best interest attorney, requesting appointment of a new (second) attorney, or vacating the order of appointment because you can no longer represent your client. The lawyer needs to talk to the child about his or her concerns, try to delve deeper into the concerns, and try to understand why the child is taking a position that seems contrary to his or her interests. The child is the client. Thus, if a lawyer is appointed to represent the child's position, that lawyer has a duty to explore this information with the child, including information the attorney obtained through an independent investigation.

If an attorney needs to request a best interest attorney appointment (or redesignation as one), the attorney may have to walk a fine line because the attorney may be prohibited from disclosing confidential client information. The attorney also needs to distinguish between the child's position, the attorney's assessment of the child's best interests, and whether the child's position is one that would put the child in harm.

In many situations, the attorney as "counselor" becomes far more important when representing a child than the attorney as advocate. The child may have lived in a harmful or detrimental situation for so long that the child knows nothing else. The child may truly love a parent who is not good or healthy for that child, and feel loyalty to that parent. The child may need counseling, therapy, or other treatment to get to a place where the child feels emotionally capable of making an informed and healthy decision. A lawyer cannot ethically present a position that is not grounded in fact or law; thus, the question becomes whether the lawyer can communicate with the child to educate him or her about options and have the child see the practical outcomes moving forward, particularly when it is difficult for the child to understand or foresee the future consequences.

If the lawyer is unable to help the child become educated and healthy to a point where the child can take an informed position in his or her best interests, then the lawyer must request a best interest attorney. However, the lawyer may be prohibited from sharing any confidential or privileged information learned during representation of the child with any subsequent best interest attorney. The lawyer must also remember to consult the ethics rules. Model Rule 1.14 of the ABA Model Rules permits a lawyer who reasonably believes that a client has diminished capacity and is at risk of substantial harm to take protective action, even if it means disclosing certain information to protect the client's interests. Is a child who is taking a position that may be contrary to his or her interests a surefire indication that the child has diminished capacity? This may be a fine line the attorney has to walk.

Another issue is distinct when working with a child versus adult client. If you represent an adult client, you share all documents with that adult client. If a piece of paper, including a pleading or a letter, comes in your door, you will send a copy to your adult client. Your file belongs to your adult client. When you represent a child client, this may not be prudent or in your client's best interests. I rarely share this information *directly* with my child client. In many cases, it will cause the child significant distress. In most cases, the child will not understand the document. The child is typically not a "party" to the case, so they do not necessarily need to respond to everything that is filed. You, as counsel, will determine which documents require your child client's response. Because the client is a child, the client will not be able to sign or verify a response; thus, most responsive filings will be related to the law or be organizational, taking positions on deadlines and process. You need to determine whether your jurisdiction mandates that you share all documents you receive with your child client. However, you need to weigh that against your child's best interests, accounting for their age and level of participation directly in the litigation. A particularly harsh pleading may traumatize the child.

d. Pursuing Positions

As a child's attorney, I feel obligated to try to bring closure to this chapter in the child's story as efficiently as possible. Whether I am appointed to protect the child's best interests or pursue a mature child client's position, I feel obligated to have a discussion about my advocacy well before any trial date. Each case and each child is different, but I typically time my discussion with the parents' lawyers for a week or two after I believe my independent investigation is starting to yield the same information. For example, when I hear the same story or similar statements from multiple sources, I am comfortable that the information I am receiving is accurate. Going to trial and surprising the parents and their lawyers with my position on issues does not serve anyone (particularly if the parents do not have a legal mechanism to obtain this information from me during the road to trial); it particularly does not serve my child client, who needs the parents to work together (or, at times, in parallel to one another) instead of fighting against each other. I try to hold a joint phone call or meeting with the parents' lawyers to disclose my positions on issues and provide them with information from my independent investigation, particularly because it is nearly impossible to send daily updates to the lawyers on the information I gathered that day. By giving the lawyers sufficient basis for my positions and clearly articulating my positions, they know what information I lack, where they need to help educate me further, and how they need to advise their client. My pretrial positions may include some additional feedback not relevant in the trial, such as, "From what I am hearing, Mr. X is dismissive of little Johnny's fears, and perhaps he should consider engaging in a class that helps him communicate with children better." The goal is to leave a family in a better place than where I found them.

It can be unnerving to share a position with counsel in advance of trial. You may get questioned, and it is inevitable counsel may argue with you and try to persuade you that you are taking the wrong position. Therefore, I am reluctant to take any position before conducting a thorough independent investigation and feeling confident that I have sufficient admissible evidence to back the position I am taking. I lose credibility if I do not have support for my position. However, I likewise lose credibility if I spend a lot of time and a lot of money investigating a case, without ever helping anyone to reach a resolution. It is a rare occurrence (perhaps only 5 percent of cases) when I take no position before trial. In those cases, it is often not helpful to take a position because it may harden the positions of the parties, create argument or posturing, or shut down any negotiations. In some cases, no matter how sound my position, it will never help parents settle. Having said that, it is unfair to go to trial without expressing my thoughts, even if I do not have a fully vetted, comprehensive position.

Conversely, you may simply not have a position to express. You are not the judge, and there are cases where it may be impossible for you to determine the best overall outcome for your child client. You have limitations. For example, you may need help from a psychologist in assessing your client's attachment to a caretaker, but have no funds or cooperation in obtaining that help. You may need your child to be in therapy, so you have a treatment provider with whom to speak; however, if the parents do not agree and there is no emergency need for it, you may not have these data during the litigation to help you decide what position may be best for your child client. If you do your job, investigate, present evidence, stay on task, and, perhaps, distance yourself from the lawyers who are busy trying to sway your opinion, then you need to trust in the process. You need to trust that the judge will look to you. Although they may not get an "answer," you should nonetheless be able to present everything clearly and in a manner that will let the judge do his or her job. You can summarize the evidence for the judge and lead the judge to the most appropriate evidence for your child client. You can cut through the garbage.

e. Finding Witnesses

You have an obligation to seek out witnesses who have relevant information to share with a judge that supports your client's position (or the position you will take on behalf of your client). A key question often plagues me, however: If I am an advocate, acting under a court appointment, must I put forth *all* witnesses that have something relevant to say, or only those that support my position? What if the child's therapist is adamant the child client not live with her father, yet you support the child living with the father? Should you still put the child's therapist on the witness stand if that witness has legitimate information to share with a court, and then examine the witness (being your witness, it would be difficult to cross-examine the person) to bring out why you disagree with him or her? Or, as an advocate for a particular position, should you simply omit any witness who does not have information supporting your position? What happens if you speak with a collateral witness and know what they may say, but that same collateral did not cooperate with speaking to the other attorneys in the case? By virtue of your unique role as the child's attorney, more people will voluntarily speak with you and be more candid in sharing information. You will have information that others in the case may never have. Do you have an obligation to share information about every collateral witness with whom you speak so that the other lawyers may call those people as witnesses, even if you choose not to? That is, what information can you keep from the others in the case and from the court as your own work product to help you formulate a position and how much, because of your unique role as child's attorney, should you share with everyone?

I tend to err on the side of sharing with the attorneys, unless it would be detrimental to my child client. I see my role as more of a problem solver who can harness the experience of other attorneys and experts to try to solve this child's problem. I have, in the past, called witnesses who do not share the same position as my child client or me. If my position is grounded in the evidence, I should be able to bring that forward to the judge. I do not want to prevent the judge from having relevant and important information just because the witness's conclusion may differ from my own. Particularly if the witness may have information that will fill in gaps for the court, is unique to this witness, and cannot be elicited from others, or if the witness has a perspective different from any other, it may be important for the judge to hear from that witness. I am not a decision-maker. I may take a position for my client, but I do not make the ultimate decision as to what happens to this child.

f. Retaining Experts

What happens if you truly believe that a case requires an expert for a judge to make a well-reasoned decision, but you have no ability to hire one because of the cost? This is another area of practice that requires significant advance planning. As the child's attorney, you may or may not have an obligation to designate any expert you intend to have testify as a witness in court. You need to be cognizant of what information you may be obligated to share with both parties in advance of any hearing or trial. You will also need to plan whether you must file a motion with the court, requesting the court order one or both parties pay the fees associated with retaining this expert, and how who pays their fee may affect this expert's work product if you ultimately do not call him or her as a witness.

What happens if one party retains an expert, such as a custody evalua-tor, and the other party will not cooperate? What happens if you support this custody evaluator doing a full assessment? Ideally you should ask for cooperation, recognizing that you have no authority to impose it. If you must, file a motion with the court requesting cooperation and participation in any assessment.

g. Pursuing Interim Measures for the Child

If you are representing a child, there may be emergencies that need to be addressed faster than a typical court process. An emergency could include anything from a child's access to a capable parent being blocked, to a child not being registered for the fast approaching school year, to a child needing emergency medical treatment. Your child client may need to be put into therapy. The child may need to undergo elective medical procedures. He or she may even need protection from a parent taking the child out of the jurisdiction if there is a reasonable basis to believe the parent may not return with the child. If one of these situations arises, you should reach out to the parents (through counsel if they have lawyers) to ask whether each party consents to the interim measure the child needs. If someone disagrees, it may be incumbent upon you to file an appropriate motion with the court to institute some type of temporary or interim measures pending a final custody resolution.

The ethical conundrum may become whether you are supplanting your judgment for a parent. What happens if neither parent believes there is a need to obtain elective dental surgery for the child right now? Do you pursue it through a motion simply because a dentist is recommending it, contrary to both parents? What if it is only one parent refusing the treatment? Even if you are an advocate for a child's best interests, you are not the child's parent. However, if you are obligated to represent a child's best interests (and not their stated position), you may need to act, including filing motions to institute temporary or interim measures.

h. The Line Between Advocate and Decision-Maker

The line between being an advocate for a child and making decisions for your child client may be a fine line, as was already discussed previously. If you are an attorney advocating for a child's best interests (versus a child's wishes), at what point do you cross the line between being that advocate and being akin to a parent with legal custody? If your child client is in emotional distress and you conclude the child needs therapy, how much evidence do you need to support this position? What happens if one parent disagrees? What happens if both parents disagree? Do you file petitions with the court requesting therapy for the child? What type of evidence do you require: a doctor's recommendation, the child making certain statements, or a teacher suggesting therapy for the child? If you pursue therapy for the child client, contrary to the parents' wishes, are you trying to supplant the parents' judgment with your own? Granted, a court is the final arbiter, but at what point are your requests frivolous (not based in sufficient admissible evidence)?

You are the child's attorney. You are not their parent. When the AAML promulgated its guidelines for representing children, this may be one of many reasons why it recommended any attorney for a child represent the child as a pure advocate for the child's wishes, not as a best interest attorney. An attorney advocating for a child's best interests is, naturally, taking a position on what is best for the child. Thus, the question becomes how you, an attorney, are any more competent to make this decision than a parent. In fact, one may argue you are the least competent to make this decision: You are not the parent or legal guardian, a judge vested with the authority to make a decision as to who has legal custody, a mental health professional who can make a real assessment as to the child's mental health needs, a teacher who can make an assessment on the child's educational needs, or a doctor who can make an assessment on the child's health. Tread carefully. Talk to colleagues. Engage the parties in discussions. Know your rules and your ethical practices in your jurisdiction.

i. Standing to Pursue Certain Relief—Civil Protective Orders, Restraining Orders, Motions to Modify Custody, Etc.

Standing to pursue certain relief is also addressed in other sections in this handbook. To pursue relief, you need to have the authority to be able to do so. Your order of appointment should clearly articulate the boundaries within which you operate, either directly or by referencing clear guidelines or mandates you are required to follow. If your order of appointment is unclear, ask for it to be clarified. Look to statutory authority and case law to determine your boundaries. May you intervene in existing cases for which you are not appointed? Does appointment in one case affecting the child open you up to intervene in other cases? What happens if there are other cases that directly affect the case for which you are appointed? Do you have an affirmative obligation to bring this to a judge's attention, and if so, how? Must you file paperwork or notices with either court in which there is a pending action? What happens if you interject in a case where you are not appointed? What happens if the court issues an order, and you decide it is the wrong decision?

Do you appeal? Do you file a motion to reconsider the judgment? What happens if neither parent wants to pursue matters further? What happens if a parent files an insufficient pleading? What if the parent forgets to plead a material change of circumstance in a custody modification matter? If you believe there is a material change, do you say something? Do you suggest the parent amend their pleading? Do you file your own pleading? If your child client is in danger, do you file for a protective order on his or her behalf? What happens if such a request is in a different court? What if it is in a different state? Are you obligated to retain counsel in a jurisdiction where you are not licensed to file such a case on your client's behalf?

The short answer is typically as follows: Look to your appointment order, know the case law, and know your jurisdiction's statute. Call the bar counsel's hotline in your state. Consult with the parents, their counsel, and, when in doubt, other experienced child advocates to determine the best path. Do not have *ex parte* communications with the court. Do not file motions you have no authority to file. Do not make matters more difficult. Your first line of defense may not be court—it may be the police or child protective services, if necessary. It may be the aunt that you interviewed two weeks ago who may have standing to intervene where you do not. Do not overstep your authority. You are a lawyer. You are not a judge. You are not a parent.

§2.04 WORKING WITH MENTAL HEALTH PROFESSIONALS

a. Child's Therapist

If a custody case is acrimonious enough to warrant a child having his or her own attorney, it is usually acrimonious enough for the child (and perhaps his or her parents) to see a therapist. Your child client has a confidential relationship with his or her therapist. You need to know the law in your jurisdiction that permits you to discuss matters with the therapist, under what circumstances the therapist can then discuss matters back with you (including disclosing confidential information), and what permits the therapist to then discuss the same confidential information with others, including a court.

The first place I always look is my court order of appointment. Does the order mandate a therapist's cooperation in speaking with me. If so, recognizing I also have a confidential relationship with my client, to what extent do I share information back with the therapist? If my order of appointment mandates the therapist to cooperate and speak with me, is that a waiver of the child's privilege with their therapist, or must my conversation with the therapist remain private unless and until that privilege is properly waived? If the child's privilege is waived, must the therapist then turn over documents or testify in court? There are a lot of moving pieces when it comes to a child's privilege and their confidential relationship with a treating professional. What happens if the child is treated just across the state line in State B, and State B has different rules about who can speak with the therapist, and your order of appointment is from State A?

I have had situations where a therapist, recognizing the acrimony in the family, refused to take notes and then, when they got the eventual call from a lawyer, told the lawyer that they could not remember anything useful about the child or family. I have had situations where I, as the attorney, was given the authority to waive the child's privilege with his or her therapist, and, when I did, the therapist still refused to communicate under other regulations and ethical guidelines. I have had some therapists who cannot wait to talk and have likely jumped the gun by disclosing far too much far too early to the wrong individuals, all because they felt that they wanted to help the family. I have also had situations where the therapist may nonetheless be subpoenaed to testify about nonconfidential information, such as the therapist's personal observations of the parents in the waiting room.

Any time you dive into issues of obtaining privileged information, and potentially threatening another individual's professional license, things get more difficult. Whenever a therapist (or teacher, swim coach, or neighbor for that matter) receives a phone call from a lawyer, the protective walls go up. I try to comfort the therapist as best I can, but I cannot give the therapist legal advice. I cannot tell them whether they can or cannot talk to me. Whenever I first reach out to a therapist, I try to do so in writing (e-mail, fax, etc.) and with a copy of any relevant documents verifying my authority to speak with him or her (my order of appointment, waivers, releases, etc.). I have had therapists argue that even my order of appointment, which clearly mandates the cooperation of mental health professionals, is insufficient for them to speak with me. I try to recognize that this professional may have been working with my child client for some time and may be the best advocate this child has in the future, once I am long gone from that child's life. I clearly talk to the child about the fact that I speak with his or her therapist. I try to set ground rules for how it is that I can gather this information, but the information can be kept secret from others. If I am tasked with waiving the child's privilege (or not), I talk to the child before doing so. I always talk to the therapist about whether the child may need therapy going forward. I try to recognize that even if the child does not remain in treatment with this professional, the child needs to have a trust in and relationship with some professional in the future.

If, after spending time with the therapist and understanding the child better, I believe the child is being treated by the wrong person, I will typically voice that concern, but always with some type of plan in place. In many custody cases, one parent (not both) put the child into therapy, or one parent met with the therapist first and told the therapist all the horrible things the other parent did. If I suggest that the family may want to explore new therapeutic options, the parent who feels slighted (whether they have a basis to feel slighted or not) will immediately agree with me, but for the wrong reasons. I also need to tread lightly, recognizing the child may have a good relationship with the therapist and be deriving some benefit from the therapy. I do not want to overstep and try to supplant my judgment for that of the child's legal custodian.

Therapy is a very personal thing for a child. It may be their safe space. It may also be a venue in which you can communicate with your child client. I once represented a child who would not talk to me. He simply outright refused. I established a good relationship with the child's therapist, who was doing good work. In doing so, I broached the topic of whether it would be appropriate for me to be present in one of the child's sessions. My goal was not to breach the child's confidence or make therapy an unsafe space, particularly because he was not communicating with me, but to see if there was a path down which I could travel to seek the child's input. The therapist talked to the child about my participation in one session. The therapist got the child's agreement and laid the ground rules. The therapist started the session with the child and brought me in for about twenty minutes of the session, at which point the child communicated more to me than he had in the previous two months. In this situation, it helped. However, this situation was rare. There were other considerations before my participation in therapy. I needed that good rapport and support of the therapist. The therapist needed to have been reassured in his professional judgment that my intrusion would not negatively affect the child. I also needed to consider how the parents felt. At this juncture, the parents were not even permitted into the child's therapy sessions, and yet, I was. It was a difficult pill for them to swallow. There was significant work before my participation. Again, however, this case was the exception, not the rule.

(i) *Case Study*

Two children were abducted by their mother about six years ago. The children were young at the time, but are now mature preteens. They were never told what happened during the approximately one year they traveled from country to country before being returned to the United States and their father. The children are now in therapy. How do you work with the therapist?

In this situation, the therapist may be key. The children are now in a situation where you are clearly back in court (and they have a lawyer), and they are older and need to understand *why* things are happening. They are also more aware (and able to go on the Internet and learn, on their own, the story of what happened years ago). Not only do they need support understanding their story, and what was likely a void in their narrative for years, but the children probably also have other issues to address, including their relationship with their mother (who has been absent) going forward, as well as their father (who did not tell them what had happened for years). They also need to express their feelings about any potential changes to the custodial and access arrangement that is now back before the court. Given their lack of narrative for so long, there is no possible way you, as a lawyer, can adequately communicate with them about this, how they feel, and what they are thinking. You need the help of the therapist desperately in a situation like this.

Everything the child is thinking is going to be shaped by the emotion he or she feels surrounding these revelations and how the child processes this new reality and story. There will be issues of trust, filling in gaps, reconfiguring old stories to make those old stories comport with the reality, revisiting their understandings of their entire lives to date, and how to address this at one of the most vulnerable times in a child's young life—right before becoming a teenager and entering middle and/or high school. In fact, you may need the therapist more than the therapist needs you. It is in these circumstances where you may even ask whether, in a family with limited resources, if one professional needs to step aside, who should it be? Often times, it may be the lawyer.

b. Parents' Therapist/Counselor

If your jurisdiction's best interest factors include the health (physical and mental) of all involved—child and parents (and possibly others)—you need to have information about the parents' health. If you are satisfied with a statement from a parent as simple as "I see a therapist to address my stress related to this case" or "I take medication for high blood pressure," perhaps that is all you need. However, for you to have a fuller picture, you may wish to gather information directly from the parents' treatment providers—therapists, counselors, or even doctors. There are significant amounts of red tape if you want access to these records. Federal and/or state law may protect the records. The parent will have an expectation of privacy in his or her health records and have a privilege with the provider that only the parent can waive. There may be hoops through which you need to jump if you attempt to subpoena any records—waivers, additional waiting periods, special notice, etc., which are often found both in federal law and your state statute.

Your order of appointment probably does not permit you access to records for anyone but your child client. When in this situation, I typically approach the parent, through their lawyer, and gauge whether the parent is agreeable to either signing a waiver or any release forms required by his or her doctors, therapists, or counselors, or if the parent is agreeable to requesting the records directly and providing them. I prefer the former. It gives me more control to ensure that I actually receive all the information and the parent did not self-select what I see.

If the parent refuses access, the question that arises is, "Why?" This is a question you can ask and explore with the parent. I do not like putting the parent on the spot with my request. If I am given permission to meet with the parent without his or her counsel present, I always ask the parent—and suggest that the parent speak with his or her lawyer about this issue—before agreeing to waive privilege or providing the documents. Even if the parent's lawyer is sitting right next to the parent while meeting with me, I will defer to the lawyer. I do not want to give the parent legal advice. I also want the parent to understand this complicated issue before responding to me.

There have been circumstances where the parents engaged in couples' counseling, and one parent wants me to speak with the counselor or review their records, whereas the other parent does not. My job is not to trick anyone into turning over documents that are protected, or to put anyone's professional license in jeopardy. There are sometimes incidents where the professional does that on his or her own. In several situations, I have reached out to the mental health professional to see if they were willing to talk, particularly if there was a question as to whether the type of relationship that existed between the professional and parent was one covered by some privilege. In more than one instance, the mental health professional, overly concerned about talking to a lawyer, instead wrote a letter that ultimately exposed privileged information. Again, it was never my intention to trick the person into violating some law or ethics rule. I try to tread carefully and respectfully.

It is also complicated when a parent's mental health professional, who never met my child client, starts opining on the child's health based on information the parent shares. I have also seen situations where the child's therapist, after observing the parent in a waiting room or after a discussion, has opined on the parent's mental health. If the child or the parent is not the patient and has no privilege, the question then becomes whether that professional lacks a valid legal excuse for avoiding a conversation with you.

c. Evaluators

(i) *Psychological Evaluation*

It would not be a family law case without at least one person accusing another of having some type of mental illness. It seems separations, custody cases, divorces, and the acrimony attendant with them create armchair psychologists in all of us.

If a person's psychological or mental health is important to the court's resolution of your child client's best interests, you may need to pursue a psychological evaluation. Most typically, you may need to request an evaluation of a parent or caretaker. However, there may be circumstances where you need to request one of your own client, particularly if the child has been exhibiting certain behaviors or having certain difficulties (at school, socially, with friends, etc.). You need to have a full picture of that child's mental and emotional health so that you can help a court determine what caretaker is best able to provide for that child's mental and emotional needs. Recognize that psychological evaluations may not be free in your jurisdiction (and if they are, they may not be comprehensive). You should examine what type of evaluation needs to be done—do your homework. Understand what goes into a psychological evaluation and what data will be revealed. Do not put your child client through a battery of tests (or any person, for that matter) unless it is necessary and will be useful. Weigh the utility against the cost, as well as your ability to actually obtain a solid reliable evaluation by a reputable professional. A bad evaluation may be worse than no evaluation.

Consider that an evaluation may simply be more data points to help this family piece together a comprehensive solution. Know that you may need to make a request for an evaluation of the court; there also may be a hearing. Be prepared to suggest professionals who you feel are best equipped to do the evaluation. Ask both parents in advance for consent/permission; if either agrees, then have them join your request with the court.

(ii) *Custody Evaluations*

Custody evaluations involve mental health professionals evaluating a family —the child *and* the parents—and making a recommendation about custody. Custody evaluators will interview the parents, child, and possibly other individuals (teachers, doctors, etc.), much like you will as the child's attorney. They will observe the child with the parents. They will review any relevant documents. If their background permits, they may conduct psychological testing of the people in the family. They will, in the end, form an expert opinion that can be presented to the court.

If a custody evaluator is involved in the process—whether to conduct a full evaluation or not, and whether they were hired by one parent, both parents, or appointed by the court—it is likely that someone will ask you to speak to the evaluator. I am always hesitant. I will ultimately reach out to the evaluator, but I will make it clear from the first conversation that I do not feel comfortable sharing any of my observations, insights, or information. Do not do anything to sway or bias their evaluation. Furthermore, the worst thing for my role as the child's attorney is to have a custody evaluator testify in court using my words or basing his or her opinion on my views. I am not a mental health professional. I am not an evaluator. While I ultimately take a position, that position is based on a legal analysis and is substantiated by legal arguments and admissible evidence.

I practice as a child's attorney in a jurisdiction where I am prohibited from giving a written report or oral testimony; therefore, it would be tantamount to violating my guidelines to contribute, in any way, to what may ultimately be my words being put into evidence as if I had some expertise or was a witness. I am happy to listen to the custody evaluator, letting him or her impart information to me. At most, I have told evaluators the names of collaterals who the parents have asked me to speak with, almost as a comparison to the collateral list that the evaluator was given by the parents.

d. Intermediaries

(i) *Conflict Coaches*

A family may be working alongside conflict coaches—mental health professionals who are assigned to each parent to help the parent be a better communicator in a conflict situation. Coaches can participate with a family as part of a larger collaborative process, or separately. They are not mediators. They may speak to one another directly, then meet with their individual clients separately. They may try to resolve interim problems and create solutions on an issue-by-issue basis, or they may work toward finalizing a full parenting plan. If this type of process might work effectively for the family with whom you are working, you may want to reach out to the lawyers/parents with this suggestion. Coaches help to resolve problems, but they also help parents learn communication skills.

(ii) *Parenting Coordinators*

Parenting coordinators are dispute resolution professionals who are specially trained to work with parents to help them assess problems, educate them, help them manage their case, and, at times (if the jurisdiction permits), make decisions, without abrogating a parent's legal custodial rights. They help parents communicate. This professional may be specially appointed by a judge or privately retained. They may or may not be permitted to speak with you. If they are able to speak with you, your insight may help them to help the parents see things from a child-focused perspective, particularly if the parenting coordinator has not or will not meet with the child.

§2.05 PRIVILEGED AND CONFIDENTIAL COMMUNICATIONS

Your child client will (depending on the jurisdiction) share an attorney–client privilege with you as his or her counsel. The purpose of the privilege is to encourage your client to be candid with you. An informed attorney is the best legal advocate. No one can compel you to share confidential information communicated to you by your client. This is an absolute protection, and the client has the right to assert or waive this privilege. The privilege applies to confidential communications (not the underlying information). As the child's attorney, you must also abide by and protect the child's confidentiality.

Model Rule 1.6[6] of the ABA Model Rules of Professional Conduct states that you cannot disclose information you obtain in representing a client, unless the client gives informed consent or there is some exception. The most significant exception that you may come across when representing a child is to prevent reasonably certain death or substantial bodily harm. Although you are not either parent's lawyer, you may be put in a position of educating a parent about your attorney–client privilege with your child client and your role to protect their confidential communications with you. It will be complicated to explain the legal nuances between privilege and confidentiality to your child client.

You should keep your child client's communications to you confidential, only disclosing information as permitted by your jurisdiction's ethics rules. Your ethics rules should permit you to disclose information to protect your child client if he or she is in danger. During your representation, you may want to use your child client's confidences to pursue settlement or to inquire about things your client told you. You will need to walk a fine line. For example, if your child client tells you his mother stopped giving him prescription anti-depression medication, you may want to confront the mother.

---

6. Model Rule 1.6 states the following:

(a) A lawyer shall not reveal information relating to the representation of a client unless the client gives informed consent, the disclosure is impliedly authorized in order to carry out the representation or the disclosure is permitted by paragraph (b).

(b) A lawyer may reveal information relating to the representation of a client to the extent the lawyer reasonably believes necessary:

(1) to prevent reasonably certain death or substantial bodily harm;

(2) to prevent the client from committing a crime or fraud that is reasonably certain to result in substantial injury to the financial interests or property of another and in furtherance of which the client has used or is using the lawyer's services;

(3) to prevent, mitigate or rectify substantial injury to the financial interests or property of another that is reasonably certain to result or has resulted from the client's commission of a crime or fraud in furtherance of which the client has used the lawyer's services;

(4) to secure legal advice about the lawyer's compliance with these Rules;

(5) to establish a claim or defense on behalf of the lawyer in a controversy between the lawyer and the client, to establish a defense to a criminal charge or civil claim against the lawyer based upon conduct in which the client was involved, or to respond to allegations in any proceeding concerning the lawyer's representation of the client;

(6) to comply with other law or a court order; or

(7) to detect and resolve conflicts of interest arising from the lawyer's change of employment or from changes in the composition or ownership of a firm, but only if the revealed information would not compromise the attorney-client privilege or otherwise prejudice the client.

(c) A lawyer shall make reasonable efforts to prevent the inadvertent or unauthorized disclosure of, or unauthorized access to, information relating to the representation of a client.

How do you do this, without letting the mother know her child "ratted" on her? You could ask about what medications the child takes in her house (and ask the father the same question). What happens if the mother gives information that contradicts your child client's statements? You should continue the conversation with the mother, carefully framing questions so as not to give away your child's statements. You should speak further with your child client. You should talk to the child's doctors, psychologists, and others (e.g., school nurses, guidance counselors) to try to resolve what information is accurate.

While in court for a hearing or trial, you may be obligated to state your child client's position to the court. Some jurisdictions may mandate this disclosure even if the child does not want the disclosure. You need to explain this carefully and clearly to a child client. It may make little sense to the child that his or her words to you are "secret" and you will not tell anyone what they say (unless you need to protect the child), but then, in the next breath, you tell the child you will stand up in court and tell a judge, lawyers, and the child's parents what the child "wants." If I am required to state my child's preference in court, I usually do so in my closing argument. If my child client's preference does not align with my best interest position (when I represent a child's best interests), I will often tie the fact that my child feels one way to the ultimate reason why their preference is not in their best interest (e.g., they were put in the middle, they were "brainwashed," they were manipulated).

After you speak with your child client about secrets, privacy, confidentiality, and privilege, your child client may fear talking openly with others, such as doctors, therapists, and their parents. Your child will need to understand that you will keep their information secret, but that they should feel free to talk to anyone. You do not want to cause your child client to close up. Although you have an obligation to maintain their confidential communications, the child should feel comfortable sharing anything with others in their lives (e.g., their doctors, therapists, parents, teachers, coaches). Depending on your client's age and maturity, you need to artfully attack this quirk, which may seem nonsensical to the child.

In addition to explaining the nuances of complex legal principles to your child client, you need to make sure that the parents understand they share no privilege with you, and you will not be obligated to keep anything they say as confidential. I include this in my initial protocol letter, introducing my process and myself.[7] If the parent has an attorney, I will not speak with that

---

7. *See* Appendix 3B for a sample letter.

parent unless their attorney is present or has given me clear permission, in writing, to speak with his or her client alone.

a. Child's Privilege with Other Individuals

Your child client may also share a privilege with other individuals, such as their therapist. When you communicate with these individuals, things may get tricky. In the case of a therapist, for example, it is often the parents who waive the child's privilege so that others can gather information from the treatment provider. In some jurisdictions, particularly in the thick of a custody case, you, as the child's attorney, may be the only person who can waive the child's privilege. Assuming you have the right to speak to a treatment provider with whom your child client shares a privilege, you will need to tread carefully. Unless the child's privilege is waived with each of you independently, then each of you may end up talking in circles, not able to fully disclose relevant information to one another. It is always uncomfortable when a child's therapist is mandated by court order to discuss confidential information with me, but I cannot reciprocate when the therapist asks me questions about what my child client has disclosed to me. It is equally uncomfortable when I have information that may help the child's therapy, but cannot share it with the therapist because it is privileged.

b. Collaterals' Lack of Privilege or Confidentiality with You

Like your communications with a child's parent, other collateral witness communications are not privileged. At times, collaterals may refuse to speak with you unless you promise to protect their information from others. This request is rare. Many will want to share information with you. Many only have information that they got directly from one of the parents. The best collateral witnesses have their own personal observations of this family. Those who really care about the child will speak openly with you. If the collateral is wary of sharing information, the question is, why? Are they scared of one of the parents? If they are scared, how so? How will that affect the child? Is the child also scared of a parent? You cannot force a collateral to speak with you (although, if useful, you may be able to subpoena that collateral to a deposition or to trial). If a collateral is concerned and refuses to speak with you, ask that person if there are others with whom you should speak to gather information, or another source of the information they would otherwise share (e.g., records, other witnesses).

§2.06 THE CHILD'S ATTORNEY AS EXPERT WITNESS

The ABA Standards are clear that a child's attorney is a *lawyer.* The AAML Guidelines are even narrower and define the child's attorney as a pure advocate for the child client's position. Some jurisdictions use mental health professionals as "guardians *ad litem*" for children. Some still use lawyers and will have the lawyers testify or write a report to provide guidance to the court. If a lawyer testifies as an expert, that lawyer will need to qualify as an expert in a specific area of specialized knowledge. If the lawyer testifies as fact witness, then the lawyer clearly needs to have exposed himself or herself to enough of the child's life to present factual observations. If the lawyer is summarizing admissible evidence through their testimony or in a written report, that lawyer still needs to weigh that role versus the role of representing the child client, maintaining that child's confidences, acting in the client's interests, and meeting all the ethical guidelines required of the lawyer.

If you testify, you will likely be cross-examined. Good practice dictates that from the day you are appointed as the child's attorney, you should keep impeccable notes, including dates, times, and precise words said. You may want to ask permission to record certain conversations with collaterals, or, if permitted, take depositions of those collaterals, to form the basis of your testimony or report. Is your testimony or report seen as an opinion? A summary of your position on behalf of your client? A proffer of evidence?

Rule 3.7[8] of the Model Rules of Professional Conduct prohibits a lawyer from acting as an advocate in a trial when the lawyer is likely to be a necessary witness, unless the testimony relates to an uncontested issue or the nature and value of legal services in the case, or the disqualification of the lawyer as an advocate would work substantial hardship on the client.

If your jurisdiction requires you to write a report, know the guidelines and format for your report, as well as the limitations for the information you include in the report. If your jurisdiction does not require a report but

---

8. Model Rule 3.7 says the following:

(a) A lawyer shall not act as advocate at a trial in which the lawyer is likely to be a necessary witness unless:

(1) the testimony relates to an uncontested issue;

(2) the testimony relates to the nature and value of legal services rendered in the case; or

(3) disqualification of the lawyer would work substantial hardship on the client.

(b) A lawyer may act as advocate in a trial in which another lawyer in the lawyer's firm is likely to be called as a witness unless precluded from doing so by Rule 1.7 or Rule 1.9.

permits you to write a report, you need to weigh the utility of doing so. Will your jurisdiction provide immunity if a party sues you for malpractice? Will your report add anything that cannot be obtained from some other means? Does your report provide any detail that you cannot otherwise discuss with counsel and/or the parties on a phone call?

§2.07 MALPRACTICE AND IMMUNITY

Some jurisdictions provide child's attorneys with quasi-judicial immunity from malpractice suits. Whether your jurisdiction provides this immunity typically hinges on whether your role is as an arm of the court (with judicial functions) or purely as attorney for the child (with a traditional attorney–client relationship). A child's attorney's role can be confusing, particularly because it is a court-appointed role and, in some jurisdictions, one where the court not only decides if an attorney will be appointed but who the attorney is that takes on this role. Courts may establish guidelines for child's attorneys and mandate background requirements before they can accept court appointments. The ABA Standards make clear that, ethically speaking, the child's attorney is an attorney and owes no allegiance to anyone but the attorney's client. Before agreeing to your court appointment as a child's attorney, review your jurisdiction's rules about whether you are entitled to immunity from a malpractice suit. Also, remember that attorneys who represent children in their parents' custody lawsuit may have different obligations, guidelines, and rules than do attorneys who are appointed to represent children in neglect, abuse proceedings, or adoption suits.

An attorney who is obligated, through his or her court appointment, to investigate a child's situation and further report directly to the court creates confusion as to whether that attorney's allegiance lies with the court or the child client. The ABA Standards make clear that the child's attorney is not an expert witness. In some jurisdictions, judges have become dependent on these "independent investigations" and reports; therefore, they request reports in the form of a pretrial brief with a proper pleading format, if a formal report (akin to an expert's report) is prohibited. Is this appropriate? Does this step of providing a written (or oral) report open up a child's attorney to malpractice and attorney grievances for violating ethical obligations, or does it make an argument (when that jurisdiction is silent) that the attorney should be given quasi-judicial immunity? What if the child's attorney represents the child's best interests, and not the child's wishes? Does that open up the attorney to malpractice? Is an attorney given some type of *parens patriae* power that truly belongs to the court?

The best advice I can give to a child's attorney is to have good malpractice insurance that covers this very unique attorney role and to know what type of limitations exists in your jurisdiction. If you are uncomfortable providing a written report or giving oral testimony, even with clear guidelines, do not do it, and do not accept appointments as a child's attorney.

§2.08 REPRESENTING CHILDREN IN HAGUE ABDUCTION CASES[9]

a. What Is a Hague Abduction Case, and How Is It Different from a Custody Case?

This book focuses on representing children in contested custody litigation. Chapter 6 of this book focuses on representing children when the family is global, spanning continents and cultures. When a custody case turns international, it may be common that the Hague Abduction Convention is part of the overall litigation. A Hague Abduction action is separate from the custody case, and it may act to stay the custody case in which you are appointed as the child's attorney. The Hague Abduction case may or may not be brought in federal court. The Hague Abduction case's only issue is whether the child will be returned to that child's habitual residence or not. The Hague Abduction case will not involve a best interest analysis of the child. However, as you will see in Chapter 6, a child's attorney nonetheless can take certain roles in a Hague Abduction case.

b. What Is the Role of an Attorney in a Hague Abduction Case?

If you were appointed as a child's attorney in a custody case and a simultaneous proceeding was filed to return the child to his or her habitual residence under the Hague Abduction Convention, you are not automatically counsel in that second court case. It may be that the judge in that case, if the issues are such that require the child's voice to be heard, will want a lawyer for the

---

9. For a discussion on the 1980 Hague Convention, please also see *The Hague Abduction Convention* by Jeremy Morley, specifically Section 2.10, published by the ABA. Also, see Chapter 6 of this book for a more detailed explanation of representing children in a Hague Abduction Convention case.

child; you may be the logical choice, if you are admitted to practice in that court. At times, the Hague Abduction petition may be filed in an existing custody case under the same case number; if you are already appointed as the child's attorney, you may take on this role in both cases.

Your role will be very different in the Hague return proceeding. You are not part of that case to assess what is best for your child client. You are to go in with the assumption that the child's best interests are served by having the child's "home court" resolve custody of the child. The Hague Abduction Convention operates to promptly return a child to his or her habitual residence, and there are only a few exceptions that can be proven (some with a high burden of proof) to give the judge the discretion to not return a child. Your role will be more facilitative at times, helping the court assess certain exceptions to return and obtaining evidence to prove basic requirements for the petitioner's case, such as "Where is the child's habitual residence?" or "Was the parent actually exercising their custody rights?" There are no guidelines that dictate the role of a child's attorney in a Hague Convention case. Therefore, you will need to ask the court to provide a very clear order of appointment so that you have no issues with access to the child, the child's records, or collaterals. If the Hague Abduction case is brought in state court, the judge may default to any guidelines for counsel in custody cases. If it is brought in federal court, then the judge may not know what to do and may rely on you in exercising your discretion as the child's attorney.

§2.09 REPRESENTING SIBLINGS

A lawyer cannot represent a client if representing that client will be directly adverse to another client.[10] When two siblings wish to "achieve fundamentally

---

10. Model Rule 1.7 of the Rules of Professional Conduct states the following:

(a) Except as provided in paragraph (b), a lawyer shall not represent a client if the representation involves a concurrent conflict of interest. A concurrent conflict of interest exists if:

(1) the representation of one client will be directly adverse to another client; or

(2) there is a significant risk that the representation of one or more clients will be materially limited by the lawyer's responsibilities to another client, a former client or a third person or by a personal interest of the lawyer.

(b) Notwithstanding the existence of a concurrent conflict of interest under paragraph (a), a lawyer may represent a client if:

(1) the lawyer reasonably believes that the lawyer will be able to provide competent and diligent representation to each affected client;

(2) the representation is not prohibited by law;

incompatible outcomes," then a lawyer cannot represent both as an advocate. The lawyer may be able to represent the siblings' best interests if their attorney can adequately protect both of their best interests.[11] A lawyer cannot continue representing a child if the lawyer would be materially limited in advocating for a position because of a duty of loyalty to another client. The nuance, when representing children, is whether there is any potential conflict when you are representing the child's best interests and the siblings have voiced different positions to you. The ABA Standards do not believe this presents a conflict of interest, but this situation nonetheless warrants care and caution. It will often require additional consults with the children (together and separate), consults with additional collateral witnesses, and an even more careful review of the materials, particularly if the siblings' positions differ dramatically or their reasons for the differing positions are more muddled or controversial. Ultimately, the best interest attorney will advocate what is best for the children, collectively and individually, but needs to provide sound evidence as to the position the best interest attorney will take on behalf of the children.

a. Working with Another Child's Attorney

Your child client's sibling may have his or her own separate legal counsel. Although you may have similar goals (to protect the children) and similar approaches to the other lawyer, you are not co-counsel. Thus, you need to be certain you do not share your client's confidences with that lawyer. It may seem counterintuitive at points in the case and may be counterproductive at times, but your ethical obligations do not yield to camaraderie with counsel for the other child.

§2.10 GETTING PAID FOR YOUR WORK

Unless your jurisdiction provides for direct payment from the court, county, or local government, you will need to ensure that appropriate provisions are made for your payment between the parties in the case. Ideally, you would like to have all payments clearly addressed in your order of appointment,

---

(3) the representation does not involve the assertion of a claim by one client against another client represented by the lawyer in the same litigation or other proceeding before a tribunal; and

(4) each affected client gives informed consent, confirmed in writing.

11. Rule 1.7 of the ABA Model Rules of Professional Responsibility specifies to what conflict of interests rules a lawyer should adhere. The ABA Standards for representing children in custody cases also addresses the conflict of interest issue at ABA Standards IVA2.

including any retainer obligation between the parties, the rules you must follow in billing and applying said retainer, your obligation for providing billing statements or invoices, whether you may delay the start of your work to wait for the retainer, your hourly rate, the percentage each party pays to you, what steps you may take or rights you have to obtain additional supplemental retainers or payment of outstanding balances, and some type of guarantee that any unpaid balance will be entered as a judgment against the parties.[12] Some states have statutes requiring child's attorneys to report at periodic intervals to the paying party or the court as to their work, fees, and costs.

a. Fee Sharing Between the Parents

If your child client's parents are obligated to pay you for your time, your fees will be divided in some proportion between them. If one parent bears the larger burden of the retainer or fees, they may feel entitled to use more of your time. If the parents share equally in your fees, the parent who is more concise, has fewer concerns, or spends less time with you may feel slighted and argue that they should not cover half of your fees and not get half of your time. You have no obligation to commit equal time to both parents. You do have an obligation to commit *adequate* time to both parents to ensure you gather sufficient information to represent your child client. Practically speaking, it is easier to work with parents when they believe that their voices are being heard. At times, parents see you as a judge more than another attorney in the case. Although some lawyers, parents, and even judges will refer to you as a neutral in the case, you are not necessarily "neutral"—you are child-focused. You may take a position on behalf of your child client, either in the child's best interests or what the child states as a preference. This position will place you at odds with one, if not both, parents. Your positions may hold more weight than a parent's preference in the court process because you come at the issue from the child's perspective, not the parent's perspective.

b. Potential Bias If Paid by One Parent

If one parent pays 100 percent of your legal fees, that parent may feel as if they have a right to dictate your ultimate position and the work you do to get to that position. The parent is, however, not your client. When you represent adult clients, they may have a third person pay their retainer. That third person may believe they have a right to call you and dictate terms, provide

---

12. *See* Appendix 3C for a sample motion for fees and Appendix 2 for sample appointment orders.

information, and get information from you. When you represent a child, the person who is paying you is most likely a party in the case, not some third person who may be more nuisance than stakeholder.

c. Nonpayment

Your order of appointment needs to be clear on fees. If it is not, file a prompt motion to alter or amend the order asking for clarification on your fees. It is important for the parties to understand their financial obligations, but also for you to be able to collect your fees should a parent not pay. The clearer the order, the better opportunity you have to be fully paid. Be certain to check your state statute and court rules that may dictate how you are paid, as well as your reporting obligations. You may be obligated to keep monthly invoices. There may be requirements as to the level of detail you include in your billing statements. You may need to file attorney fee affidavits or motions with the court to request payment of your fees. You may need to register with the county or local business authorities to be able to receive payment. Be certain to ensure clarity from the outset so that you are able to collect your fees throughout the case, or ensure collection when the case concludes.

d. Dischargability of Fees in Bankruptcy

The majority view of bankruptcy courts is that fees for a child's attorney should not be discharged in bankruptcy. Courts have traditionally read 11 U.S.C. § 523 (the exceptions to bankruptcy discharge) fairly liberally to include fees for a child's attorney within the exceptions.[13]

§2.11 COMMUNICATION WITH PARENTS

a. Self-Represented Parents

If a parent is self-represented, that parent may see you as his or her own lawyer. They will ask you legal questions. They will rely on you in negotiations. In some cases, self-represented parents may be confused about your role, may try to avoid you if the court has ordered them to pay you, may refuse to return your calls, and leave your e-mails unanswered. If you have two self-represented parents and you are the only lawyer in the case, the court may place a higher burden on you when presenting the case at trial.

---

13. *See In re* Blaemire, 229 B.R. 665 (1999).

You must ensure evidentiary rules are followed, issue subpoenas and discovery, and present all the facts proving the case to the judge. Although this is your obligation regardless, if there are other attorneys involved in the case, they typically cover some, if not much, of what you would otherwise present, thereby lightening your load. Do not rely on other lawyers to do your job.

You need to be extremely careful when speaking with a self-represented parent, particularly because you are *not* their lawyer. You should take all steps to protect yourself, such as having another person sit in on any meeting, whether it is another attorney or staff. Typically, your first meeting with a parent is in person, whether that parent is self-represented or has counsel. If that parent has counsel, be certain to include counsel in this first meeting or obtain written permission to meet with the parent without their counsel. This initial meeting is more the parent imparting information to you, rather than you providing information to the parent. After the initial meeting and your subsequent independent investigation, you should get to a point where you would like to negotiate some type of settlement for your child client. You should consider negotiating with both parents simultaneously so that both parents hear the same thing from you and do not mistake or misinterpret your positions. You may also want to try to do this in writing. A highly emotional parent may feel that you are attacking them when you are simply questioning them, presenting options, and trying to resolve a good holistic outcome.

I recognize it is not always possible to communicate with both parents together at all points in time after your first fact-gathering meetings. You may have to deviate from this protocol once or twice when both parents are self-represented, live in distant parts of the city, refuse to communicate with one another, or are difficult to reach, but who nonetheless seem to want to resolve matters. You may need to have phone calls with both parents separately, trying to negotiate a final solution (knowing they did not read their e-mail, lost their cell phone, did not pay their Internet bill, and would not or could not go to the local library). You should consider drafting carefully crafted settlement documents and spend the necessary time and effort mailing them back and forth with elaborate cover letters covering your ethical obligations. It is not typically advisable to negotiate with self-represented parents one-on-one, without any record or observer, and without the other parent present. However, there are rare situations where finances, time restrictions, or other extenuating factors may make these one-sided meetings necessary.

Give significant thought to everything you do, write, and say before communicating any information.

At times, mediation skills may help when working with self-represented parents. You are not necessarily a neutral because you are counsel and will be taking some position on behalf of your child client, but you can give the same caveats and warnings that are given at the beginning of a mediation session, cover the same ethical principles in the initial letter you send to both parents, and reiterate the principles again and again, verbally (with witnesses) and in writing. Try to remain transparent and do as much as you can with everyone together, to the extent this is possible. With the blessing of both sides, you may act as scribe when they have reached an agreement.

Be certain to review the ABA Model Rules of Professional Conduct, Rule 4.3 on Dealing with Unrepresented Persons.[14] The presumption is that an unrepresented person, particularly if the person is not experienced with legal matters, may easily misunderstand the lawyer's role, believe the lawyer may have some allegiance to them, or assume the lawyer is disinterested, even when that lawyer represents another person in the case. You cannot give legal counsel to a self-represented litigant. You need to be extremely cautious as to what you say to a self-represented litigant, out of concern they may misunderstand you, believe you are representing their interests, or feel compelled to agree to something without understanding the law and their own interests.

b. Parents with Lawyers

Be certain to inform everyone, from the outset of your role in the case, that you will not communicate directly with a represented parent unless that parent's lawyer has given you permission to do so *in writing*. Be careful to not draw an inference against a parent when a lawyer refuses to give you permission. There are a variety of reasons for granting direct contact with their client or not, ranging from cost to the lawyer simply wanting to be kept abreast of all that is ongoing.

---

14. Model Rule 4.3 says "In dealing on behalf of a client with a person who is not represented by counsel, a lawyer shall not state or imply that the lawyer is disinterested. When the lawyer knows or reasonably should know that the unrepresented person misunderstands the lawyer's role in the matter, the lawyer shall make reasonable efforts to correct the misunderstanding. The lawyer shall not give legal advice to an unrepresented person, other than the advice to secure counsel, if the lawyer knows or reasonably should know that the interests of such a person are or have a reasonable possibility of being in conflict with the interests of the client."

A potential problem you may encounter is when a lawyer does not give you written permission to speak directly one-on-one with his or her client, but the client keeps reaching out to you. This may happen for a variety of reasons, but most commonly if the client is trying to save on costs. Periodically, clients may also be unhappy with their own lawyer and want your help in convincing their lawyer of some settlement arrangement or course of action. Regardless of the reason, the answer is simple and clear—you are not the parent's lawyer. You are prohibited from communicating with the parent if that parent is represented.

This ethical dilemma becomes more apparent when you visit your child client at a parent's home, and the parent is present. Rarely, if ever, will their lawyer be present. It is awkward, artificial, and uncomfortable if their lawyer is there. It is not uncommon that the parent will pull you aside during this meeting, even if the meeting is only to speak with your child client, and share information with you. Be sure to again remind the parent of your ethical obligations, then report directly to the parent's lawyer afterward as to what had happened.[15]

§2.12 COMMUNICATION WITH THIRD PARTIES/COLLATERALS

You are rarely going to get the best information from parents or your child client. Parents have an agenda. They are emotionally involved; although their story may be accurate, it is also shared through their own emotional lens and own recollection of how they felt when things occurred. Children communicate differently than adults. Some child clients may be preverbal. Some child clients may have been manipulated or have social, emotional, or mental health issues that shade their communication. You would have to be an extraordinarily skilled professional to truly comprehend everything a child client is sharing. You will typically be unable to understand the full story without background information to provide context and to help you weigh the words of everyone else. Some collateral witnesses are more helpful than others. Some may mirror the emotion shared by a parent. Some may use the exact words a parent uses. You must always clarify the source

---

15. Model Rule 4.2 of the ABA Model Rules of Professional Conduct states "[i]n representing a client, a lawyer shall not communicate about the subject of the representation with a person the lawyer knows to be represented by another lawyer in the matter, unless the lawyer has the consent of the other lawyer or is authorized to do so by law or a court order."

of the collateral's information. Some of my collateral interviews are very short because there is relatively little that they have personally observed in the child or family's life. Typically, the best collaterals are those without any agenda—teachers, doctors, therapists, etc.

a. Finding Collaterals

Some collaterals are easily identifiable. If a child is of school age, they will have teachers and guidance counselors. They may have daycare providers, nannies, or babysitters. They will have friends (and their friend's parents), neighbors, coaches, instructors, and other adults instructing their life.

My first source of referrals is my child client's parents. I ask for names of schools, then I reach out to the principal to ask if they could connect me with teachers and guidance counselors. (I have also needed to speak with attendance keepers and school nurses.) I ask for names of therapists, doctors, and other medical professionals. I ask for the parents to give me a list—no matter how long—of people who can help me "parse through the issues in the case and get to know the family better." I ask the parents to prioritize the people on the list with the people who have the most relevant information and most personal observations listed at the top, in case I run out of time to call every single person. I want to call the most helpful people first. I will typically ensure I touch base with everyone on the list, unless it is impossible. If I ultimately take a position that is contrary to the position of one or both parents, the parents find it easier to swallow if they know I spoke to the people they believe are important.

I will talk to my child client about the people on their parents' lists, unless doing so would upset the child or be counterproductive. I will typically ask my child client about who may have information to share with me to help me. Sometimes, the child may ask me to speak with their friends—something that I have never done, and would not consider doing, without a discussion with that friend's parent. Whenever I speak with a collateral, I also tend to ask them with whom I should speak to give me more information.

b. What Are You Looking For?

Ask any collateral open-ended questions from the beginning of your conversation, and stress that you would like to know their personal observations. There may be some collateral witnesses who will have specific details (whether it be of a parent's drinking, a family fight, a medical problem, or something else). Some collaterals will have an agenda—they are a parent's friend or grandparent—and will try to plead their allegiance by describing the family's situation in similar, if not identical, words as the parent with whom they are aligned.

I always tend to find "neutral" collaterals to be the most useful. When I say a person is "neutral," I mean they are typically in the family's existence solely for the child client. These collaterals include pediatricians, daycare providers, teachers, or coaches. They will have the best personal observations and be most factual. Other collaterals, you will find, often share information that is mostly, if not entirely, from one of the parents.

Do not be discouraged if you reach out to a collateral and the only information you get is that your child client is "doing well." You may go into your investigation expecting a scathing report that helps you damn one parent, but reports of a happy and/or healthy child client are wonderful and tell you just as much about the family situation.

When you talk to collaterals, if you find they are useful or have important information, you should broach the topic of them testifying at trial or in a *de bene esse* deposition. It is never too early to put this idea in their head, in a very sensitive way. Even if your trial date is several months away, you may say, "Thank you so much for sharing this information. From what you said, I think a judge would be very interested in also hearing this information. If I need you to speak directly to the judge at the trial, would you be able to come to court?" If the collateral is within your jurisdiction, you can issue them a subpoena to have on file with their employer. You can give them the trial dates and see what date of trial is best for them, so you know whether you may need to request permission to take this witness out of order at trial. It may be that another lawyer would like to call this witness as well, and may have already discussed testifying with the witness, but never plan on another lawyer doing your job.

c. Inquisitive Collaterals

Without fail, at least one collateral per case will ask you about the details of the case. The most common question you will receive is a question asking what the judge is likely to do with the child. Some collateral witnesses will ask what another person already told you. You may get concerned when a collateral appears to be far too invested in a case that is not their own. Often, it will be your child client's grandparents who involve themselves in this manner. Typically, these same collaterals are also the people who call the pediatricians, want to sit in on meetings between the parent and you, and are perhaps also covering the retainer for their child in their child's custody case. Sometimes, a nanny may ask about the potential outcome, and this may be more out of concern for their job security. Teachers may ask the outcome, or other questions, to gauge just how much trouble this family may be in the future. Be hesitant to provide details to collaterals. The details are not typically confidential in any way. Be concerned about how the collateral may use the information or whether they may distort the information in some way and create additional issues where there were none. Politely deter the collateral; thank them for all of their help and for supporting the child in this difficult time. Never opine on the outcome of a trial. Instead, promise that you will do your very best to gather information so that the judge can make the best decision for the family.

d. Noncooperative Collaterals

Often, a collateral will insist that they will not speak with you unless you can guarantee some confidentiality between the two of you, or you will promise to not call that person as a witness at trial. You cannot promise either thing. You may question, however, why the person is insisting on these promises. Do they simply have a concern about taking sides, or are they genuinely scared to confront the person about whom they will speak ill? What does their concern tell you about the key individuals in the case and the impact of these adults on your child client? Assure the collateral that you are not asking the person to take sides or even speak ill of anyone. You are merely asking them to provide personal observations, not opinions.

It is not uncommon that therapists will be concerned about speaking with you unless they have all the requisite paperwork to guarantee they have the necessary permissions and releases. Start this process early. It is also common for teachers and schools to shy away from speaking to you. Nearly half of the schools to which I reach out have no idea there is a custody case ensuing. The school is surprised when I first make contact with them. For the other half, the family tends to be so overly acrimonious that the school has the family on their radar; the school may be concerned about speaking to a lawyer because the next step is typically being subpoenaed to court to speak to a judge. They are nervous about how this will affect their school (finding substitute teachers, disrupting schedules, etc.), and they are nervous about how this may affect their future ability to interact with this child, who will inevitably remain at this school, at least for the immediate future.

Initiate contact with the schools (the current school and past schools) by reaching out to the principals with your order of appointment, simply identifying your involvement, and asking if any of the teachers or guidance counselors may have insight into your child client's day, routine, and well-being. I have volunteered to go to the school to meet with people (including my child client) and try to work with the school to not overwhelm the staff at key times in the year (first day of school, midterms, winter break, summer break, etc.). If the school refuses to speak with you and refuses to provide any documents, issue a subpoena for documents and review the school records. Speak with beforecare and aftercare providers. Speak with your child client's friends' parents. See if you can get the same information without pursuing the school. If you cannot, subpoena key individuals from the school for deposition or trial. Ask the parents and other collaterals whom at the school may have the most pertinent interaction with your child client.

e. Sharing Information from Collaterals

I have no obligation to report back to the parents or their counsel after every conversation I have with a collateral. My conversations with collaterals are, for the most part, not confidential, and I have no problem sharing the information. I will never share my personal notes that I keep from each conversation with a collateral. I insert comments on demeanor, impressions, and my own thoughts and questions into my notes—things I consider my work product. However, I will happily field phone calls from lawyers or parents to discuss my conversations with collaterals (except for those who do hold a confidential relationship with my child client, such as a therapist). I make very clear and comprehensive notations about all the people with whom I speak when I provide descriptions in my billing statements. I will, periodically, send an e-mail to everyone simply noting the people with whom I have spoken and asking if there are additional collaterals with whom I should speak. I will offer my availability to schedule a call with counsel to discuss the collaterals and my conversations with them.

If a collateral provides a very specific concern, I may reach out directly to counsel immediately afterward to discuss. For example, I had a principal express significant concern about a mother and her interaction with that principal, and the mother's threats to sue the school. The principal was very defensive and was, perhaps, arguing their case against the mother's presumptive lawsuit to me. I reached out to the mother's counsel immediately after that call to alert them to this concern, and to my concern that the mother's negative interaction with my child client's school may be affecting my child client.

Why do I reach out to counsel to update them on my conversations with collaterals when I have no obligation to do so? The parents are likely paying me for this investigation. Sharing information will help push negotiation forward. Sharing information could provoke a conversation that shows where I should look for more information. I am also not subject to discovery, so sharing information is, in many ways, my attempt to prepare everyone for what may come out at trial. Hopefully by being transparent and helping everyone see the larger picture, I can reach a more comprehensive resolution for the child client.

I also share information with my child client about my conversations with the collaterals. Be cautious that you do not distress your child client and that you reflect things accurately, and in a sensitive way, to your client. If I can have a good conversation with my child client, it may help them remember additional important things that could help me present a better case.

f. Expert Third Parties

Your case may require an expert to consult and possibly testify. One of the most frustrating parts of being a child's attorney is the lack of funds to retain experts. You will need to use court-provided resources, you may need to request that the parents contribute to the cost voluntarily, or you may need to file a motion with the court and request that the court order funds to permit you access to an expert. The most common expert with whom I need to consult is a child psychologist. Even if I am not seeking a full evaluation of the parties or my child client, I may need to ask questions, such as, "Why is my child client doing this?" or "How do I ask my child client about Y?" or "I am thinking about a schedule for my child client, but what is the best schedule for a child of this age when the parents live X miles apart, and have these particular communication issues?"

§2.13 SCOPE OF APPOINTMENT

a. Appointment Orders Versus Child Hiring Attorney

Ideally, an attorney for a child is appointed by the court and is appointed early in the case. A court order provides for more authority, more power, and more guarantees for a child's attorney. It will often streamline processes for the attorney to seek information independently of a subpoena, have access to child protective services files, and be able to access otherwise privileged information. It will provide more guarantees (or at least a mechanism for enforcement or contempt) that the attorney will have access to the minor child. It will typically also have provisions for payment in the case. The lawyer's appointment should not be seen as a substitute for other investigatory services, such as a custody evaluation, a child protective services investigation, or law enforcement investigation.

There may be situations when a child has the need for an independent attorney when a court-appointed attorney might be unsuitable. If a parent is calling the child as a witness at trial, the child may need an attorney to prepare the child for the court proceeding. In some jurisdictions, once a child reaches a threshold age, the child can seek a custody determination on his or her own accord. In those situations, the child may wish to consult counsel. Older children are savvy enough to know that when people engage in court proceedings, they have lawyers. The child, however, will no doubt have little to no ability to find a competent lawyer, get him or herself to the lawyer, reach out to the lawyer to schedule an appointment, or fund their own representation. The Internet makes a lot of the child's research more easily accessible. In addition, because more children now than ever before are part of custody disputes, children often have more than one friend who can provide feedback to the child about working with a lawyer or participating in the process.

If you, as a lawyer, are contacted directly by a child, the first question that may come to mind is, "Is this really driven by the child, or is it driven by the parent?" or "Is this e-mail ghostwritten by a parent pretending to be a child to ask questions of me?" More common than not, a parent may reach out to you after their older mature child has expressed certain concerns to them, such as not wanting to visit the other parent. In jurisdictions, such as Maryland, that permit a child of a particular age to file a custody action in certain situations, there may be more opportunity for you to have this type of fact pattern walk through your office door.[16]

Be certain that you review your order of appointment as soon as you receive it. If it lacks clarity or does not specify your role, authority, payment, and the duration of your appointment, you may want to seek the court's

---

16. Md. Code Ann. Fam, Law 9-103 permits a child, age 16 or older, which is already subject to a custody order, to file a petition to change custody. The action may be filed in the child's name.

intervention to clarify these points in an amended order. The order should be clearly drafted so that a third party, such as a daycare provider, coach, school, or doctor, can easily understand your role and their obligations to provide guidance to you. If you begin work under an order of appointment and you find the order is insufficient—for example, you were appointed to represent a child for a very limited purpose, but that role needs to be expanded as you have learned more about the situation—you may need to file a motion with the court asking the court to clarify or expand your order of appointment.

Your jurisdiction may include, in its order of appointment, a mandate that the child be made available to you, or you have access to certain information, confidential, privileged, or otherwise. Some jurisdictions may provide for this access by way of a second complementary order. Regardless, it is important for a child's attorney to have such access by way of court order, if the law of your jurisdiction permits it.

b. Nonappointed Attorney's Role

If a child reaches out to you directly, or that child's parent brings the child to meet with you as the child's attorney, recognize you may be met with challenges, from securing payment to being seen as a "hired gun" to not having access to certain court or other records. Recognize you may have no authority to intervene in the case, and if you do, you need to secure the court's permission to intervene on behalf of the child. If you cannot intervene, you will be in the periphery of the court proceedings in many ways. You will not have guaranteed access to collaterals, teachers, doctors, or even the child. You will have no guarantee of payment. You may be reliant on the child's parent (if a parent supports the child's representation by counsel) to facilitate access, financing, and meetings. This may make you too reliant on that parent and give that parent power (or the expectation of influence) they should not have.

Tread carefully if the child hires you directly. Without a court order providing you with access to information or the ability to intervene in the court case, you may have limited ability to adequately advise your child client and may ultimately prove more harmful to the overall process than helpful. Without any ability to independently verify the child's assertions and potentially receiving only limited information, you may have an unintentional bias or an incomplete picture when you ultimately advocate for the child. If you take on this role, you will be representing the child's stated position, not their best interests. Your own client, however, may be unable to provide releases for you to obtain information or the legal standing for you to participate in the case. In that regard, you may ultimately serve as a mere educator and advisor to the child to help him or her understand the process. Be certain to not overstep your role.

c. Addressing Noncustody Issues (e.g., Child Support)

Know your limitations as a child's attorney. If you are appointed to represent a child in a custody case, then your appointment may be limited to only the custody case; it may not give you the bandwidth or permission to address ancillary issues, such as child support. In my jurisdiction, I have no authority to address child support. However, there have been situations where my child client has expressed significant concern about being able to continue in an expensive activity, and I may express a position to counsel that the parents should facilitate my client's participation in the future. If there is a companion case, such as a Hague Abduction case, a protective order case, or a child support case—all of which will affect your child client, but will not be addressed by a custody court and are outside of the scope of your appointment order—you should research whether your jurisdiction will permit (or require) your involvement in any way. Your involvement may simply be to educate your client and to work with the parents in negotiations to settle certain issues, and not to work within the court process itself. If the court permits your participation in the companion action or to address the issues that are before the court alongside the custody issue, know the law, and be assertive in asking the court to ensure you have a clear order of appointment that covers precisely what is needed to facilitate your expanded involvement, including your additional fees, and your access to additional information, records, and people.

d. Appeals

You need to understand whether your appointment as a child's attorney mandates participation in any appeal and whether you are permitted to file an appeal on behalf of your child client if you feel one is appropriate and necessary to protect your client. Furthermore, if the child's attorney is not an appellate attorney and feels incompetent to handle an appeal, that attorney must seek to be replaced or discharged. You will need to properly educate your child client if an appeal is filed or the child wants to file an appeal. Ensure the child understands the delay, timeline, obligations, and limitations, as well as the possibility for remand and perhaps another trial.

e. Terminating Your Appointment

I have, on occasion, been appointed by a court to represent a child client, with the notation that I need not begin work until a retainer is paid. If a parent refuses to pay the retainer, I am stuck in a position of either asking the court to vacate my order of appointment or to enforce the terms of the order and mandate payment of my retainer. I typically file a motion that requests both as alternative outcomes.

In Maryland, my appointment as a child's attorney ceases after 30 days from the entry of the final custody order (and this is spelled out clearly in my order of appointment). After the 30 days passes, I am then done. I may never hear from the family again. Periodically, I will receive a piece of mail from the court, evidencing to me that the family is back to modify or enforce the custody order. It is rare for the court to reappoint a child's counsel a second time if the family returns at some point in the future.

At times, I have been appointed for a more minimal role for the child (in Maryland, you can be appointed merely to waive or not waive the child's therapeutic privilege); then, I learn that a different attorney was appointed a few years later for the child to advocate on their behalf at all hearings. Is this in the child's interest? Should any child who was represented by counsel, by default, continue to have counsel when new issues arise in the future? Who pays for this ongoing attorney role? Should the child always have the same lawyer with whom they will work, or is it acceptable to have an attorney in one stage of the case, and then another attorney years later when the family is back in court? How does this affect the child? Should the attorney ensure the child knows to reach out to the lawyer in the future if something has happened? What obligation or authority does a child's attorney have, in the future, to approach the court to be reappointed if they know the case has reopened?

If my child client is old enough to use e-mail or text message, I will ensure they know how to reach me directly. I will never refuse to return a call or message from a child client, even years after my representation/appointment has ended. I have been fortunate that no child client has reached out to me more than a month or two after the case concluded. If the child reaches out to me a year or two later, I will need to weigh what next step I must take. I may speak with the child and then reach out to the parents' lawyers (or former lawyers) or to the parents directly. If the child shared concerning information, however, I may need to reach out to someone different—child protective services, the police, a teacher—or even review my jurisdiction's rules as to whether I have the ability to file something in court on behalf of the child client (and request that my fees be paid and I am reappointed as counsel). Some jurisdictions permit any competent adult to file for a protective order or some other necessary action on behalf of a minor. Some do not.

§2.14 Other Lawyers Working with the Child's Attorney

If you work in a law firm, it is common for you to work alongside another attorney whenever you handle a difficult case, particularly one that is in litigation. You may need help preparing witnesses and exhibits, drafting briefs, arguing motions, or with any other variety of tasks. If you represent a child, you may need help from a colleague within your firm. You may need a lawyer to be available should you be traveling. You may need help with briefing a particularly complicated issue. The question will be to what extent may that co-counsel be involved if they are not the appointed attorney in the court's order. To what extent will that attorney expose you to malpractice claims or liability if they do not meet the criteria, set by the court or jurisdiction, to represent a child? How will another adult's involvement affect the child in this case?

There may also be times when you want an observer to be present when you meet with your child client or with either parent, such as a paralegal or secretary. You may plant this person with the intention that if something happens, you feel protected by having a witness to the other person's bad acts, or a witness that you did not perform any bad acts of which you may be accused. You need to weigh the impact of this person on the situation, including if your child client has this additional person involved in their life. You will also need to weigh putting this person in the crosshairs of being called to testify in court as to what the mother said or father did during any given meeting.

If your jurisdiction permits you to involve another attorney as co-counsel in your child client's representation, even if that co-counsel is not named in the order of appointment, you will need to delegate the tasks appropriately to this other attorney. You will want to ensure that the child understands this attorney's role if this other attorney meets with the child. You will want to ensure you do not act in a manner that confuses or concerns the child by including another individual in their life. If this attorney is not designated in the court's order of appointment, then that attorney's ability to speak with collaterals (e.g., doctors, therapists, social workers, child protective services investigators) will be limited because the order of appointment often gives permission for third-party collaterals to speak with you.

A co-counsel attorney may best be able to help by organizing the file, drafting pleadings, doing research, finding resources, and being a sounding board. If you are the court-appointed attorney, it is your responsibility to ensure that this child's interests are met. It is your job to ensure the child is not confused or put in a difficult situation by having two adults involved, instead of one. Having another attorney on which you can rely is extremely useful; however, in practice, it should be more limited, and more in the periphery, than in a typical litigation case. You must also understand your jurisdiction's ethical rules in supervising others within your firm, particularly in a case like this when they have no court order dictating their work with this child client.

§2.15 COMMON SENSE

When I represent a child, there are some basic, commonsense rules that need to be followed. It may make your job a little more difficult. It may mean involving additional people. It may mean more expense and inconvenience to you and others, but they are good practices you should follow.

a. Do Not Drive Your Child Clients in Your Automobile

I do not want to be the person responsible for my child client if I am in a car accident. I refuse to drive my child clients anywhere. This means driving out of my way to see them. It means having a parent possibly hovering nearby while you meet with your child client. It might mean you need to get creative. I simply do not want to risk being behind the wheel if the unthinkable happens.

b. Do Let Someone Know Where You Are When You Do Home Visits

I always try to schedule times to see my child client in their home environments, where they may act more naturally (or, if they do not act more naturally, then that, in and of itself, tells you something). Even if I am visiting with a child client in the nicest, most affluent, suburb, I always tell a family member or friend the address where I will be going, the time I will be going to that address, and approximately how long I think I may be at that address. If something was said or done in the case before my home visit that causes me additional concern, I may even check in with the family or friend when I arrive and check in again when I leave, with instructions on what to do (i.e., call the police) if I do not check in within a certain timeframe of when my home visit should have ended. I may even use a cell phone app (e.g., Glympse) that will use GPS to send my location to another individual for a period of time I choose.

c. "Pushing" Parents to Settle—Playing the Strong Arm

I always am careful to not push anyone to settle. A settlement should be free, voluntary, and uncoerced. However, I am aware of the fact my voice in this process has some weight, I may have information that no one else has, and I will ultimately take a position on behalf of my client (whether it is their own position or my best interest analysis). I am also aware of the fact that settling a case is nearly always what is best for the child. Therefore, there are times when I do use my influence in the case to push toward settlement. Do not be afraid to do so.

In some cases, things may be so clear-cut and my position so well defined that I will very clearly articulate it and do so as early as I am able. I will generate options. I will pursue options I believe are best for the child. I will volunteer to draft the parenting agreement or consent order. I will call for "two-way" meetings with the parents. I will push for alternative dispute resolution processes. You need to also recognize that you have a "dog in this fight." You are not a neutral—you are child-focused. Be careful that the parents and their lawyers do not mistake your role as that of a mediator, or else they will become concerned when you assert yourself because you did not set their expectations right or they misunderstood your role.

d. Do Not Be Your Child Client's Parent or Friend—You Are Their Attorney

You are an attorney. You are not the child's parent. If you see a parenting deficit, then you need to address it with the parent or the court or both. Although you are a counselor and advisor to the child, there is a line between that role and the role of a child's parent. If your child client is skipping school, should you tell him or her they are behaving badly? Maybe. If your child client is skipping school and then professes they are going to Harvard like their older sister, do you correct them and tell them that their bad behavior will make it difficult? At some point, your counseling becomes parenting—something may be lacking with your child client's actual parents. Be careful you do not cross the line into parenting your child. It could affect your relationship with your child client. They may be less candid with you. It is a difficult position. Each child and each circumstance will be different, so you need to weigh how best to reach your child client.

You should also not go entirely opposite of parenting the child client and act as if you are their friend. You are not their friend. They may treat you like a confidante. They may tell you things about friends, their significant others, their sexuality, their bullying, their grades, or their drug or alcohol use, which are well beyond what they would tell their parents. You will be bound by your ethical rules of disclosure (or nondisclosure). You will not want to breach their confidence in you. However, you are not their friend. You may support this child, but you may not condone everything they do. There may be times when you grow extremely fond of your child client. You may find yourself caring deeply for your child client and feeling very emotional over the circumstances in which they find themselves. These cases are difficult. You need to strike the right balance in your role.

e. How to Take a Position That May Have Less Negative Consequences for Your Clients at Home

It is extremely frustrating to know that, once you take a position on behalf of your child client, your child client may then go home and be put in a difficult situation. The child may be subjected to cross-examination about what they told you as their attorney. A parent or sibling may try to get your child client to recant what that parent or sibling believes the child client told you. A parent may punish your child client for what they perceive the child told you. It is very difficult to know that your child client will have to live with certain consequences after you take a position. If you take a position too early in the litigation process, it may favor settlement; however, it could also work against your child client and put them in the crosshairs for the rest of the case up through trial, with a parent trying to manipulate the child to influence the outcome of the case. If your child client's situation is very difficult, you should weigh whether you need to pursue some type of temporary relief on behalf of the child. If your child's situation is dire, then you hopefully have already pursued some temporary relief for the child (and if you have not, then do so).

You never can predict a parent's reaction. I have had child clients call me, crying hysterically, asking why I hate them and their mother/father so much. I have had child clients tell me they hate me for putting them through this situation. I would much rather have the child client say those things and direct those feelings toward me if that is what it takes for them to preserve their own situation and sanity.

If a court issues a final order, I always try to reach the child client first. I try to ensure that the child has some type of mental health services available to him or her before I start taking positions that may upset the status quo. I also reach out to the child's support network, including their teachers and guidance counselor, and ask them to watch out for the child and contact me if the child may behave oddly, miss school, be sick, have a slide in their grades, etc.

f. Know the Law—You Should Not Advocate for a Position Unless That Position Has a Basis in the Law

You are a lawyer. You do an investigation. You may take a position. You clearly have opinions on what you think may be happening with the family. You may have "gut feelings." You may even voice your opinions in settlement negotiations. If you have represented enough children, you will start to sound like a child psychologist when talking to counsel and parents in these cases. However, you are a lawyer. You present evidence to a court. You are not a witness. You are not an expert. You need admissible evidence to support the position you take on behalf of your child client. If you have a "gut" feeling about the father (or mother), find the evidence. It may take some more digging, but your gut feeling is not admissible in court.

g. You Are a Lawyer: No *Ex Parte* Communication, Even If You Are Court Appointed

Follow your ethics rules. This includes the rule against *ex parte* communication with the court. Even if the court has appointed you, you still must follow your ethical obligations.

h. Do Not Lose Your Cool, and Be Clear About Your Role as Child's Attorney

Without fail, in nearly every case where I represent a child, at least one of the other lawyers refers to me as a "neutral." When you represent a child, you are not neutral. You have positions and views and opinions. You will argue your case just like the other lawyers. Your positions may ultimately be contrary to one or both parents. It is a difficult place to be. In many ways, you have the same job as a judge, but rarely with the same protections. The lawyers will argue their cases to you, knowing your view may hold great weight in a judge's eyes. Lawyers may see you as arbitrator or mediator. If you have a settlement meeting, counsel and the parties may expect you to play the role of a neutral intermediary, trying to foster communication between the parties. To the extent you are able to do this without compromising your role as the child's advocate, then that is acceptable. However, do not let counsel fall into the trap of seeing you as a mediator. It will skew their views and expectations. When you begin asserting yourself and stating your opinion in the settlement meeting on behalf of the child client, you will inevitably upset someone, if not more than one person. They will feel attacked. Tempers may flare and voices may rise. Do your best to not engage in any yelling or screaming between the parties. Once voices rise, no one truly hears the message; your communication will be distorted or lost. Ensure that everyone knows if you hold a settlement meeting or a discussion, you have a role and that role is not as a neutral.

INVESTIGATION AND INFORMATION GATHERING 3

§3.01 INDEPENDENT INVESTIGATION ON BEHALF OF THE CHILD

A child's attorney is at a disadvantage in trying to assess where the truth lies. A parent or third party may have influenced the child (intentionally or unintentionally), therefore affecting the information the child shares with you. Perhaps the child is too young to verbally communicate. Perhaps one of the parents (or both) is prohibiting you from meeting or talking to your child client. Somehow, you must learn about this child, his or her life, and resolve to represent the child's interests when your own client may be unable or unwilling to provide valid and accurate information. (Note that even the "inaccurate" information you receive from your child client gives you a glimpse into their life and situation.)

When you represent a parent, the parent determines his or her goals after you counsel him or her. You then advocate for that position, whether you completely agree with it or not, all while competently counseling the client on options and outcomes. When you represent a child, you are playing in an entirely different ballgame. You are left with little direction. You have two parents, each pulling you in different directions. It is absolutely imperative you be permitted to conduct your own independent investigation, with cooperation from third parties and both parents, to reach a fair conclusion.

77

If a parent refuses to cooperate in sharing information, that refusal also gives you information about the child's situation.

a. Information Gathering from Papers and Documents

When you begin representing a child client, start by gathering information from the parents. They began this litigation. However, realize each parent has an agenda. Each parent has certain goals in this litigation. Therefore, just before speaking with either parent, review any documents. Obtain copies of your child client's school and medical records. You may have this authority under your order of appointment. In other jurisdictions, you may need to subpoena these records. In still other jurisdictions, you may need to rely upon the parents to subpoena or provide the documents. At this initial information gathering stage, do not forget to request that each school or medical provider fill in a business records certification. It is embarrassing and difficult to backtrack closer to trial and ask for this paperwork. Request documents early in your representation because many schools or doctors will take a while to compile the papers and send them to you. You do not want to be stuck one week from a trial date, unable to obtain documents. If your order of appointment permits you access to your client's records, then reach out to each school or doctor and provide a copy of your order. (More recently, I have done this by e-mail, but have also written formal letters and faxes.) Be certain to include both current providers and schools *and* past providers and schools.

The third party may be reluctant to provide documents. There may be concerns of HIPAA or privilege if there are medical records. The fact that you are a lawyer may frighten the third party into refusing to respond, or having his or her lawyer respond. If you must, petition your court for an order permitting you access to these records. Ensure the order is clearly written. Draft a proposed order for the court to help in this regard.

A slightly more difficult task is when you seek out a parent's records. In the most contentious of custody cases, it is not uncommon for at least one of the parents to have mental health, medical, or drug addiction issues. You may wish to see records verifying these conditions or explaining the treatment plan the parent is exercising (and whether they are following through with it). The treatment provider may require that any request for records come directly from the parent/patient. Consider asking the parent to sign a release form permitting you access to the records. If the parent provides you with copies of their records, question whether the parent is providing you with full records or is self-selecting the information you receive about his or her treatment. It may be possible to petition a court for these records and convince a judge of the records' utility, particularly because many jurisdictions include a parent's health as a factor in determining a child's best interests. Depending on the issues in the case at hand, you may find that a thorough interview of the parent will suffice, and you do not need any verifying records.

When you begin requesting records, get creative. Do not overlook beforecare, aftercare, summer camps, or other activities. It may be pertinent to know what parent signs a child in and out of an activity, or whether the activity maintains a log of the time the child checks in and out to assess whether a parent is routinely tardy. I have subpoenaed Uber and Lyft records when a father insisted that he used those means of ensuring his daughter got to school, but there were concerns that she was chronically late. Do not overlook mental health records. The law will vary by jurisdiction. In Maryland, as the child's attorney, I have the sole authority to waive a child's privilege with his or her mental health treatment provider and therefore have access to these confidential records. In other jurisdictions, however, I may need both parents to sign a waiver or release form to access the records.

Finally, do not overlook past treatment providers or schools. It is easy to focus on the child's current circumstances, which are, admittedly, most pertinent. However, requesting historical records may give you context to the child's life and potential issues, and help you pinpoint milestones for the child, particularly so you can see if the child is hitting benchmarks or has deviated from their norm.

Once you have the records, you are only through half of the battle. Many records will be incomprehensible, either because they are handwritten or because they address information that is well beyond your education and experience. You may need help understanding the records. Consult with a medical professional or other expert to help you decipher the records. Speak to the person who wrote the records to get a clearer picture of their content. Start the record gathering early in the process so that you have sufficient time to depose individuals, do informational interviews, or issue discovery.

b. Information Gathering from the Parents

My very first meeting is typically with each parent because they are in need of my help in resolving their custody issues. I need to understand the issues before the court. I typically hold these meetings in an office, whether it is my office or the parent's lawyer's office. I have even had initial meetings at the parent's office, if that suited my schedule, the parent's schedule, and was not out of the way. This first meeting is complicated by the fact that, if a parent is represented, you may not speak with him or her unless that parent is accompanied by his or her attorney *or* the attorney states, in writing, you are permitted to meet with their client without their presence.

When I go into a first meeting with a parent, I have often reviewed all the court pleadings and have some understanding of any existing custody order and legal positions that have been taken. I usually do no more research into the case than that, opting to let the parent educate me on what is important to the family and where I should focus my time. I insist each parent provide me, by the end of our first meeting, with a list of important people who I should contact to continue my investigation.

I start my parent meeting by asking very open-ended questions, such as, "What is going on?" It is very telling to listen to a parent direct the conversation toward what is important to him or her. You will get a solid sense of whether the parent is hyperfocused on the child or the other parent or some ancillary issue. I always ask the parent to talk to me about the child, including his or her interests. I need information so that when I meet with the child client, I can begin establishing rapport. I candidly ask parents what they believe will happen when I meet with their child for the first time. I ask what the parent has already told the child about me, if anything. I may need to suggest ways for the parent to talk about me to the child.

Usually at the end of the first meeting, I discuss schedules so that I have a concrete date when I can visit the parent's home, preferably with the child present. Although a home visit is not mandatory in my jurisdiction, and it may be impractical or impossible (due to distance, circumstances, or the child's existing custody schedule), seeing the child interact with his or her parent in their daily setting can speak volumes and provide much more information than any words the child says to me. Home visits present significant challenges in some ways. You are going to a stranger's house, encroaching on their territory, perhaps driving a significant distance (sometimes to an undesirable or dangerous neighborhood), and passing judgment on the home environment. Although custody evaluators may spend significant time scrutinizing the child's bedroom or whether there is a can of beer in the refrigerator, I focus less on those items and more on the interaction between child and parent on their home turf. I can usually size up a parent's home by a quick glance—is it clean, is it suitable, does the child have space to do homework and eat, and where does the child sleep? I do not like comparing one parent's home to the other parent's home. One parent may simply have more money than the other. A child may be equally happy (or happier) in a small home or an apartment.

When I visit a parent and their child at their home, I need to be respectful, courteous, and careful. I always tell someone, whether family or friend, the address where I will be, and I check in before and after my home visit. Although I have not yet had any problems during a home visit, I need to take all reasonable precautions when entering a stranger's home. When at the home, it is not uncommon to see other people. Many separated couples have to live with their parents or other relatives or have a roommate. In situations like this, I often like to see the child's sleeping accommodations—do they have to share a bed with another sibling, a parent, or a cousin? Depending on the child's age and gender, this may be relevant to your investigation. If there are other people in the home, who are they, and should I also speak to them (at the home visit and/or separately in a meeting)?

It can be awkward sitting around talking to the parent or child at the house because that often does not give you a sense of what is normal for the child. During my home visits, I have participated in homework, snack time, throwing a football in the backyard, preparing for swim lessons, family game time, cooking dinner, or any other routine activity for that family. I usually do a home visit shortly after the child arrives home from school, so as not to interfere too directly with dinner, homework, or bedtime. It is also one of those times of the day when it may be more difficult to fabricate the "ideal" environment—a child will come home exhausted, want a snack, want to decompress, throw their shoes by the front door, etc. There are times when the parent wants to sit down and talk to you, but I typically discourage that because I do not want the child to overhear adult conversations about the litigation. The child or parent often invites me into the child's bedroom, where I can ask the child to show me their toys, homework, or computer. Children often love to show off their environment. If they do not, you need to assess why. Is the child shy or embarrassed?

c. Maintaining Balance Between the Parents

When representing a child, one of the more difficult things is to ensure some type of balance in the information you are gathering. You may get an inaccurate understanding of the family if you speak primarily to one parent and their witnesses. It is important that your information gathering cuts across both parents somewhat equally. I qualify the word "equally" with the word "somewhat" because you will never be equal in the amount of time you spend with each parent. You will typically find one parent or his or her lawyer will call you much more, have more information to share, or have a tendency to communicate differently. You may end up visiting with your child client more when the child is with one parent than the other. Once you have sufficient information to start forming a position on behalf of your child client, it will be common for one of the parents to disagree with your assessment and start blaming you for spending more time with the other parent.

Another difficulty is determining what information you should share with the parents. It can be overwhelming to copy in a parent and their lawyer on every single piece of information you gather, or call or e-mail them after every conversation you have with a third person. I typically get to a point where I feel as if I have spoken with enough people and read enough documents that I can begin sharing what I have learned and drawing inferences about each parent and the child. At that point, I typically try to hold a conference call with both parents' lawyers. On that call, I usually speak very candidly about the information I have, where that information leads me, and what positions I am beginning to form. I also use that conference call to ask the lawyers where they believe I have a deficit in information, where else I should look, and to help me brainstorm ideas on the next steps in the case. My goal is always to try settling the case. Two agreeable parents are better than a custody trial. If one or both parents are unrepresented, it is usually difficult to have a joint conference call. In these cases, I may do separate calls with each side, understanding the risk in being blamed for exhibiting some bias or having each side hear my thoughts in a slightly different way.

Another consideration is cost. If one parent is paying you more money (whether by court order or not), the nonpaying parent may use that to his or her advantage and increase his or her communication with you. A self-represented litigant may try to use you as his or her own lawyer. A parent who has high legal bills from his or her own lawyer may try to plead with you and exclude their own lawyer, particularly if your hourly rate is lower. If one of the parents cannot pay you, or has failed or refused to pay you (even if court ordered to do so), it may be difficult to not appear to have some type of bias against that parent. If you must file a motion for that parent's contempt for failing to pay you under a court order, it may make it very difficult to get that parent to cooperate with you moving forward. I do not typically restrict a parent's communication with me. If that parent wants to share information and feels that the information is necessary to me having an informed position, I will listen. I am simply transparent with both sides that this is my process, and I do what I can to share all information I gather with both sides. If I must pursue fees during the course of litigation, I rarely take a side as to who should pay those fees, instead letting the parents argue over "bad faith" actions and who ran up the other's fees. I carefully review all of my bills and ensure everything is reasonable. I permit the parties sufficient time to ask questions about my bills before seeking payment through the court.

d. Information Gathering from Mental Health Professionals

Mental health professionals are one of the most important resources for a child's attorney. However, you are likely to hit the most obstacles trying to speak with or gather information from a mental health professional, unless the person was hired to conduct some type of forensic evaluation of the family. Your first line of defense is your order of appointment. The court order appointing you to represent your client *may* include provisions permitting you access to your child client's mental health professional. Even if it does, that court order still has limitations, such as if the mental health professional is out of state. Some mental health professionals will not speak with you or provide you information unless both parents sign releases/waivers. What happens if a parent refuses? Should you draw some negative inference from this refusal? Will your jurisdiction permit you to go to court and request a court order permitting you access?

I have also found that, even if you have access to the mental health professional, the treatment provider may still be unwilling to cooperate in providing information, either over a concern they could be sued, they could affect their patient's treatment, or they will be called to court as a witness. The mental health professional may begin asking you legal questions, even though you are not their lawyer. If you are fortunate enough to have a good treatment provider working with your child client, this person will be invaluable to discuss theories and observations. The person may provide much needed support for when you need to talk to your child client about the litigation, and for checking in to ensure your child client is processing things in a healthy way. I have even met with my child clients in their therapy sessions, with the therapist's approval and set guidelines for my involvement. If you are having difficulty with the child opening up to you, this may help.

There may come a time in a case where you feel that your child client's treatment provider is not providing the necessary support to the child, and the child would be better served working with a different professional.

You may need to discuss with the parents or their lawyers whether replacing the therapist is appropriate. There may also be a situation where your child client is not being treated at all, but you believe treatment may be helpful—not only for the child's well-being, but also for gathering information on the child's views and health. You will need to decide whether and how to interject on behalf of your client.

Another resource may be either parent's mental health treatment provider. It is unlikely you will have direct access to either parent's mental health records, even though, in most jurisdictions, both parents' health is a relevant consideration in determining a minor child's best interests. You may want to question both parents about any mental health ailments and their treatment regimen. If you have any concerns that a parent has a significant issue and, more importantly, that their issue is not being properly treated (or the parent is not following appropriate medical advice), you will want to ask the parent to provide information about their treatment and their follow through.

Depending on a parent's behavior and any concerns that may arise in your independent investigation, you will need to weigh whether to ask the court to order a psychological evaluation of a parent. If you ask the court to order a psychological evaluation, you must consider the cost. Your child client will be unable to pay and you, as their lawyer, may have no information about the parents' finances; therefore, you have limited ability to present information to the court that the family can ensure payment for this evaluation. Be sure to clearly articulate the type of evaluation you want the court to order and the purpose of it. If you have a mental health professional in mind who can provide such an evaluation, you should suggest this to the court. Also, recognize that evaluations may take time to complete. If you have a trial date, you will want to ensure the evaluator starts the process early enough to secure data that will be available by the trial date.

The best situation is for both parents to agree to some type of neutral evaluation and pay for it. If a child custody evaluation is being conducted, you need to weigh your role in the evaluation. You are counsel for the child, not a trial witness. You may have significant information from your own investigation. Whenever a custody evaluator is involved in my client's case, I speak with him or her. I try to gather information from the evaluator, and I may share information on the sources of my information. However, I do not share my opinion or position on the case. I also do not share the information I obtained from certain sources, in case I unconsciously share the information in a biased way. I do not want to affect the evaluator's neutrality. I also want to get independent information from the evaluator that confirms (or not) my thoughts on the case and family.

e. Information Gathering from Third-Party Witnesses

Besides mental health professionals, you need to review as many of the child's records as possible. The best-case scenario is when the records confirm that the child is doing well and not under any stress. The records, however, can pinpoint changes in the child's life. For instance, you might pinpoint a particular month when the child's grades slipped and be able to correlate that slip in grades with a stressor in the child's home life. Be sure to request historical records for the child, so you have a barometer as to the child's current well-being.

I routinely speak to people at my child client's school. I typically reach out to the principal shortly after being appointed, sharing a copy of my appointment order. I ask the principal if I can obtain copies of the child's records and be put in touch with the child's teachers, guidance counselors, and others who may have pertinent information (school nurses, attendance clerk, lunch monitor). Depending on the circumstances, I may go to the school and meet with several people on the same day, or I may simply speak with them on the telephone. A child may use school as a safe haven from a tumultuous home life, so it may not be evident to the school that the child is having any stress. I ask whether the child has an individualized education plan, any accommodations, any learning disabilities, or other issues. I ask about the child's socialization, interaction with his or her peers, and any negative (or positive) classroom behaviors. When I review the school records, I pay special attention to absences and tardiness.

I also routinely request my child client's medical records. In most cases, the medical records alone are of little value. I do not have a medical degree and cannot decipher some of the chicken-scratch in the records (although records are now more routinely typed). However, on occasion, the medical records are very important. They can show a pattern of the child's health issues, who cares for the child, and whether this child is going to have ongoing issues in the future, needs to be in proximity to good medical facilities, or needs to have a parent who is extra attentive to their medical needs. It may also give insight into the parents. If a parent accompanies the child to their medical appointments, the doctor or technician may record the parent's behaviors or comments directly in the record.

In my investigation, I often speak with other collateral witnesses who may have personal observations of the child, his or her siblings, and parents, such as the child's coaches. I may ask to speak with neighbors if the child is active in the neighborhood. I will typically want to speak with the child's friends' mother or father, who may, at times, be more of a surrogate parent to the child in times of stress. Grandparents, aunts, uncles, and other family members may have interesting observations. They may also have a vested interest in one parent obtaining custody over the other, so they have an inherent bias.

I also like to speak to stepparents and any other adult with whom the child may reside. In some households, the stepparent takes on more of a parenting role than the legal parent of the child client. It is important to understand the household dynamics. Stepparents may often mimic their spouse's position; however, on occasion, they have excellent personal observations of things the child has said or done when in their house that have given me that key piece of information to break through to my child client and understand their situation. Stepparents may have less personal investment in a particular access schedule between parent and child. Some stepparents may have a different view than their spouses over what schedule is best for the family as a whole. Your child client may have difficulties with the stepparent. It is not uncommon that a child may view their stepparent as stealing their parent, taking away too much of their parent's time and attention, bringing new children into the mix that compete with the child, or stepping too far into the role as the child's parent. In other situations, the child may actually trust the stepparent more than his or her own parents and confide in this stepparent, leaving that adult with more useful (and less biased) information than the parents.

No matter the collateral witness with whom I speak, I must be prepared to answer questions. The witnesses may ask what documents have been filed in court, what position each parent is taking, what will happen, and what I think a judge may do. Some collaterals, usually coaches or teachers, will ask advice: what to do if mom or dad behaves a certain way, what to do if they have witnessed the child acting oddly, whether to intervene if they see the parents fighting at a practice or recital, or what to say to the child if the child is crying or distressed. They may ask whether they are allowed to tell the child client we have spoken. I typically tell my child client, during my initial meeting, that I will be reaching out to people in their lives; if I know precisely who those people are, I will name them to the child client. Therefore, the child should not be surprised if their guidance counselor tells them I am speaking with them.

When receiving questions from the collateral, I will answer truthfully. I cannot give them advice. I am grateful for their support of my child client. If they have additional information to share, I would be grateful to receive it. Both parents are working hard to resolve this for the child, and the lawyers and judge will work equally as hard to figure out the situation. Avoid giving too much detail about the case, potential outcomes, court filings, etc. It may serve to create more stressors for the family when this collateral then goes to speak with one or both parents after your call. However, I typically bend this rule when speaking with a person who is treating my child client. I may need this person to understand more of the dynamic and the possible outcomes so they can help me work with the child and to prepare the child for the eventual trial and final order.

(i) *Case Study*

You represent a six-year-old boy. You receive a telephone call from your client's teacher, who tells you your child client is hitting classmates at school. The teacher is concerned about contacting the parents because they have lodged accusations against the teacher in the past, claiming she excluded one of them from meetings, information, and reports. The teacher wants to know what to do.

This is a difficult situation. You need to be completely clear with the teacher that you do not represent her. Most likely, her institution has legal counsel that can work with her with regard to the accusations the parents have been making. You need to refocus this teacher—she is giving you very important information pertinent to your child client's representation. She is giving you a glimpse into the parents' personalities and how they interact with one another and with important people in the child's life. She is also giving you information about the child. I would ask the teacher questions: What is causing her to be concerned about reaching out to the parents? What have the parents done in the past to cause this concern? How has the school had to address this issue in the past? How is this affecting the child? What is happening in the child's environment right before he hits a classmate? How has the child been interacting with classmates generally? Is there a pattern as to when the child acts out versus when he does not?

Continue to ask the teacher questions to gather data. You cannot advise her as to what step she must take, and I am cautious to not act as the conduit between a third party and the parents—that is not my job. However, the fact that a third party is putting me in this role indicates the parents need some process in place to help them communicate with one another (and, sadly, with third parties).

f. Information Gathering from Experts

What happens when a unique issue arises and you do not know where to turn? What happens if the parents' attorneys do not designate the necessary experts that you believe must be presented to the court? You may have the obligation to subpoena or call an expert as a witness if you feel that person is important to the judge's determination of your client's best interests. The major obstacle I have encountered is paying for an expert. A child's attorney needs to have an extensive network so that he or she has sufficient contacts to pick up a phone and ask some questions of appropriate professionals. Most of us have good colleagues who will spend a little time, at no cost, speaking about a case. However, we cannot expect our colleagues, however generous, to get involved in a case at no cost. Psychologists, foreign law experts, educational consultants, therapists, social workers, and a variety of other experts cost a lot of money. You may have to ask the parents to voluntarily pay for the experts' fees, or you may have to go to court and request the court order the parents to pay for the experts' fees.

If the expert is your expert, as counsel for the child, despite a parent paying the fee, the work product doctrine should still apply. You may feel pressure to disclose information from the expert to the parents, particularly the one who paid the expert. The expert may be unfamiliar with the work product doctrine and feel some allegiance to the paying parent. Be transparent with everyone from the outset. If this is your expert, protect their work product, unless required to disclose the information because you intend to call the expert as a witness at trial. During the negotiation process, you will likely share information from this expert, regardless of whether they will be a trial witness, in an effort to move the case toward settlement. However, if the expert is retained for you to consult on case strategy, this person is your consultant.

g. Obtaining Records

If your appointment order does not give you access to your client's records (e.g., school, medical, dental, therapeutic), subpoena the records or seek a specific court order for access to those records. Alternatively, if you trust either parent to obtain full and complete copies of your child client's records, you may also request the parents obtain the records. However, you will be beholden to their timeline, not yours. You also may not be certain the records are complete because the records arrived at your desk through a third party and not directly from the record keeper.

h. Information from Child Protective or Social Services

If you are representing a child when his or her parent is suspected of neglecting or abusing the child, there is likely a report with the state or county social services agency. Consult your state laws as to what access you are permitted to this report. At times, it may require a court order. In other instances, you may need to obtain the parents' written consent or release. You may need to go directly to the social services agency office and review the paperwork in the office. You may be limited in whether you can duplicate or use any of the papers in a trial. I have found it is typically a fruitful effort, but a lengthy process, to gain access to a social service case file. One of the first questions to ask of the parents, their lawyers, and any third party (particularly educators or medical professionals who may have an obligation to report any suspicion of abuse or neglect) is whether they are aware of any social service investigation. If you are familiar with the attorneys who work with social services in your jurisdiction (in one of my jurisdictions, it is the county attorney), reach out to that person at the very onset of your case to make an inquiry.

(i) *Case Study*

You are representing three siblings. The youngest child was, unfortunately, severely injured and suffered brain damage while in the care of his mother and her boyfriend about four years ago. Child Protective Services (CPS) investigated the mother and boyfriend and recommended the child be placed in the care of that child's father, with the mother's agreement. The two older children remained in her care. The mother has now filed a motion to modify custody, asking for custody of the youngest child. She says it is not in that child's best interests to be separated from his siblings. Dad claims that mom has "not cared" about the child for four years and only now seeks a modification because the government learned the child was with the father; thus, they started sending the child's government stipend to the father, and not the mother.

How do you determine what happened four years ago? You will need to approach CPS. My first step is to review my order of appointment. If my order of appointment does not permit me access to any CPS records related to this family, I need to ask the court to modify the order or enter a new order related to CPS. I have had situations where the judge told me he had no authority to do this, so be prepared with references to any case law or statutes. When the judge informed me, in open court at a status hearing, he could not give me permission, he also stated only the parents could give me access to the CPS records. Therefore, I asked, in open court, if the parents were willing to give me that access. Fortunately, they both agreed. Had they not, it may have reflected poorly on those parents. I received signed waivers from both parents and was able to provide those waivers to CPS.

Once you have written authority to speak with CPS, the next challenge is reaching the appropriate person within the government agency. In one county where I practice, I simply reach out to the county attorney and provide a copy of my order of appointment; she requests the CPS file for me, and I go to the CPS office and review it. In another jurisdiction where I practice, it is not as easy. I spent about one month tracking down the caseworker. I fortunately had the case number from one of the parents. When I finally tracked the down that person, the person had control over her own files and was willing to provide a copy, but had little flexibility to meet me. I spent several hours traveling around, trying to meet with the caseworker, on several days until I finally received a copy of the file. In yet another jurisdiction—one where I do not even practice—CPS willingly spoke with me with a vague order appointing me as the child's attorney. Each jurisdiction is different. Pursue every avenue. These records can be extremely useful. Some of my jurisdictions mandate I review the file at CPS's office, I make no copies, and I take no notes. Other jurisdictions will readily hand me a file and permit me to take it with me.

Finally, once you obtain the file, how do you use the information in court? This may be the most challenging part of this multistep process. In many jurisdictions, you may be prohibited from sharing anything from the CPS file. What if you found that one detail in the file that drives home the point you need to make to the court on behalf of your child client? I gathered that information in a recent case while reviewing the CPS file. Because I could not offer the CPS file into evidence, I cross-examined the parent on the witness stand about the details, as they related to that parent's behavior. Fortunately, she admitted the transgression. What would I do if she failed to admit it, despite previously admitting it in a CPS investigation? I would know that she was perjuring herself. I would need to ask for a break/recess, and I would typically approach her counsel and inform the counsel of what I knew. With any luck, counsel would work with me to either clear the record or risk knowing I would be taking a strong position against the perjuring parent. If you have access to the CPS file early enough in your investigation, then issue discovery, ask to speak with others who may have observed some of the behavior outlined in the CPS file, or issue subpoenas to witnesses or for documents. If you can obtain information that pieces together the admission by the parent in the CPS file, then know you will need to start that process early in your case.

(ii) *Case Study*

You represent a thirteen-year-old boy. His swim coach, with whom you spoke as part of your investigation, calls you to say your child client seemed stressed the other night when he observed his parents fighting in the vestibule of the swim practice. What do you do?

If the coach is simply calling to give you more data, that is wonderful. If the coach is calling because she wants you to intervene, then you need to weigh your next step more carefully. In that regard, you need to dive into what happened with this "fight." Ask questions of the swim coach: Did she observe the fight? How did the child react? Did the child say anything to her? Did others observe the fight? Was this a verbal disagreement? Did it get physical? Did the police need to intervene? Was the child observing from a distance or with one of the parents? Ask the child, although revisiting the fight with the child may add additional stress. Ask the parents. Talk to others who may have observed this fight. Does this fight rise to the level that you have some further obligation to the child, such as reporting to a social services agency, or filing a motion with the court to temporarily change custody? Regardless of the level of the fight, do you, as the child's attorney, need to take additional steps outside of the normal court process to try to prevent this from happening again? Is that your role?

As lawyers for parents, we often call opposing counsel to request they ask their client to stop some obtrusive or disturbing behavior. As the lawyer for your child client, you should act no differently. The conversation may be more awkward if a parent is self-represented. However, you should, at all times, act like the lawyer and give your child client the representation that you would give to his or her parent.

i. Limitations in Information Gathering

If you are a court-appointed child's attorney, your role will be dictated by the rules and laws that create this type of quasi-judicial position, as well as what is outlined in your court order. The laws and order should refer to the type of information you are permitted to obtain, any shortcuts to requesting that information without need for subpoenas or waivers, and guarantees that the court will support you in doing your due diligence in representing a child. If you were hired as private counsel for a child, you may have more roadblocks. You do not have the protections and guarantees afforded in a court appointment order. You are relying solely on the parents' cooperation in securing information for you. If the court permits your appearance on behalf of the child, you may have the authority to seek court orders giving you more access to information and people, but those court orders may require hearings and significant time.

j. Working with Custody Evaluators and Others in an Investigative Role

You may not be the only person who is investigating the child's best interests. Custody evaluators, doctors, the school, child protective services, or health and human services may all be investigating the child's circumstances and seeking out certain information. You may have more information than any of these other investigators, however, because of your unique role and broad access to information. Others may need to rely on self-disclosure by the child and parents. You need to weigh whether or not you share information with these other investigators. For instance, if a school is investigating a child's learning challenges to create accommodations for the child, do you share information you received from the child's doctor that may be relevant (recognizing the privacy issues involved with medical records)? Or, do you trust that the parents will cooperate for the child's interests and share all relevant information with the school? Although your role is to protect your child client's interests, you need to speak with your client, ensure your client understands what is happening, speak with the parents, and never supplant your role as attorney for that of a parent. You are not the child's parents. A parent's cooperation with other professionals and evaluators can shed light on that parent's willingness to address a child's best interests and help you with your overall position.

If you are sharing information with a forensic evaluator, you may taint the evaluation. Does the information you are sharing have your implicit (or explicit) bias? For instance, are you reflecting the contents of a phone conversation accurately (where you may, even subconsciously, leave out some of the content, or reflect it in a manner that was unintended)? Or, are you simply telling the evaluator, "I spoke with X, Y, and Z," without making any recommendations to the evaluator as to who they should speak with? Is your statement that you spoke with these individuals equivalent to your recommendation that the evaluator also speak with them? What if you are working with a family where one of the parents simply works better with you and does not trust the evaluator, which is limiting the information that parent is providing to the evaluator? You need to walk a very fine line. You cannot intervene in a forensic evaluation.

k. Out-of-State Information Gathering

It is difficult to gather documents and information from people over whom you have subpoena power. It can be frustrating, difficult, and, at times, impossible to gather information from people out of state or out of the country. This frustration is evident when you attempt to speak with a child's therapist whose office is in another jurisdiction. Each jurisdiction may have different rules as to when the mental health professional can speak to a third party. Schools may be more willing to turn over documents voluntarily, unless the school was involved in complicated litigation in the past, making the school reluctant to help you. A doctor will be suspect when an out-of-state lawyer contacts him or her.

Ultimately, you may need to rely on the parents to help you gather information out of state if your court order of appointment is not voluntarily respected. You can retain local counsel, register your order of appointment and seek to enforce it, or open a miscellaneous action to issue subpoenas or notice depositions, but it may be costly. Start gathering your information early. Not only are parents usually more inclined to help the child's attorney early in the case (before the child's attorney has started forming opinions or taking positions), but also starting early provides more time to maneuver through any legal hurdles you run up against.

(i) *Case Study*

You represent a five-year-old girl who resides primarily with her mother in Tennessee. You are not in Tennessee. In fact, you are not even in a state bordering Tennessee. How do you meet with your child? How do you gather information about the child's home life, family, and friends?

The logical answer is you need to travel to Tennessee. I have been in situations where a court will not appoint a child's attorney unless that attorney is willing and able to travel to the other jurisdiction where the child will be visiting or living. However, it is easier said than done. Travel costs money and takes time to schedule. You should ask the Tennessee parent for photos (recognizing they could be staged), videos of the child in activities, information about the neighborhood, and information about the child's activities. You should do independent research on this location as well. How are the schools? How long must the child drive to get to activities? Are there family or friends nearby? What does the child's daily life look like in Tennessee? It is important, in answering these questions, that you focus on something more specific than Tennessee. In some communities, it is important the child's attorney focuses on the very street on which the child will live. Some streets in the nicest, most expensive cities are less child friendly and more dangerous than some streets in poverty-stricken rural areas.

Can you hire someone to conduct an assessment of this area of Tennessee (e.g., a social worker, custody evaluator)? Can you talk to people in Tennessee? Will the schools give you information or talk about their programs? Will the third parties give you information specific to this child, or general information? How do you then get these potential Tennessee witnesses to court in your jurisdiction? Do you need to plan ahead for telephone or videoconference testimony?

l. Court Case Search

If your court permits a search of its files, you should consider searching for parents, any stepparents, and any other adults with whom your child client may live, to see if any of these individuals had past legal (including criminal) difficulties. The challenge you may encounter is determining whether the individual you are searching and the individual you find are one and the same. Depending on the issues in the case, you may want to determine whether a private investigator is necessary, either to run a background search or to survey the situation. If a parent is refusing to disclose his or her address, that may cause you concern.

In a recent case, the father refused to disclose his address to the mother because his fiancée was in a safety program with the state because of past domestic violence; thus, her address was shielded from public inspection. This created an interesting dynamic—my child clients' mother did not know the address where her children were staying, but neither did the person who sought harm against the children's new stepmother. This led to further investigations on whether stepmother's past abuser could resurface and potentially put the children in harm's way. The situation was uncovered because of a search through court files related to the stepmother, including a file for a protective order that she sought against the individual who sought to harm her.

§3.02 MEETING WITH THE CHILDREN

The child is your client. In nearly every case where you represent a child, you will want to meet with that child. The older the child, the more prominent a role the child's voice will take in your investigation. Even if the child is young and has no understanding that you are his or her attorney, you are still likely going to want to meet the child. If, however, you believe meeting the child may cause the child more harm than good, discuss this with the child's parents and justify to the parents and the court why you chose not to meet with your child client. It is possible that meeting with your child client will yield nothing. It is possible that logistics prevent you from meeting with your client (e.g., your client lives in a different country, is hospitalized, is in residential drug treatment, is in boarding school). It may be that technology is unavailable for you to have a distance meeting with the child. It may be that your presence can cause harm to the child. Perhaps the most pertinent information will never come from the child but from third-party collaterals, such as doctors or teachers.

This is going to be your decision—whether to meet with the child and at what stage in the case, where to have the meeting, the agenda for the meeting, who brings the child to the meeting, and who else might be at the meeting. You may need to give up the ideal for the practical. Before meeting with your child client, gauge what information others shared with the child about your role. Your child client may come to any meeting with a preconceived notion about who you are and what you will do for him or her. Depending on a parent's predisposition, the child may be biased for or against you, before even meeting you. Even if you explain to the parents how they should approach your introduction, it may never happen precisely as you had envisioned.

a. Initial Meeting[1]

My initial meetings with my child clients are often awkward. My child clients typically fall on one end of a spectrum during this initial meeting. Either the child is relatively quiet and withdrawn or the child wants to overshare information as if he or she is arguing the case for what they want. I will occasionally find a child client who is somewhere in the middle—relieved to have someone with whom he or she can talk. I have had child clients who

---

1. *Representing Children in Dependency and Family Court: Beyond the Law*, by Rebecca M. Stahl and Philip M. Stahl, publishing in 2018, Chapter 5.

are far too young to understand I am a lawyer, that I am *their* lawyer, and that their parents are even in custody litigation. In those situations, I am often introduced as "mommy and daddy's friend, Melissa." It is difficult to not draw some loose assumptions based on the child's demeanor during the first meeting. Are they quiet because mom brought them to the meeting, and they are afraid of being questioned afterward by mom? Are they overly aggressive in posturing because they are meeting you, for the first time, with their sibling (who you also represent) and they are afraid their sibling will take an opposite view?

Some of the most difficult aspects of meeting with a child client involve understanding their nonverbal cues and communication, as well as interpreting what the child client actually verbalizes. If a child client says they want a "2-2-5-5" schedule, does that imply a parent discussed precise custody outcomes with them and used this very specific terminology? A child is very suggestible. A child's responses are influenced by internal and external factors, including their parents, siblings, family, friends, teachers, coaches, and even movies, television, books, songs, or simply how the child processes information. If you lead a child to a particular outcome, that child may very well follow; thus, you need to be keenly aware of talking to the child in an open-ended fashion. You need to speak simply and at the child's level. You do not want to confuse a child and cause the child to alter his or her response or answer a completely different question than what you are asking. I often look at whether a child's words mirror the parent's words, so I will ask open-ended questions of a parent too. If both a mother and the fifteen-year-old daughter complain of the father by saying he is "lazy" and "refuses to work" and "yells" and "steals money" and a myriad of other accusations, particularly using the same exact words as one another, unprovoked, you may wonder if this is a conclusion that the child client drew directly from the parent.

The child client's upbringing, health, mental and emotional issues, disabilities, culture, religion, and any trauma that may have affected him or her influences a child's communication. Observing a child client may provide more information than taking the child's words verbatim. If a child has gone through a trauma or abuse, be aware of how you act. Are you wearing perfume that may trigger a memory of the child's abuser? Do you have the same inflection, accent, or tone as the parent who consistently punished the child? Do you have the same hair color, wear a similar hat, or don the same jewelry as a particular person in the child's life that will affect how the child reacts to you and communicates with you? It may be impossible for you to know these factors going into your initial meeting with your child client. However, be attuned to the fact that you, your own biases, and your own way of being could affect the child and how that child communicates with you. Your biases may also affect how you frame questions to the child client. You want to be keenly aware of these biases (these outcomes that you are already formulating in your head based on your independent investigation), and be certain that these biases do not lead your child client toward an answer or statement that is simply inaccurate or only a partial truth.[2]

It is also easy for adults to believe a child may be lying if the child's story changes, but a child's story may change for a very simple reason—memory. A child may have different memory storage, different recollections, a different way of interpreting memories, or may have repressed memories. It may be very difficult for a lawyer to work with a child who told a clear story and then seems to forget it. It may be necessary for the child's attorney to ask for the help of mental health professionals. Be certain to observe the child's breath and their body language, and follow your instincts. You may not have the background, as a lawyer, to interpret all the child says; however, if you are attuned to communication issues, you can find a path to get you closer to an answer.

One thing works well for me whenever I meet with a child client: I do not take notes. I do not write. I do not have paper in front of me. I merely talk to the child. As soon as my meeting is done, I draft notes based on the meeting, including a lot of inferences I draw from the meeting that the child may not have verbalized. If I have to get into my car immediately after the meeting, I audio-record my notes so that I do not lose my thoughts. By not taking notes, I can be fully present and engaged with the child. It allows you to focus on observing the child.

Finally, recognize that you are not there simply to gather information. You have other roles when you represent a child. Your key goal is always to protect the child. As their counsel, you can assess where their concerns and stresses lay, and determine how you can shield them from the parent's hostilities. You are also an educator—educating the child about your role, the process, and having realistic expectations. After meeting your child client, particularly a verbal child client, you can use your other research and the information from your investigation to interpret your child client's communication and behavior. Each child is different. For some, it may take you five

---

2. *Id.* at Chapter 4.

or ten minutes to get a full picture. For other children, you may meet with them five to ten times and still feel lost. Your role and your presence may be distressing factors for the child; you need to recognize this and assess your insertion into this child's life. Your child may reflect memories that are of events that never actually occurred, and it will be your job to figure out how this fits into the bigger puzzle.

(i) *Introduction*

When appropriate, I begin the meeting by talking about myself. No matter how skilled the parent, they may not fully comprehend my role and may misrepresent my role to the child. I will often ask the child what they already know about me, so I hear it in their own words. I will need to tailor my introduction to the child client based on his or her age and maturity—something I may know little about, unless I have already done enough investigation to get a solid sense. A child's view of court may be based on movies or television. More commonly today, it is based on their friend's parents' divorce. In addition, it is helpful to set conversational ground rules with the child. Let the child practice answering questions and give the child instructions, such as giving the child permission to say they do not know an answer, say they do not understand a question, and correct you. You should also affirm to the child you are not part of their family and therefore do not know what has happened to them.[3]

Children will see you as an authority figure who has all the answers. They may feel uncomfortable when they do not know an answer or do not understand the question, so they may make up answers or guess at an answer. If you phrase a question too narrowly, the child may feel it inappropriate to refuse to respond, even if they cannot respond given your framing. Children may guess, assume, or fit information they have into a picture they think you expect from them.

(ii) *Answering the Children's Questions*

The child client may have a lot of questions, ranging from exploring my role as their attorney to helping them understand the potential outcomes in the case. I have had child clients ask me who filed the court case, what that parent is requesting, and why they need a lawyer. I typically try to explain my role as being another person, in addition to the judge and their parents'

---

3. Karen Saywitz, Lorinda B. Camparo, and Anna Romanoff, *Interviewing Children in Custody Cases: Implications of Research and Policy for Practice*, 28 BEHAV. SCI. & L. 542 (2010).

lawyers, to help figure out what will work best for the child. I try to explain that I can bring a unique perspective to the discussion because I can listen directly to my child client and help figure out the situation from his or her perspective.

Some children are resentful that they need to spend time meeting with a lawyer instead of spending time with their friends. Others are excited to have someone in their corner. I typically end my meeting with my child client (usually with older children) by ensuring he or she has a way to contact me by text and/or e-mail. When a child is younger and not able to initiate communication with me directly, I try to find a safe person (e.g., a school guidance counselor, teacher, coach, or someone else who will see the child routinely) and encourage that person to contact me if something seems unsettled with the child, or to act as a conduit to ask the child if the child would like help contacting me.

It may be difficult to discuss privacy and confidentiality with your child client. This is a difficult concept for even lawyers to truly understand. A child may easily misinterpret and believe that you are asking them to lie to others or keep secrets. The child may not understand why you keep things private, but they can speak to others about it. It is a fine distinction, and one that needs to be carefully addressed at the child's level.

(iii) *How Much Should You Disclose About the Court Filings?*

As with most legal questions, the answer is, "It depends." A child may have a lot of questions about what has been filed in court, what both parents are arguing to the judge, and what both parents want. As a lawyer yourself, you are aware that the assertions in a pleading may differ from reality. There is a lot of posturing in court pleadings. If the child client has already read the pleadings, you must address that issue head on. Especially if the child client is older, try to explain the role that lawyers take in litigation and legal maneuvering. I have even fallen on my sword and explained that, in a lot of cases, lawyers just make things worse, so the child should not blame his or her parent; rather, we are working to fix things so the lawyers will all go away and stop interfering in the family. I have never actually shown court filings to my child client, but am fairly straightforward in responding to the child client if he or she asks pointed questions about the court case.

Being direct and being artful are not mutually exclusive. I can be honest and direct, but still ensure the child knows that mom was feeling scared when she learned that Elizabeth stayed home alone so that dad could go play soccer; thus, mom wanted the help of a judge to figure out if there is a better way to have the parents work together for Elizabeth. Elizabeth would be extremely upset if I were more blunt and told her that her mother is suing her father for being neglectful and not taking care of Elizabeth. Being so blunt may also put the child client in a position of trying to defend one or the other parent.

How you word your communication to the child is the *most* important thing for your child client. He or she must understand what is happening in their own language, at their level of information processing, and considering all the things that have already happened in their lives (living in a violent neighborhood, through a catastrophic natural disaster, through a war zone, with a family member that is an addict, with bullying, possible abuse, fighting parents, moving around, different cultural ways of communicating, a learning disability, etc.). The way you answer these seminal questions may directly affect how a child client answers your questions and may, if you are not careful, give you false information from the child client.

b. Observing the Children with Their Parents

More often than not, I meet my child client and I leave the meeting more confused than when I entered it. I always come away from meeting a child with a healthy dose of skepticism. I have heard children lie to me. I have had children so confused they do not even know the truth. I have had children so scared to tell me the truth that nothing I can say or do will pacify them. It is rare that my child clients will share everything with me during the first meeting. It takes time to build rapport. One of the most useful visits with a child client, which I often do on a second or third client meeting, consists of observing my child client with his or her parents. I had one case where my child client would sit in my office crying that her father hated her, ignored her, and made fun of her. I went to see the child with her father and found the complete opposite to be true. Not only was the father attentive, loving, and involved, but also the child was completely at ease with the father and equally affectionate. Their interactions could not have possibly been a lie, given what I had seen. By observing the child with her father, I had a new perspective on what the child had said and began hypothesizing why she may have relayed certain impressions to me that seemed false. I could then use that to investigate further and speak with additional collaterals.

When I observe a child with his or her parent, I often try to conduct the observation at the parents' home. This allows me to see the family in their home environment. One of my favorite times to see the family is right after school. I can see the child's routine—getting backpacks unpacked, getting a snack, getting ready for a sport, helping fix dinner, etc. It lets me be a true observer in what is a common daytime occurrence. The family is not as able to fabricate a scene for me. It is hard to clean up the chaos that is usual when a child gets home and drops his or her belongings on the floor.

When you visit a family's home, however, you must be respectful. Exercise common courtesies and respect family rituals. For example, I represented a child whose father was an Orthodox Jew. If I visited their home on Friday, I could not disrupt their meal preparation so that they could have everything prepared before sundown. The child would need to shower before sundown, and the family would need to ensure lights and electronics were off before sundown. I could not conceive of asking them to change their routine so I could be accommodated.

(i) *What Happens If a Child Is Prohibited from Seeing a Parent?*

There may be instances where one of the parents has little or no time with the child under an existing custody order. This may make it difficult for you to ever see that child and parent interact. If that parent is seeking more time with the child, how do you know if the child is truly comfortable with that parent? You may have to rely on professionals to help. If the parents can reach a temporary détente to permit the absent parent to have some access to the child, you may be able to conduct your observation; however, you could be put in the role of a supervisor and a therapist, depending on the reason the parent has little to no access. You also run the risk of seeing something that gives you less than an accurate picture. If a child has not been around that parent for a while, will the parent act overly emotional? Will the child feel uncomfortable—not because the parent did something wrong, but because the child's attachment to the parent has been weakened?

(ii) *What Happens If a Parent Has So Little Time You Cannot Find a Time to See the Child with the Parent?*

Unfortunately, you must be flexible. I have found representing children to be more intrusive on my schedule than representing their parents. I never want to interfere with my child client's school or activity schedule, I want the family to maintain their routine as best as possible, and I want to have meetings with the child in environments less fabricated than my office. Because of this, I am routinely working on evenings, weekends, and driving halfway across the state. I have driven to bad neighborhoods where the news reported a gang shooting two days earlier. I have returned from my holidays early to capitalize on my child client's winter break. I have driven across the state to visit a child client at a residential drug treatment center. It is not glamorous work by any means. Although you could demand a parent bring the child to your office at a certain date and time, I have learned an office meeting usually does not yield the best information and may ultimately create the most chaos for the child, who is already enduring a significant amount of stress. Based on the difficulty with meetings and the required flexibility, I will routinely only take one or two child representation cases at a time; it is far too difficult to manage the schedule out of the office with my other cases if I were to be involved in more.

c. Locations of Meetings

The location is entirely dependent on the child client. I typically ask both parents where the child may feel most comfortable. I usually stress to the parent that I do not want the parent, grandparent, or anyone else hovering or nearby. It is not uncommon that each parent will suggest his or her house as the best place. Depending on the situation and what I have already learned, I will agree to meet the child at the house; however, I will often also meet the child in other venues throughout my representation, and will insist that I am alone with the child (and not supervised by nanny cameras). Some children are more comfortable around their own belongings or a favorite pet. However, depending on the family's circumstances, the child may also be intimidated in being at a parent's home, and the parent may be oblivious to this fact (or, worse yet, knows the child is intimidated and wants the venue to affect the child's meeting with you).

If I am meeting in a public location, I often ask whether meeting near the child's home community is comfortable for the child. If I meet the child at a coffee shop or ice cream parlor near their house, it is convenient; however, they may also see their friends, which may create discomfort for the child. I have accepted invitations to meet with my child clients at their birthday parties, sports games, school plays, recitals, and therapy sessions. I will often reach out to the school, failing all else, and ask if the child has a free period, gets to school early or late, or if there is a convenient place for me to meet them on campus. When I questioned whether the child client has friends and socially appropriate interactions at school, I have observed them during recess or homeroom. I have even observed my child clients from afar while they are on the school playground, simply to see how they interact with their peers. If the child refuses to talk, you may want to talk to their therapist and see if it would be intrusive to sit in on the therapy session.

Clearly, some venues are more appropriate for discussion time and some venues lend themselves more to your observation of the child client. Always try to see the child in his or her parents' homes. Only on rare occasions will that be inappropriate or not feasible. Seeing a child's bedroom can be very instructive. Ask the child client to tell you about their toys, games, and photos. I had one child client point to a photo of her dad on the dresser at her mom's house. I asked her who was in the photo. She said, "my friend." I pushed and asked, "Isn't that your father?" She then whispered, "Yes, but in this house, I call him 'friend.'" The father, in that case, had concerns that the mother was urging the child to call the stepfather "dad." I would not have gotten the same interaction but for my visit to my child client's bedroom.

Perhaps the best thing about visiting with your child client is that you get to dress down. You will sit on floors, on the grass sidelines at a football game, on swings in a playground, and walk across sticky floors at an ice cream parlor. It typically will not work to wear a business suit to meet with a child client, nor is it practical for the simple reason that the child needs you to get down (sometimes literally) to their level. You have authority. You are a lawyer. You are a direct conduit for this child to a judge. Yet, this child needs to feel comfortable with you, not intimidated by you. There are the rare occasions, like when I represented a teenage girl, that wearing heels and a skirt were not only acceptable but a topic of conversation. However, in nearly every case, I want to be considered more akin to a friend and confidant than a business person.

You also want to ensure the environment has few to no distractions.[4] During a first meeting with a young child client, we met in an office conference room. The child had attention-deficit hyperactivity disorder, and this was a new environment for him. He was literally bouncing off the walls. He stood on rolling chairs and even climbed onto the table. There was absolutely no way he would verbalize anything to me until he was done exploring. I merely let him explore. I never ultimately had a conversation with him; however, I learned a bit about his behaviors, which gave me context to his grades, friends, and the way each parent could address the child's behaviors.

---

4. *Id.* at 549.

d. Building Rapport with a Child

It may be impossible to build rapport with a child. There may simply be situations where you will be unable to have a child trust you. If this case warrants your presence, the chances are the parents are in a very high conflict situation. The level of acrimony will no doubt have bled through to the child, causing the child to have a fundamental hesitation to speak candidly with an adult involved in this process. Having said that, the best way to build rapport with the child is to not push the child for information. Let the child move at his or her own pace in getting used to your presence in this difficult situation. This requires time—something you may be lacking. You may not need to see the child for large chunks of time. However, you will need to start seeing the child consistently and in different venues. Although I have the right to ask to meet with my child client at my own office, I often find my office a difficult place to meet with a child. It is possible that a child is most comfortable and forthcoming when near his or her parent, a sibling or a family pet, or at the family home—all situations that I view suspiciously given the influence these parameters may have on my child client. Nonetheless, you need to start somewhere.

I will always want to meet with my child client alone. If I represent siblings, I will want to meet with them together and apart. I will want to meet with the child with both parents. I will want to blend in. I will not push. I will often attend my child client's activities—extracurricular events, sports, recitals, and plays. There is often a fine line where I ask myself whether I can actually bill the child's parents to sit on the sidelines of a soccer game, but I can envision some circumstances where this may be a legitimate expenditure. Am I also observing the parent interact with the coach, other parents, and the child? I have had situations where my child client is reluctant to talk to me. In some rare occasions, if there is a therapist or counselor involved with the child, I gather information from that professional; then, if appropriate and permitted by the professional, I may attend the child's therapy sessions. I have often shared meals with my child clients, as well as ice cream, birthday parties, and even school days (as long as my appearance at the child's school does not cause the child additional stress and set our relationship back).

The purpose behind seeing the child on several occasions in several different venues with several different people is to help provide a reality check. Are the child's actions matching the child's words? I need to ask this because, even when the child seems forthcoming and comfortable around me, I always question whether the child is being truthful. A child may be lying, and not even realize they are lying because it has become commonplace for their own self-preservation. They may be relaying their truth to you, but it may not be an accurate picture of their reality. You are a lawyer, not a psychologist, and understanding a child's communication may be extremely complicated.

e. Having Others in Meetings with a Child

At times, including others in your meetings with the child client may be unavoidable, whether it is for efficiency, security, or malpractice issues. You may have been appointed to represent a child when a trial is fast approaching and you have little time to meet with the child on multiple occasions, in multiple venues, with multiple people. If you are representing siblings, it may be nearly impossible to schedule sufficient meetings to see the siblings separately.

In a nonideal world, you need to make a judgment call. You may want to have another person around for your own security. Is the child known to be violent? Is the child traumatized so that your presence or words could cause the child additional trauma, and this warrants having a mental health professional present? Will the child lie about something you said or did to cause your law license to be put in jeopardy? Are you concerned about being alone with the child out of fear the child may harm him- or herself or have an accident? Would you ever consider driving the child client in your own car? Is the child so young that the child must have others around for the child's own safety or needs? Is the child sick and requires a parent or guardian to be nearby? Is the child in residential drug treatment and requires a treatment provider to be nearby because the child has previously attempted self-harm? Are you representing the child and his or her siblings and need to see how they interact with one another? Are you afraid that having a more dominant sibling may create difficulty for the other to speak his or her mind? Ultimately, you need to consider all possibilities and recognize that there is often no "right" answer.

I often try to meet with my child client in a neutral location (e.g., a restaurant) for my initial meeting. If I represent multiple siblings, I often do the first meeting with everyone together. My first meeting is often a time to discuss who I am, what I am doing, what the rules are, and what is happening. I then answer questions for the children. This meeting is often introductory.

I rarely get into significant substance. I simply let the child client begin the process of understanding who I am and feeling comfortable with me. At times, having a third party, including a sibling, may make an otherwise awkward first meeting more comfortable.

f. Children of Different Ages

I rarely make blanket assessments of a child based solely on that child's age. One child at age five may be more mature than another child at age nine. Children's cultures, upbringings, mental health, emotional and physical health, and community all affect their ability to communicate. If the child has experienced trauma, loss, or abuse, that child will also communicate and behave differently. I will often meet with both parents and review any papers I am given before meeting with my child client, if for no other reason than to have some foundation for how best to communicate with this child. I have represented children as young as infants and as old as age 17. Maturity and circumstances, more than age, affect the child and the ultimate outcome or position you take on behalf of that child. You not only need to tailor your discussions with your child client to their unique circumstances, but any potential outcome will need to be specific to that child and their needs.[5]

(i) *Case Study*

You are appointed to represent a four-year-old child. The child does not understand the terms "lawyer" or "confidentiality," or who you are. How do you advise your client?

There have been cases where my child client never really knew I was their advocate. They believed me to be a friend of both of their parents. At times, I have never even talked directly to my child client about the custody case. Furthermore, I am often relieved when the child client does not know his or her parents are in court. For slightly older children, I talk to them about judges and lawyers. I ask them to explain what they think about those people first. I always try to couch the role of lawyer and judge in terms of people who help their mom and dad. Older children often know what lawyers are, and some have tried to educate me about "one-party" consent and explain why they felt it appropriate to record one of their parents. Quite a few older child clients—particularly those with smartphones and Internet

---

5. For a discussion on child psychology, particularly related to children of different ages, please *see Representing Children in Dependency and Family Court: Beyond the Law*, by Rebecca M. Stahl and Philip M. Stahl, publishing in 2018.

access—have researched the law and the courts and found informational websites online explaining the process. Some of the children want to know precisely what their mom and dad said to the court in documents or when they have gone before a judge. Without fail, you have to assess your audience: How will the child client respond? How much should the child client know? If you do not answer the child client's questions, will he or she get the information from somewhere else? I recently worked with a fifteen-year-old child who seemed to have a really comprehensive understanding of the legal system and claimed that it came from a pre-law class at his high school. Just as with adult clients, you need to explain the process and what happens. Many children will be interested in knowing about timelines—when will all of this be done?

Confidentiality is also an important issue. To a child who does not understand the issue of confidentiality, it may sound like you are asking them to keep secrets from their parents. A child needs to understand that you keep their secrets, but that they can talk to whomever they want. The child also needs to understand the exceptions to confidentiality: You will always step in to protect them if you think someone might hurt them. You need to be careful how you couch the exceptions to confidentiality out of fear that a child may not be forthcoming about very important information crucial to your investigation if you may tell a parent or the authorities.

g. Educating Children, Answering Questions

A child's attorney is not just an advocate for the child's interests or his voice. A child's attorney, much like a parent's lawyer, is an educator. The child may have a lot of questions for you. The child may have been told certain things by his or her parents. They may not want to disclose who said what or where they heard the information. I have had child clients refer to discreet legal rules, such as knowing that the State of Maryland requires two parties to consent to being recorded; when asked how they came to learn of this rule, they tell me they learned it in school. I had difficulty believing a local public school taught a child that they could not record their mother without the mother knowing. I also coupled this with the fact that the child's father had shown the child all the pleadings in the case and felt obliged to answer the children's questions (with his own filter).

You will educate your child clients about complicated processes, such as reunification therapy, understanding the role a lawyer takes in posturing in a legal pleading, and understanding the parent's underlying motives in filing a lawsuit. Children will understand things based on the filter through which the information is shared. I have also had to answer more interesting questions, such as why my client's mother would not keep kosher (she was Catholic) when the child wanted to keep kosher because her father kept kosher.

I have had child clients ask me to talk to their teachers about why they did not get a grade that the child felt he or she deserved. I have had child clients ask me to make their parents understand why they behaved in certain ways or said certain things. I often go into meetings with my child client nervous about what question may be presented to me. I will rarely, if ever, meet with my child client without having first spoken to both parents and their lawyers, or having reviewed the court papers. Even if this information is unnecessary to an intelligent conversation about the case, it helps me prepare for what might arise in my conversation with my child clients. I have had to tell my child clients, "I do not know, but I will talk to X, and I will find out and I will be back in touch." If I have to leave my client with no answer, I promise I will be back in touch by a certain date, because the lack of an answer may often leave the child in distress. Children need certainty and clarity. They need to know they have a place to go to talk about this, to ask questions and receive answers.

h. Reporting to Child Protective Services

Know your jurisdiction's mandatory reporting requirements before entering the case. I have represented children in a lot of cases where the parent feels the child may have been abused at the other parent's home. You are probably not a professional that can say, with any certainty, that abuse has or has not happened. Much of the "abuse" I have observed in my cases is subtle. A mother reports that the child said something about the father touching the child while bathing the child. A father reports that the child consistently has bumps or scratches on his head when he returns to the father. While the mother was unloading the dishwasher, the toddler opened the screen door and ran toward the street. Is the "abuse" or neglect observed? Who disclosed the "abuse" or neglect? Was it the child (how old is the child, what did the child say, etc.)? Did a third party observe something? What professionals are involved already that can lend some guidance?

If you are sufficiently concerned and believe that there may have been abuse, then report it, or determine whether another person has reported it. You may also want to bring others into the situation. You can ask the court to order a home study. You can speak to the child's therapist, pediatrician, teacher, or guidance counselor about their observations and anything the child may have said to them. Some pediatricians focus on detecting abuse of a child. For this pediatrician to distinguish between abuse and another injury, they need to examine the child. If you submit photographs taken by a third party, the pediatrician may be unable to make any assessment or draw any conclusion.

If a child has been abused or neglected and a third-party professional has confirmed this, then there needs to be an assessment of who was at fault. For instance, if a child's injury was not observed until several days after returning to the other parent's home, was it Parent 1 or Parent 2 that caused the injury (or neglected the child in a manner that permitted the injury)? Is the nanny at fault? Is an educator or coach or doctor abusing the child? Although it may not be the norm, is it possible that the parent reporting the abuse is the one who is actually abusing the child? Is the abuse/injury a way of one parent trying to strategically manipulate the custody litigation?

i. Working with Children with Special Needs

Special needs may range from mild learning disabilities to profound cognitive impairment. Your child client may have developmental delays, occasional panic attacks, or even serious psychiatric problems. When you work with a special needs child, you should become an expert on that child's specific needs. Does the child require you to communicate through visuals, through a third party, or as if you are their imaginary friend? Will they understand what you say? Will you understand what they say? Can or will the child communicate verbally? Has the child been diagnosed (and diagnosed properly), or is the child someone you suspect of having a special need but the parents have not yet recognized that need? Communicating with a special needs child has unique challenges, as does advocating for what is in their best interests. Will the child have needs met better by one parent over the other? Is neither parent equipped to meet the child's needs? How is this child's needs affecting the larger family, including other children (who may also be your clients)?

You may believe you are an "expert" at representing children with special needs. However, these needs—and how each family's dynamics affect the child's needs and the parents' responses to that child—vary dramatically situation to situation. Just as with any child, despite having a process, you need to be flexible and attentive.

Does the child have specific medical issues (heart defects, muscular dystrophy, cerebral palsy, dwarfism)? How are these being treated? What professional do you need to speak with to further understand the child's medical issue, how the family is addressing that issue, how it affects your interaction with the child client, and how you formulate a position on behalf of the child? Is the child being tested, having long hospital stays, or needing expensive equipment? Does one parent better provide accommodations? Does one parent deal with frequent crises better, along with the uncertainty and worry? What does the support system look like in each parent's house?

Does the child client have certain behavioral issues (e.g., attention deficits, fetal alcohol spectrum disorder, Tourette syndrome)? Does the child require certain behavioral interventions or discipline tactics? What strategies does each parent employ? How does each parent discipline the child? How does each parent address the chaos that may ensue in his or her house? How does this child's behavior affect the child's education? How does it affect the other children in their house?

Does the child client have a developmental disability (e.g., autism spectrum disorder, Down syndrome)? How is each parent advocating for this child? What other people must you speak with to understand the child's disability, the parents' role in addressing it, and whether the child is getting the resources necessary to thrive? You may find it helpful to speak to the school, attend meetings related to the child's individualized education plan, talk to the child's treatment professionals, and research the child's communication and behavior with their particular disability. If you understand what to look for, you may be better able to observe things that could give you clues into what may help your child client.

Does the child client have learning disabilities (e.g., dyslexia)? Does the child client need to follow a structured plan, proposed by a professional? Does the child need accommodations? Your child client may suffer from self-esteem problems. Will the parent work at home with the child? How are the child's grades?

Does the child client have mental health issues (e.g., anxiety, depression)? Have you talked to the child's mental health professionals? Is the child in therapy or being treated? If the child is not being treated, then why? Do the parents acknowledge the child's health issues? Is medication necessary? What are the parents' views on medicating the child, particularly in contrast to the treating physician's views?

Be sure to fully investigate your child client's situation. If you speak only to the parents and no one else, you may have a completely different picture of what is best for a child. One parent may claim that he or she is a better advocate for the child, but that same parent may be so severely distressed and overwhelmed that their advocacy is not helping the child's daily situation. Some parents may minimize a child's special needs or refuse to admit the child has special needs, because humans crave normal. Humans want to fit in. When in doubt, engage a professional.

j. Child's Report of Abuse

As previously mentioned, you should tell your child client that your communication with him or her is private and you will not tell anyone else, although the child can talk to whomever he or she wants. You also need to tell the child that if you think they or someone else might be in danger, you will tell someone to protect that person. In most cases, the child will gloss over this statement. However, some children may internalize it, and you will need to ensure that it does not cause a child to hide important details from you.

If a child discloses something to you that is abusive, you need to act. If it is a past act and you do not feel the child is in present danger, then it may be appropriate to report the abusive act to the appropriate authorities so it can be investigated. If the child is in present danger, you may need to take additional steps, such as filing an emergency motion in court to ensure the child is in a safe place.

Your child client may also disclose past abuse of a sibling, which may warrant a report. If the child says anything that indicates any person is in present danger, you need to report it, whether it is to the police, child protective services, or some other authority in your jurisdiction. If the person in danger is not your client, you can only report it; you cannot file motions or pursue relief in your custody case on behalf of that other person, who is not your client.

It can be frustrating or scary if a child reports something to you that indicates abuse or neglect. The child may not identify it as abuse or neglect. They may minimize the parent's behavior. You need to be certain to investigate while recognizing that you are a lawyer, not a social welfare investigator, police officer, or a judge. You need to become familiar with what behaviors may indicate abuse or neglect. You need to recognize that an abused or neglected child may have a different way of communicating or reflect stories differently than what happened in reality. They may talk about their circumstances as if they are telling a story or talking about a friend. Their sense of time and place may be skewed or inaccurate.

In addition to a child who may be harmed by another person, you need to be sensitive to a child who may be harming him or herself. Why is the child harming him or herself? Is it a cry for help? Is it experimentation based on something a friend has done or something that was seen in a movie? Is it indicative of something happening (or not happening) in the family home? A child who is self-harming may need help, ranging from periodic therapy to a full assessment and hospitalization. When you represent a child who has harmed himself or herself, it is often telling to observe how the parents have addressed this issue. Did they minimize it? Did they explain it away? Is their behavior in line with what professionals may be saying in the case (the child's therapist, a doctor, etc.)? Rely on professionals. If the child needs to be hospitalized but the parents are not acting, you may need to act. You may need to push follow-through on the recommendations of professionals. You need to understand why there is no follow-through. You may need to file a motion to obtain help for the child. If the parents are the root cause of the child's self-harm (through words or actions), you may need to assess whether your jurisdiction permits you to seek a protective order on behalf of the child if the parents are not acting to protect the child.

k. Case Study: Hearing What the Child Is Not Saying

You represent an eight-year-old girl. She is a middle child, and she consistently tells you her father ignores her. You know the father has claimed that mom has told the children negative things about him, making them not want to see him. Do you believe the child?

Your job is not to blindly believe your child clients. In fact, you should not blindly believe your adult clients either. People who are in stressful situations cannot communicate clearly. For most people, experiencing a familial separation and reconfiguration can be one of the most stressful situations they will ever experience. They may use different words to describe things. They may omit information (intentionally, particularly if it does not support their side of the events, or unintentionally). They may say what they think you want to hear, or say what they think one of their parents wants to hear. They may behave a particular way to protect a parent or ostracize a parent. They may do all of this subconsciously and without any malicious intent.

How do you actually know what a child is saying? Investigate, investigate, and investigate. You need to talk to others, and you need to see the child's nonverbal cues. You are a lawyer. You may not be a communications specialist. You may be entirely unable to take a child's nonverbal cues and put them into context. It may be you are not meant to represent children. However, lawyers do have other professionals at their disposal—therapists, psychologists, psychiatrists, parenting coordinators, coaches, custody evaluators, and many more individuals who can help us interpret our child client's motivations, goals, and inner thoughts. You will need additional education, which you should continue through reading and training. You need to engage other professionals routinely to learn about child communication. You need to observe the child in a variety of situations so that you can accurately describe to others the child's behavior. How is the child's body language when sitting next to her siblings? What about the child at home with her father?

What happens when the eight-year-old child who said her father ignores her was seen happy and relaxed playing football with her father in the driveway when you arrived for a home visit? What happens when you interview the middle child's two other siblings and, without provocation, both tell you that the father ignores the middle child? Is this a coincidence? Do their stories indicate the middle child told the truth? Or, is their story fabricated for your benefit? Observe. You may get more from observing your child clients than listening to them many days, particularly if the child is younger and less verbal.

l. "Parenting" the Child

I have had difficulty representing some children when I see the child engaged in self-destructive behavior that needs correcting but, at least during the thick of the litigation, no one is providing that child any guidance. It is extremely frustrating. To what extent should you give the child client direction or life lessons? In other words, should you parent the child client? I think the short answer is a resounding "no"—you are the child's attorney. However, when we represent adults, we often provide insight or thoughts about how the parent is approaching something in their life that may make things easier. The parent, however, is an adult, whereas the child looks to you as an authority figure. Furthermore, if you are providing the child a life lesson, the question becomes: Why aren't the parents? Are you becoming too involved? Are you giving the child bad guidance? Should you be talking to the parents instead?

(i) *Case Study*

You represent a sixteen-year-old girl who is skipping a lot of school. Her parents are aware she is truant and have gotten messages from the school. The parents have been unable to stop her. They clearly cannot be at the school all day monitoring her, and the school seems unable to do so. After she is dropped off, she leaves. The child is at risk of being expelled. Above all, the child will sit in meetings with you and tell you that she plans on going to a good college like her older sister. How far do you go in talking to the child about the child's behavior?

I treaded lightly in this situation. Clearly, I wanted to tell the child client she was very much mistaken if she thought a good college (or any college) would admit her with her track record. However, she was my client. I did not want to judge her, ostracize her, or cause her to distrust me. Furthermore, judging and parenting, although not my role, also did not help me understand the child's perspective and *why* she was skipping so much school. Was she in with the wrong social group? Was this school the wrong fit for her? Was it peer pressure? Was she engaged in other risky or dangerous behaviors?

You need to take additional steps to see what a behavior is saying about a child, his or her family, and who may be best equipped to care for the child.

§3.03 DISCOVERY

a. Depositions

(i) *Do You Need to Be There?*

I am cognizant of the fact I am often a third attorney charging people for my time. However, I have the right to be a participant in discovery pursuant to my jurisdiction's procedures and my order of appointment. Although I will typically be present for any deposition either party wants to take (and, of course, for any deposition I notice), I will, on occasion, talk to both counsel and provide them with copies of questions I want the deponent to answer, ask if they will present the questions on my behalf, and then provide me a copy of any final transcript to review. If I choose to be absent from a deposition, I need to be certain my absence will not negatively affect my ability to properly represent my child client.

Because I am tasked with independently investigating my child client's case and often have carte blanche access to third parties, treatment providers, and otherwise confidential information, I rarely find a deposition necessary. I often feel as if I have more information (and often more candid information) than anyone else in the case. Having said that, there are times when a deposition may be necessary for evidentiary purposes. As a child's attorney, I cannot take a position unless that position is supported by evidence that I believe is likely to be admitted by the trier of fact. It can often be challenging to present evidence when you also have to balance a child's interests (e.g., trying to avoid having the child testify or having their therapist testify and destroy any therapeutic relationship the child has with their treatment provider).

I had one case where a parent told me that their child, my client, had a "bathroom issue," which raised a significant concern in my mind about the cause of this bathroom issue. I questioned third parties and the other parent about this behavior. Although I concluded that the bathroom behavior was not from some type of abuse, it was significant enough that a judge needed to know the mother had observed this behavior. It also likely warranted some type of professional interventions, either through therapy or a pediatrician. Unfortunately, perhaps because I found the behavior so concerning, when I questioned the mother on the witness stand about this behavior, she gave a very different picture and denied any behaviors on the part of the child. Had I issued discovery or taken the mother's deposition in advance of the trial, I may have been better able to preserve the evidence to present at trial.

(ii) *What If No One Has Noticed a Deposition, but You Believe One Is Necessary?*

Under my jurisdiction's rules, I am an attorney of record and have the right to participate in discovery. I have, in the past, noticed document depositions and oral depositions to preserve evidence. I have taken *de bene esse* depositions of experts that would be unavailable during the trial. The biggest obstacle in noticing a deposition as the child's attorney is the cost. Unless one of the parents will voluntarily provide for the cost of the court reporter (and possibly interpreter and office space) or your appointment order provides for a retainer sufficient to cover this cost, you may be limited in what you can do to obtain discovery. You may need to seek interim orders for costs or fees from the court if you feel a deposition is necessary to protect the child. The next obstacle is whether you have planned sufficiently far in advance to give the court time to review and order interim fees/costs. If not, you will not only be strapped for cash but for time as well and stuck in a position where no deposition could possibly happen before the scheduled trial date.

b. Issuing Discovery

If one or both parents have lawyers, the likelihood is discovery has already been issued, and it is fairly comprehensive. When I represent children, I often like to seek out information directly from outside sources, but there may be circumstances when I need it from parents/parties. I try to limit my requests. If the parents have no lawyers, I try to be very clear, with a lot less legalese, when I request the information. My goal is to obtain information, not trip up someone or pin him or her down to a position. However, as a lawyer, there is some legal strategy in taking a deposition or issuing other discovery. If others have issued discovery, review it and ensure all the legal factors are covered in the discovery requests. If they are not, issue additional discovery to protect your client's interests.

c. Responding to Discovery

My jurisdiction prohibits a child's attorney from testifying or providing a written report. Some jurisdictions will permit written reports if the reports are substantiated with evidence that is likely to be admissible under the jurisdiction's rules of evidence. (The court may acknowledge a report as being akin to a brief or a pretrial statement.) If you are in a jurisdiction where your role as child's attorney is treated like an attorney of record versus an expert who will evaluate the situation and testify, then you likely have a right to issue discovery and obtain responses; however, do you have an obligation to respond to discovery? Review your jurisdiction's rules and procedures carefully. It is possible that you will have an obligation to turn over all relevant discoverable documents, especially if you intend to rely on those documents at any trial, and they are not work product.

What happens if counsel issues you interrogatories? What if the interrogatories are not addressed to your child client, but addressed to you? In this case, your written responses would be likened to drafting a written report, which is prohibited under your jurisdiction's procedures. What if your jurisdiction does not have fully fleshed-out procedures, and you may now have an obligation to respond to discovery? Can you be deposed? Is it even proper to depose you, or should any and all discovery, including depositions, be of your client? What happens if your child client's deposition is noticed? Can you obtain a discovery protective order? On what grounds? Would you need to disclose confidential information to ensure the child is protected, such as information from the child's treating therapist? Would you, perhaps, opt to have your child deposed instead of testify in court, if it is likely the child may testify?

As a rule of thumb, any document I received from either side or any third party, unless confidential or work product, I provide to all parties and counsel. I do not share everything with my child client unless required or necessary. For example, I do not tend to share the pleadings, deposition transcripts, or financial documents with the child. These disclosures may serve to harm my child client or distress them more than educate or advise them. I will often talk to my child client in advance (and after the fact) when I speak to a third party, so the child is aware of what is happening. I do not want the child to be surprised or concerned if they hear this information from another source. The child's medical records or school records may make little sense to a younger child, but I will talk to the child if I have questions in the records or see anything out of the ordinary. I need to tread carefully in my conversations, always remembering that I am the child's attorney, not their parent. When I see the child has been tardy to school thirty-five times, is it my role to chastise the child and encourage the child to be on time? Or, is it my role to simply ask the child about the thirty-five tardies, understand under what circumstances those tardies could and did happen, and comprehend their explanation for those tardies?

§3.04 MODIFICATION ISSUES

If you are representing a child in a modification case (as opposed to an initial custody determination), you need to investigate whether there is a material change of circumstances. The burden to prove that a material change exists will be on the parent who is seeking to modify the existing custody order. However, you, as counsel in the case, will also need to address the issue. If you believe no material change exists, you may want to speak with the parent (or his or her counsel) who pled to modify custody about this impediment to moving forward with the case.

If there is no material change but you, as the child's attorney, nonetheless feel the order warrants some changes, you may want to push for a negotiated settlement, anticipating your child client may get no change otherwise. Although some material changes are evident, not all are—and not all actually play out in court as the parents anticipate they will. You need to include this as part of your investigation so that you know, strategically, where your child's case stands. It is horribly frustrating to spend time and money pursuing a modification of a custody order for your child client only to be told, by a judge, that you have no material change in circumstances and the order remains the same. Even if it is not your burden to prove in court, you need to investigate this issue so you can argue appropriately and approach the case in a way that is tailored to achieve your client's goals.

Negotiation and Settlement 4

§4.01 Taking a Position and Making a Recommendation

a. How Is a Recommendation Different from an Expert Opinion?

Every jurisdiction will require something different of you. In some states (or counties), you may be required to provide a written opinion or testimony. Your opinion may take the form of an evaluation that assesses the child's best interests. In many jurisdictions, this role is left to a mental health professional and takes the form of a custody evaluation, which is subject to certain processes and professional rules. Your report may be less of an opinion and more of a recitation of information you received during your independent investigation. This creates evidentiary problems, unless the information is presented in accordance with your jurisdiction's rules of evidence.

When you represent a child's best interests (as opposed to the child's express wishes), you also run into issues that you (a lawyer) are conducting some type of evaluation of this family, for which you are not appropriately trained nor are you qualified to give. A lawyer who represents a child's interests, even if prohibited from testifying or giving a report, will ultimately take a position. This position is presumably supported by evidence (admissible or not), which may be contrary to their own client's position.

The AAML Standards recommended that a child's attorney only ever be appointed to advocate for the child's express wishes; this is the only legitimate role an attorney can take. We are attorneys, not mental health professionals or evaluators. In many ways, being appointed to represent a child's best interests puts us in a position of making a professional assessment, often founded on information not admissible in court. We often form positions based on our child client's statements, even when the child does not testify. Yet, this "best interest" type of attorney is frequently appointed and serves a valuable role in advocating for a child, particularly when a child is not clear on his or her express wishes, is unable to articulate them, or is coached or trained to say things that may not accurately reflect the child's wishes.

Child's attorneys are tasked with independently investigating the child's circumstances and, like any attorney role, in counseling their client, which involves talking to the child about the process and outcomes. The attorney will need to carefully review all the information obtained in his or her investigation before taking positions for the child, but those positions are often the foundation of a settlement between the parents. It is, certainly, a fine line to walk between taking a position on behalf of a child client, ensuring the child client understands that position, working within professional and evidentiary rules to present that position, and opining on a child's best interests.

In negotiation, I often leave my positions open-ended. I present a lot of potential options that might work for the child, in the hope I can help the parents brainstorm. In some ways, I am acting as a quasi-mediator (yet recognizing that I am an advocate and not a neutral). It is fair for both parents and their lawyers to understand your positions in advance of going to court, even if those positions are not yet fully fleshed out. I will often abstain from giving an opening argument at trial when I represent a child's best interests, so I do not predispose the court without the court hearing the evidence and assessing the weight that it will give to any admissible evidence. I will then focus my closing argument on the evidence actually admitted. I may actually refine my position through the trial once I hear what evidence actually emerges and what does not. I do not want to look foolish at the end of a trial, when, in closing argument, I take a position that was not supported by the evidence presented. This also ensures I do a thorough job in ensuring that I can present evidence during the course of a trial that supports the position I ultimately feel is best for the child. I walk a fine line between presenting evidence to support my position and presenting all relevant evidence useful to the fact-finder. Even if a piece of evidence does not support my position, as a child's attorney, I need to ensure it is brought before the court (and, in negotiation, to the parents). This may differ from a parent's attorney and their presentation.

Note that, throughout this book, I refer to my "position." Some child's attorneys will say this is their "recommendation" as to what is best for a child. However, I believe that the word *recommendation*, although commonly used, is not entirely accurate. I do not make a recommendation. Experts will make recommendations. I take a position supported by evidence and argue that position, just as counsel for either parent argues their client's position. I also try to shy away from the use of the word *opinion* instead of *position* because it too implies I have some expertise to conduct an evaluation of my child client's circumstances.

There may also be situations where I cannot take a position. Perhaps the course of the case simply did not yield the information I ultimately determined was necessary to take a position. In a perfect world, I ask for information, get the information, and have the support of the court to order evaluations; however, this may not always happen. There may be no money. I may be appointed too late in the process to actually have sufficient time to request evaluations or studies. I may weigh requesting a continuance of the trial date against having more time to gather information; in certain situations, it may be extremely prejudicial to my child client to have a continuance. It often becomes very difficult to take a position where your gut may tell you something different than the evidence. It may be difficult to take a position where you are weighing two homes that are relatively comparable but, due to the case's facts, the child can only reside in one. In these situations, it may be that you simply lay out the facts for the judge (and in negotiations, to the parties and their lawyers), including applying all the evidence to the statutory factors necessary for the judge to make a decision.

b. How Much Information Do You Share to Legitimate Your Position, Particularly When It Came from Your Child Client?

There comes a point in my investigation when I begin hearing similar enough stories about the family that I can feel comfortable drawing certain conclusions. Typically, when I reach that point in a case, I contact both lawyers for the parents and schedule a conference call. I try to do this as soon as possible, but at least several weeks before trial, if time permits. The goal is to inform both lawyers of the information I gathered in my investigation, to present options for settling the case, and to ultimately inform both lawyers of the positions I am formulating on behalf of my client.

If I am a pure advocate, I will inform both lawyers of my client's position. It is only fair that both lawyers are warned, in advance, as to what information I may have, particularly if I am prohibited from providing a written report or responding to written discovery. It is almost always best to resolve a custody case before trial, and most of my child clients want that resolution. Therefore, I also aim to educate both lawyers, who do not have the breadth of access to information that I have, to give them unique options and to give them concrete positions so they can negotiate with their own client.

When I speak with both lawyers (either at my scheduled pretrial conference call or at any point before a trial), I share as much information as I am able to share. I often begin by summarizing the collaterals with whom I spoke, the documents I reviewed, and any interesting observations I made based on my years of experience. I try my very best, adhering to my professional and ethical rules of conduct, to avoid saying the words my child client has said to me. Only when I am permitted *and* also believe it serves the child's interests will I disclose their communication to the parents or their lawyers. In many cases, I avoid using the child's words entirely, trying my best to keep the child from being placed squarely in the middle of the dispute and fearing one or both parents may interrogate the child about what I said the child said.

I will often give the lawyers my assessment of the situation, which, in many cases, is instructed by the child's words. In these informal conversations, I tend to be more casual and appeal to the lawyers' experience working in contested custody cases. Instead of saying, "Nathan told me both parents put him in the middle," I may say, "I get the impression your clients will put Nathan in the middle." The distinction likely makes little difference overall and may not change how either lawyer presents the information to his or her client; however, if I can take any of the impact away from the child, I will do so.

In many cases where I represent a child's best interests, the child is relieved to know that they are not the decision-makers; ultimately, I figure out what is best with the help of their parents, other lawyers, and a judge. I also want my child client to be candid with me. If either parent goes back to the child and says, "I heard you told Melissa X," I lose credibility in my client's eyes; they will shut down and severely limit my ability to get useful information from them to represent their interests.

Ultimately, I cannot control what parents say to my child clients. I have had calls, voicemails, and messages from child clients accusing me of trying to hurt them or their parents. I have had child clients hate me for what their parent said I told them. This may be inevitable. A parent who may be upset at what I have had to say about the child's situation may try to persuade the child I am wrong, or to recant what the parent thinks the child told me. I may then have to be even more suspicious of my own child client's words going forward. This indicates that I may need to express my position and my investigatory information at a slightly later stage of the negotiations, after I believe I heard my child client's concerns and voice sufficiently well.

c. How Do You Address Parents Who Disagree with You Because You Do Not Disclose Client Communications?

When you represent a child client, you may be precluded, as the child's attorney, from disclosing what the child says to you (much like you would be if you were representing the child's parent). Even if you are permitted to disclose the child's communication to the parents or their lawyers, you need to weigh how you disclose the information. When a parent's lawyer knows your position, that lawyer may often push his or her client to settle in line with the position you have outlined, knowing a judge will give great weight to the child's attorney's position. It may be difficult for that parent to settle when that parent is being told X from their child and you are being told Y. Is the child lying to you? Is the parent only hearing what he or she wants to hear? What happens when the child's parent refuses to believe your position because the child is telling them something different?

It may be difficult to convince a parent of the virtues of your position if your position is primarily based on the child's own words. In these situations, I often choose to focus on the words of collaterals, school documents, and my own observations of the parents when pursuing my position. It is often difficult to ensure a child is presenting an accurate picture without independent verification, and you need to present evidence (that hopefully does not involve your child client testifying) to support your position at trial. The hope is that you have enough information to share with the parents to support the position you are taking. If you do not have enough information to support your position, you need to reconsider whether you must investigate further before taking that position.

It can be a difficult balance when a parent believes he or she has articulated their stance and information clearly, but you insist on spending their money and gathering more information, speaking to more people, reviewing more documents, and meeting their child multiple times. Representing a child can be difficult and time consuming. However, given the weight your position will have at any trial, it warrants careful investigation—which, if done well, will hopefully cause the case to reach settlement in advance of any trial.

I have had parents insist my position is not founded in reality because the child is telling them something different than my position. They want to know why I am not respecting their child and their child's opinion in this process. First, if I am representing a child's best interests, it may be that I know and respect the child's opinion, but disagree with it based on the other information I gathered. It may be that the child is actually telling the parent something different than they are telling me. A child may say what they want their parents to hear, or what they believe their parents need to hear, to protect their parents. When a parent challenges you based on what they are hearing from their child, it also raises red flags about how this came about. Did the child volunteer the information to the parent, or did the parent interrogate the child? Now that the parent spoke to the child, will the child change their story with you? If they do, what does that say about the weight you give to your child client's statements?

d. How Do You Interact with Parents Who May Be Involving the Child Too Much in the Litigation?

During your investigation, you may conclude that one or both parents are including the child far too much in the litigation. Even the most well-intentioned parents will hold their hearts on their sleeve or speak in not-so-hushed tones to a friend on the phone where their child will overhear. This may be inevitable. However, there will be cases where parents sit their child down and question them about what schedule they want with the other parent. They may show the child the court's documents. The child may be present when the parent was served with court papers. Some parents have even brought the child to court, whether it is at an initial status hearing or a full hearing, with every intention of the child speaking to the judge.

While I fully support a child understanding what is happening and having a say in their own lives, that involvement needs to be healthy and without additional pressure, stress, and influence. You are the buffer; however, even with you, a parent may remain unconvinced that the child will tell you what the parent believes the child wants or needs to tell you. In my initial protocol letter to all parties, I clearly state that parents should not discuss the case with the child and avoid behaving in a way that causes the child additional stress in an already stressful situation. This may fall on deaf ears. I may need to remind the parent and their lawyers, as well as ensure that the judge in any hearing or trial reviews a parent's bad behavior.

A parent who puts his or her needs or wants above the child will continue having difficulty differentiating the child's needs from his or her own; the parent also may behave inappropriately in other parts of the child's life. Be certain to communicate with the child. Ensure the child knows he or she can reach out to you if they feel uncomfortable with their conversations with their parents. Give the child permission to use you as an excuse: "Mom, Melissa told me I don't need to discuss this with you." You want to ensure a child is comfortable talking to a parent, but on his or her own terms with the child voluntarily sharing important information.

§4.02 COMMUNICATING WITH BOTH PARENTS/LAWYERS

a. In-Person Meeting Versus Telephone Call

There is always value to an in-person meeting. Although child's attorneys are not decision-makers, it is valuable to see a person's reactions and gauge whether you believe that the information they share is credible and trustworthy, and whether they really believe what they are saying. Having said that, it is not always possible to have an in-person meeting because of the distance, scheduling, or expense. I am more liberal at picking up a telephone and calling counsel. It is not uncommon that one of the two lawyers may be easier to work with; once your own position takes shape on behalf of your child client, there may be one of the two lawyers you more naturally gravitate toward because they are more closely aligned with your position. I always struggle with this because, even though I am asked to take a position on behalf of my client, I do not want to be perceived as taking sides. I also do not want to *actually* take sides. If I get too comfortable with one lawyer or one parent, I always fear I may miss something. If I become too entrenched with a particular position, I may feel uncomfortable considering my initial viewpoint was flawed. I try not to take any position until I am far into my investigation.

If I meet with one parent in person, I try to meet with the other parent in person to give balance to what I am doing. If one parent meets with me without his or her lawyer (with permission of that lawyer) yet the other parent has his or her lawyer in the meeting, I try to touch base with the absent lawyer by phone after meeting his or her client to give some balance. When I give a position or a summary of the information I gathered, I typically relay information to counsel simultaneously, never separately, and usually by phone conference. If I must relay a position to a self-represented litigant, I will speak with each parent separately rather than give my position and summary to them together, recognizing the acrimony between them and the possibility for fighting. Speaking to both sides separately does hold the potential for saying things slightly differently and leaving the sides with different impressions of where you stand, so be very careful.

b. Communicating with Each Side Separately or Doing It Together

I see a lot of value in having both sides of the case on a call or in a meeting when discussing potential outcomes, brainstorming solutions, and discussing my positions as the child's attorney. When gathering information, it is less important to do so—and, in fact, probably best to meet with each side individually (although some parents will be overly concerned about which parent you meet first). I often receive tidbits of information while talking to third-party collaterals, which I want to relay to one side or the other. For example, I may speak to my child client's therapist, who is concerned that the child's father is not reacting appropriately during discussions in therapy sessions with the child. The therapist gave the father suggestions, but he does not seem to be implementing those suggestions. In this case, I would pick up the phone, call the father's attorney, and have a candid discussion with him about what the therapist relayed to me about his client and what the father needs to do to interact better with his child.

In another case, I may receive a telephone call from my child client's school principal, who is very disheartened by the child's mother and her behavior toward a teacher. The mother entered school grounds and threatened to sue the teacher after a discussion about the child's behavior. Ultimately, this information is important to my future position and will need to be relayed to both parents. However, immediately, I may call the mother's attorney individually and ask what happened.

It is also not uncommon for one side or the other to take significantly more of your time than the other. You may need to continue reassuring both parents you are available if they have anything to share, so you do not give the appearance of favoring one parent simply because they are more talkative, louder, more passionate, more "in your face," or more demanding.

In summary, I typically follow the trend that if I am gathering information, then it is more productive to speak directly with one parent or their attorney. If I am generating options, settlement positions, or other sharing information that must go to both parents, then it may be more productive—and less likely to cause additional arguments—if I communicate with both sides together.

(i) *Case Study*

You represent two girls, ages seven and ten years. Their father is an Orthodox Jew and their mother is Roman Catholic. The parents share time equally with the children under a consent custody order. During your representation, you learn from the children that they are refusing to eat at their mother's home because she "won't buy them kosher food." How do you approach this situation?

In this case, my first step would be to conduct a reality check. Was the mother actually refusing to buy the children kosher food? If so, why? What things did the children communicate to the mother? What is the underlying issue? Do the children actually identify as Jewish? Were they raised Jewish in this family? How is the father instructing this dialogue between the children and mother, if at all? Is there an emergency if the children are refusing to eat for their entire time with their mother? To what extent do you urge the mother to be flexible, particularly if that does not necessarily address the underlying bigger issues? To what extent do you tell the children to be flexible? Do you have any obligation or right to even have this conversation, or must you proceed through court channels?

If the parents do not have lawyers with whom you can address this issue, how much discussion can you have with the self-represented party about what steps they should or should not be taking? Are you giving them legal advice if you suggest the mother should start buying kosher food? Are you causing more harm by dealing with the superficial issue instead of whatever larger issue underpins the children's ongoing dispute with their mother? What about the children's request for kosher food, and why they identify as Orthodox Jews, and with what religion did the children identify before the parents' separation?

In this situation, I spoke to the mother. I asked her questions, such as the following: Have the girls said why they want to eat kosher food? Have they always kept kosher? When did they start keeping kosher? What types of foods have they requested? Do you take them grocery shopping with you? Have they participated in selecting foods or making the menus in your home? What type of conversations do you have with the girls about their food selections? Have you talked to the girls about their choice of religion? How do you feel about that choice of religion?

By asking a lot of open-ended questions, I learned that the mother believed the father instigated a change in diet to "alienate" the children against her or fabricate reasons why they did not want to go to her house. She was not opposed to expanding the food choices at her house. She came to the conclusion, through my questions, that she would engage the girls more in the process of grocery shopping and menu planning. I was fortunate that the problem resolved itself the way it did. It also lent itself to providing more data points for me, such as whether the children would create additional impediments to being at their mother's house now that their desire for kosher food was met.

(ii) *Case Study*

During a home visit, your child client's mother pulls you aside and tells you that your child client is having bad bathroom behavior: He never feels clean and will clog the toilet with toilet paper. Without making the allegation, the mother raises sufficient concern that you question whether the child may have been sexually abused. You begin investigating, talking to others about this behavior to see whether it happened, what happened, and when it happened. During your investigation, the mother says that she was exaggerating. Even later, the mother claims that this behavior never happened *and* that she never claimed it did. How do you communicate with the lawyer, the mother, and authorities?

Your first obligation is clearly to protect the child. If you come across information requiring your immediate action to protect the child from harm, you need to take those steps, whether by reporting an incident to CPS and letting them investigate or filing an appropriate motion with the court (if you have sufficient admissible evidence) to warrant some type of change in the child's living arrangement or legal custody. Assuming that there is nothing concrete but for the mother's observation, then a lot of your communication with the lawyers and the parents is to continue investigating. When you are negotiating an outcome, however, it may be important to discuss what this behavior may mean and how to address it (whether through therapy, a doctor appointment, etc.). It may also be relevant to discuss the mother's communication with you. She told you something fairly significant and then denied ever telling you the very details that concerned you. This clearly shades whatever the mother has told you and causes you to question her candor. This is certainly something you should raise with her attorney. It may require some further investigation, particularly concerning the mother's ability to communicate with the father about the child's health and needs.

§4.03 COMMUNICATING WITH CHILDREN ABOUT OUTCOMES

Once you get a final custody order, your job is not done. Much like if you were representing one of the parents, you need to discuss the order and what it means to your child client going forward. In some cases, you may want to strategically schedule when you talk to the child client about the outcome so your voice is the first they hear—not either parent, with the parent's slant on the judge, the court process, fairness, justice, and expectations. Depending on the circumstances, the child client may be more anxious about hearing the outcome from a parent than from you.

One of the most important parts about communicating outcomes with a child is that you should stress they are not the decision-maker. You likely went through the variety of potential outcomes with the child before any trial or court order, but you may have abstained from talking about the likelihood of any one outcome. It may also be that the child does not have the ability to grasp the potential outcomes or understand the potential future scenarios, or the child may be too stressed to discuss them. Each child is different— even within the same family. When the child's parents are negotiating an outcome that will affect the child, the child should not only have input, but also understand the positive aspect of his or her parents communicating and cooperating. I always try to stress to the child that their parents are working very hard; both truly love the child and want what is best. I may articulate that sometimes parents are not sure about what is best and need help. Sometimes parents have different opinions on what is best, and that is okay. I have often found that the child client is more concerned about his or her parents working together than what the actual outcome may be.

(i) *Case Study*

Your child client is in residential drug and mental health treatment. She wants to return home to the parent in whose house she suffered significant setbacks that put her in treatment. She is outspoken that if a judge forces her to go to the other parent, she will run and no one will find her. How do you discuss outcomes with the child?

It may be difficult to address potential outcomes, in advance of any trial, with a child who is in a very fragile state. The first person I would approach would be the child's treatment team. I would discuss potential outcomes with that team and ask for their expertise on how the child may react to each, as well as what support can be set up for the child for the timeframe when you tell her about the potential outcomes (and then when you tell her about the actual outcome). The child clearly already made her wishes known to you, and presumably you have already explained your role (as either an advocate of her express wishes or her best interests) and the process. You may want to tell the child the potential outcomes, including the one she is adamant should not happen, with her support system in place. You are a lawyer, not a treatment provider. If the child has a relapse or outburst, gets violent, or becomes depressed or withdrawn, you do not know how to respond. She needs her treatment team. It may also be important to involve professionals when talking to any child client about potential outcomes or about the actual outcome, even if the child is not in such a dire situation as in this case study.

§4.04 INVOLVING THIRD PARTIES TO SETTLE THE CASE: COACHES, PARENT COORDINATORS, THERAPISTS, PARENTING CLASSES, SUBSTANCE ABUSE ISSUES, AND VISITATION SUPERVISORS

When a lawyer is appointed for a child, it is often due to the case warranting this additional perspective because it is overly complicated or there are special considerations. If you are involved in a complex case, it is acceptable to need help. You are a lawyer, not a mental health professional. You may need additional information to understand the impact of certain outcomes on your child client. You may need to work directly with the child's individual therapist or have a full custody evaluation of the family to determine the best outcome from a psychological perspective. You may need to suggest creative solutions for the family. You may need to involve certain therapeutic or educational services in the middle of litigation to help move the parents or child to a place where settlement is ripe. If a parent has a substance abuse problem, it is better for the child to negotiate immediate services for the parent instead of waiting for a court to resolve the issue. By negotiating interim solutions for the family, you could help the family get to a healthier place where a more creative solution can be had.

Most certainly, you should consider third-party services in your ultimate preferred outcome for your child client and advocate accordingly at a trial. However, these services should be considered to be part of a creative negotiation, as good outcomes for settlement and as stepping stones toward a full healthy resolution for this family. The key is always to settle matters amicably. Even in the cases where a child was overly involved in the litigation, was inquisitive, and requested their own participation in court, the child felt relieved and happier when the case settled. Not one child I have represented, even if they seemed to want to be actively involved, truly wanted litigation over settlement. Many were (unfortunately) fully aware of the expense and stress with litigation.

You can call upon a variety of professionals. When negotiating a parenting agreement, a mediator, parent coordinator, or coach may be extremely useful. A mediator—a third-party neutral—can help the parents discuss those issues to be resolved by focusing on their goals (instead of positions) and brainstorming creative outcomes. A parent coordinator may work with the parents, with or without lawyers, to get them to communicate better, build trust, and reach smaller solutions. The earlier you employ this type of professional, the better the situation may become.

Any process you can employ during the pendency of litigation to decrease tensions, and let the parents see that they have some common ground, may be helpful in reaching a final resolution. Using money on this type of professional may be preferable to using money on lawyers in a trial. A coach—or more accurately, two coaches (one for each parent)—will advocate for their client and also educate them about healthy and productive communication. They will essentially teach their clients to communicate better and serve as intermediaries to help move through impasses and toward solutions. Many times, solutions are right in front of everyone's face; however, the parents do not realize it because they are talking over one another, not listening, or communicating the same thing but in different words. They may distrust one another enough that they do not actually hear the words of the other and instead "assume."

It may also be necessary, particularly during the pendency of the litigation, to employ other professionals. If there are allegations of (or actual proven) substance abuse or anger issues, employing professional treatment early in the process will make for a healthier individual who can get to a place where they can have productive communication. If you are working with a family where one parent has had no or little access to their child, or where there are concerns about abduction or inappropriate behavior or abuse, agreeing to some interim supervised access may actually give additional data to everyone and start down a path to determine how the child feels about seeing this parent. Custody evaluators and reunification therapists may serve key roles in proposing and implementing longer-term processes earlier in the case to help move the family forward.

If you wait to start working with professionals until *after* any final resolution, you are setting this family back by months, if not a year or two, depending on how long it takes your court to schedule a final custody trial. Even if a parent or child does not reach a full and healthy state by the time of trial, employing professionals early will move everyone in the right direction. It will also increase the likelihood that a judge will see the utility and mandate the involvement of professionals in an ongoing basis.

§4.05 OVERLAP AMONG CUSTODY CASES, DOMESTIC VIOLENCE CASES, AND CIVIL PROTECTIVE ORDERS

Simultaneous to a custody case, one or both parties may have filed a second case requesting a civil protective order based on an allegation of abuse or violence in the household. As part of those civil protective orders, a court may order custody and/or access between the parents. The court may also issue a protective order on behalf of the child, seeking to exclude one of the parents entirely from contact with the child. In most of these situations, your order of appointment is in the custody case, not the companion domestic violence case. You may have no authority to act in the domestic violence case. You need to review your statute carefully and ensure your order of appointment is clear. You do not want to take steps in a case where you have no authority and no protections.

Having said that, you may be put in a difficult situation where your child client's interests are directly affected by a court order outside of your reach. If no one has asked to consolidate the domestic violence case with the custody case (if this is permissible), you may want to consider doing so. It may be impossible if the two cases are brought in two different courts. What happens if the protective order is in the District of Columbia Superior Court and the custody case is in Montgomery County Maryland Circuit Court?

Setting aside the jurisdictional analysis, you would need to conduct under the Uniform Child Custody Jurisdiction and Enforcement Act
(UCCJEA) and the care you need to take in not engaging in the unauthorized
practice of law, you may have an obligation to file some type of notice with
the case in which you are appointed to ensure the judge is aware of any existing case and any court order. However, you may have an obligation to at least
file some type of notice with the case in which you are appointed to ensure
the judge is aware of any existing case and any court order. The parties have
an obligation under the UCCJEA to provide this information in their initial
pleadings; however, particularly if the parents are self-represented, this may
not happen. Furthermore, the domestic violence case may begin after the
custody case's initial pleading is filed.

In the end, the judge in your case needs to have full information at his
or her disposal and may need your guidance to communicate directly with
his or her companion judge. Should you ask to intervene in the domestic
violence case? This may depend on the statute in your jurisdiction and
whether you hope to accomplish something in that case that cannot be
accomplished by simply ensuring your judge has all information available
to him or her.

§4.06 CHILDREN'S VOICES IN ALTERNATIVE DISPUTE RESOLUTION

There may be strategic or evidentiary reasons for directly involving a child
in a trial. The key role of a child's attorney is often to keep the child's
distance from the acrimony and turmoil inherent in litigation. However,
what about including the child (directly or indirectly) in the settlement
process, very specifically in mediation or a collaborative divorce? A lot
may depend on the mediator the family selects to help in the case. Mediators are not typically trained to speak directly to children, so the process
often includes trained specialists who speak to the child. If a mediator
is a lawyer-mediator, then the mediator may have no training at all for
including a child in the sessions or process because (in the United States,
at least) this is not typical. However, there may be significant reasons to
involve the child, to some degree, in the mediation process. At the very
least, if you are representing the child, you need to be included in any
discussion of settlement.

a. Child-Inclusive Mediation

Child-inclusive mediation is a form of mediation that includes the child's voice and preferences in the mediation process, usually by having a neutral third party speak with the child. This neutral third party may be called a "child specialist" in some contexts. The purpose of this type of mediation is to have the parents receive information directly from their child, while ensuring the child believes their opinions are protected and will not have negative ramifications for the child at a later date.

b. Child-Focused Mediation

Child-focused mediation is a more traditional approach. The mediator focuses the mediation discussions on the child's best interests by asking questions, exploring options, and discussing outcomes entirely centered on the child's interests. Child-focused mediators may use a child's attorney to help structure the process in a way that centers each session's agenda on the child to achieve a complete parenting plan.

c. Child Specialist in a Collaborative Case

A child specialist, also used in child-inclusive mediation, is typically a child therapist with experience in divorce and separation who gathers information about the child to bring into the dispute resolution process (in this example, in a collaborative divorce case). The child specialist is not an advocate or an evaluator and is not providing therapy to the child. They will not make a report and not make recommendations. The child specialist is trained to help put the child at ease and alleviate the child's stress related to the divorce by allowing the child to feel emotionally protected and having a voice in the process. The child specialist's training will typically include being able to identify coaching by one parent, being able to read a child's feelings and explore nonverbal cues, and then being able to productively and constructively communicate this information to the parents through the alternative dispute resolution process.

§4.07 APPROVING A FINAL SETTLEMENT BETWEEN THE PARENTS

Even though you are not a decision-maker, you are an advocate—either for the child's voice or the child's best interest. Therefore, if the child's parents reach a settlement agreement, you, as the child's attorney, need to approve of the settlement from the child's perspective. Before giving your blessing, it benefits your child client if you have a conversation with them about the terms of the settlement. You need to answer your client's questions. Your client may even present information that helps you suggest shifts in the final settlement. When you are a third lawyer in a case, there may be times when the parents or their lawyers forget to engage you fully in the settlement discussions. Be certain to assert yourself. If you see a final settlement going to the court that you have not reviewed, speak up. I prefer amicable settlements; thus, if both parents can reach an agreement, I typically approve of it. However, it is my job to bring forward any information that can call into question the advisability of the agreement.

LITIGATION

5

§5.01 TRYING A CUSTODY CASE

a. Strategy for Parenting Plans

Even when you are the third attorney with two competent opposing counsels in a case, you will still have plenty to do so that the judge receives the information needed to make a decision. In some cases, you may be the only person who knows certain details because you had more open access to records, potential witnesses, and information.

Even if you ultimately take a position in court, you will likely believe it is important to share all of the information you spent so much time gathering with the judge, even if some of the information may work against your position. When you represent a parent, you can clearly and ethically make judgment calls to present only certain information, in the best light possible for your client. When you represent a child, your strategy needs to ensure that a judge has all information needed to make the best decision for the child. It is possible that a judge will come to a different conclusion than you, which is okay. Your strategy simply needs to help the judge get to a sound conclusion.

The parents' counsel may forget even the simplest of questions, such as, "What schedule do you believe is best for your child?" Be prepared with sample calendars. If you have school business records, be sure to tab pages that help a judge find the most pertinent information. Bring a printout of the next year's school academic calendar. If you have health business records, question the parents from the records instead of formulaically handing up the documents in a pile to the judge. Make things easy for the judge. Go through your jurisdiction's "best interest" factors.

If you ultimately end up at trial, you should draw conclusions for the judge. You should be clear about your position (whether it is the stated position of the child or a position you feel is in the child's best interests). Make sure enough information is elicited during the trial to support your position with admissible evidence. You look foolish if you give a closing argument for a position not supported by evidence. Your position should not be based solely on your independent investigation; rather, it must be based on credible admissible evidence.

Be proactive in gathering sufficient documents, ensuring they have business record certifications, and preparing exhibits to question witnesses. Although I have never felt the overwhelming burden of production when litigating as a child's attorney, I always feel an extraordinary burden to ensure my position is sound and based in the evidence I know will be presented. I cannot trust either parent or their attorneys to present my case for me. It may be that they present a lot of the evidence I would have hoped would come out, but I cannot count on it. Participating in litigation involves participating in all stages. If the judge asks counsel (or the parties) to brief an issue of law, then that includes you. The ultimate conclusion on this issue of law may be irrelevant to the role you take or position you choose, but your brief may approach the issue from a different perspective. Although a parent's advocate may omit those parts of case law that do not fit their client's position, you can focus on the full picture and provide the judge with a comprehensive summary of the law. The judge may get a better overview or focus from your brief than a very argumentative brief on behalf of a parent.

Before going into court, the child should understand the position you will be taking, even if the position is not fully fleshed out with concrete details. This may be a difficult conversation if the child disagrees with you. You need to stress to the child that everyone—the parents, their lawyers, and the judge—is working hard to figure out the best solution for this child. You need to stress that the child is *not* the decision-maker. You may need to explain why the child cannot or should not be present at the trial. You may need to decide if the child should be present to testify, and how. You may need to explain potential outcomes to the child, particularly if an outcome may be unique or creative (e.g., use of a parenting coordinator, including the child in therapy, or supervised access).

At the trial, your position will ultimately be a presentation of your jurisdiction's custody factors and a summary of the evidence that supports the judge taking his or her own position. If helpful, you should prepare a proposed order or proposed parenting plan schedule for the judge to present during the trial. If you are preparing summary exhibits to use at trial, be certain to file your jurisdiction's rules for timely disclosing these summaries to the lawyers and parties.

b. Selecting Witnesses

You cannot rely on either parent to subpoena or call all the witnesses that you may need to prove your case. It may make logical sense that you be the attorney who subpoenas certain witnesses (e.g., the custody evaluator) and questions that witness on direct examination. You may need to enlist witnesses on your own. It may be possible for you to limit your witnesses to only those that each parent calls to trial. If so, you should have the opportunity to cross-examine each. It is likely you have already spoken to each witness as part of your independent investigation, so you should typically have notes on any potential witness that either parent calls at trial. Each judge will determine the order in which lawyers will present their case and question witnesses. In many circumstances, you will go last. If you have no new questions for a witness, do not waste the court's time creating new questions. However, be careful that all the questions are asked of this witness for the judge to have a comprehensive understanding of the child's life.

You will question each witness differently. You may be more aggressive or direct with some witnesses and more open-ended with others. My goal is always to get as much information as I can onto the record. Most of my witnesses will be fact witnesses, but it is also possible I will be required to call an expert witness. I may coordinate with counsel when it comes to certain witnesses. For instance, if a custody evaluator is part of the case, it may make most sense to call the custody evaluator as the child's attorney's witness. However, it may also make the most sense to call the custody evaluator first; if so, the person may need to be taken out of turn. Coordinate with opposing counsel so that the trial flows seamlessly.

If a child's therapist is testifying, you may have already established a good working relationship with that person. Thus, you may ultimately be the person who the therapist calls to ask questions about what to expect at trial, when to arrive to court, where to go, and how to prepare. I have had cases where a parent's counsel subpoenaed the child's therapist, but the child's therapist refused to talk to any lawyer but me before trial. I have also had cases where I have requested one or both parent's counsel to seek out an expert for trial when it was clear one was missing.

Finally, if the court sets deadlines by when a parent must designate an expert and provide that expert's opinion, that deadline may not include the child's attorney—particularly if the child's attorney was appointed later in the case, after scheduling and deadlines were already set. You may come across a person who should render an expert opinion at trial but that no one designated as an expert. Be strategic. Call the witness as your own because the parents may be precluded from doing so, unless given leave to amend their expert designations or reopen discovery. Be certain to follow your Civil Rules of Procedure with disclosures about the expert's opinion, even if a particular deadline did not include you.

I am always aware of the fact that, if I am calling a witness, it is highly unlikely that I had to provide discovery responses related to that witness. I am not always included in the "scheduling order" issued by the court because my appointment may have come after the scheduling or initial status conference/hearing. I am never trying to hide information from either party. I will often have conference calls with counsel before trial to ensure that everyone is on the same page. Be transparent.

(i) *Case Study*

You represent an eight-year-old boy. His mother, originally from Ukraine, wants to relocate the child back to Ukraine. Although she is a U.S. naturalized citizen and can remain in the United States, she has never held a job in the United States. The father is originally from Ukraine, but has lived most of his life in the United States. Most of his family is in this country, although he has a brother who remains in Ukraine.

As a child's attorney, you will investigate the child's best interests, including their relationship with both parents and extended family. However, it is clear from this fact pattern that you also need a witness who can educate the court about Ukrainian law. Will Ukraine respect the U.S. custody order? What happens if the child resides in Ukraine? What are both parents' rights in Ukraine? Are there any treaties or bilateral agreements between the United States and Ukraine? What happens if the child is in Ukraine and one of the parents refuses to abide by the U.S. custody order? You may also want a fact witness who can describe the community, schools, and resources in Ukraine available for the child.

Setting aside the inherent difficulty of actually finding a Ukrainian lawyer or someone who has sufficient knowledge or information about Ukraine, the other obstacle is the cost. You, as the child's attorney, may be limited in your ability to hire expert witnesses or pay for travel of other witnesses. In cases like this, after I conduct my investigation into Ukraine, its environment, and its laws and draw some conclusions, I typically approach both parents about the costs of this witness and why I believe this witness is a necessary component of the trial. If I am met with a roadblock, I may then revert to the parent who is paying my fees or the parent who would benefit most from the court understanding this information, then discuss whether that parent may pay the costs associated with the witness.

. Be certain to file any appropriate motion, notices of intent to rely on foreign law (in this fact pattern), requests for language interpreters, requests for appearance telephonically or electronically, or expert designations. Because the child's attorney is not typically bound to respond to discovery and may not be included in any court scheduling order where there is a deadline for expert designations, the child's attorney may have a bit more leeway to bring in an expert witness later in the litigation. Particularly if the child's attorney is appointed at a later stage of the court case, after discovery has already been exchanged, and conducts a thorough independent investigation, it may not be until that later date that the child's attorney realizes the necessity of a particular witness. Remember, however, that the child's attorney is still bound by the Rules of Procedure and will nonetheless need to follow all required processes to ensure the witness, if testifying, can do so without objection and without bankrupting the family. In this hypothetical, if you approach one parent, and not both, to ask if that parent will retain the expert, recognize you are making a judgment call placing you squarely at odds with the nonpaying/nonretaining parent, making a clear statement that you are siding with the position (at least on this issue) with one parent. If the paying/retaining parent you approached would derive no benefit from this expert, they are unlikely to retain him or her.

c. Deciding Whether the Child Should Testify

You should remind yourself routinely that, more than anyone else in the entire case, this child is the one who must live with what the court decides. There are a variety of reasons why a child should never go near a courthouse, but also some good reasons why they should, including that the child may truly want to testify and there may be no other source for the information that is crucial to the judge's ultimate decision.[1] There seems to be an unwritten rule in many U.S. family courts that if a child sets foot in a courthouse, that child will be forever affected to the child's detriment. A child may not always be harmed if he or she participates directly in the proceedings.

As the child's attorney, you are in the best place to assess whether this particular child may (1) be useful to the proceedings, (2) have information necessary for a custody determination, and (3) be harmed by being directly involved in the trial. It may be that the child's presence, as a witness, will lack all utility. Particularly if a child will refuse to speak, be too stressed to speak, has been coached by a parent, or is going to lie, then the child's presence may actually harm the process more than help it. However, the child may be the only source of the most important and necessary information. You, as the child's attorney, cannot testify. There may be no custody evaluator, no doctor or therapist, no excited utterances, no school reports, and no other way of ascertaining a child's objectives and views. In a legal system where one of the factors in a custody best interest analysis may be the child's views or opinion, how else do you elicit the information for the court?

A child's attorney must always weigh the necessity of the child's testimony against whether testifying may harm the child. Will testifying cause the child to feel as if his or her loyalties are stretched? Will testifying put too much stress and anxiety on the child, causing him or her to become physically ill? Will knowing that the child is testifying cause one or both parents to lobby the child, further entrenching that child in this litigation and making the child feel responsible for his or her parents' dispute? The general unwritten consensus within the U.S. family courts has been that a child should rarely, if ever, be directly involved in the litigation; often, the child is appointed an attorney for the primary purpose of ensuring the child is kept out of the litigation. However, the practical reality in the United States is that, in many courts, judges rotate on and off the family court bench; they may have little or no experience (or training) ever speaking directly with a child, let alone questioning a child as a witness. If a child is to testify, it is incumbent upon the child's attorney to take whatever steps are necessary to

---

1. Also refer to the discussion in Chapter 6 about the importance of the child's voice in cases that involve other countries and how that may affect your decision as to whether your child client should testify.

minimize the potential for harm to the child and maximize the veracity and reliability of the information the child will provide.

If your child client is directly participating in the litigation, you must prepare the child for their participation. You also should prepare evidence as to the child's maturity and competency so that you can guide the court, as is permitted, when it comes to appropriate questions to ask the child. The child's attorney must also understand that if they are appointed to represent the child's stated positions and not best interests, and the child wants to testify, the lawyer has an obligation to abide by the child's directives. This will add additional steps to the lawyer's preparation, including extensive preparation of the child, communicating with opposing counsel, and communicating with the court. You should consider filing a motion or notice with the court indicating that the child would testify, or speak with chambers to ask the judge's preference for how the child should testify. Do not simply show up on the day of trial with your child client in tow.

The child's attorney, in his or her preparation, should also consult with other professionals, such as the child's therapist (if any), about the impact testifying will have on the child. The lawyer should determine whether evidence can be obtained from other sources or whether the child's testimony is integral to presenting the child's case. Furthermore, the lawyer must counsel the child client about the impact of testifying, expectations, and the potential for cross-examination.

Periodically, you may be surprised when one of the parent's lawyers either appears in court with the child or issues a subpoena to the child to have him or her appear and testify. You must decide how to respond. If the child simply appears in court, is the child missing school? Is there an appropriate time for the child to appear, such as the end of the school day? Did you have sufficient time to prepare the child for being in court? Do you need to adjourn or ask for a continuance to prepare the child? If opposing counsel listed the child as a potential witness on any pretrial disclosures, do you have grounds to continue the trial date?

If you receive a subpoena for your child client to appear in court (and perhaps even bring along documents such as child client's journals, calendars, school projects, photographs, yearbooks, etc.), you need to know how to respond. In these situations, start by speaking with mental health professionals who are involved in the case. How will testifying affect the child? Should you file a motion to quash on the basis that this will unduly harass or distress your client? Should you contact counsel and ask for an alternative method to be used to preserve the child's testimony, such as a *de bene esse* deposition? If you are close to trial, do you need to request a continuance? Is the child client of an age and maturity where you feel they can testify? What will the child say? How will they react? What stress will they experience? Can you get an agreement between counsel and the court as to how the child will be heard (in the courtroom, closed court, who is present, what questions are asked)?

(i) *Options for an In Camera Interview*

If a child must be exposed to the court process by directly participating, you should take as many preliminary steps as possible to ensure that the child client feels safe and secure. One of the steps would be to ask that the judge conduct an interview of the child in camera, in lieu of in open court. Many judges who consider talking to a child in a custody case will do so in chambers or an empty courtroom, with no parent, lawyer, or other person present. The concern of the parents and their lawyers are always aligned with whether or not this type of interview—the information of which may be the basis for the court's custody order—should be done on the record and with lawyers (at least) present. The other concern may be whether the judge has had sufficient training to be interviewing a child in an age-appropriate way or whether an interview, which may last twenty to thirty minutes at most, would actually yield reliable information on which a judge can base his or her decision.

Your preparatory work can help the situation. You will want to speak with the judge's law clerk or assistant to ensure you understand the judge's procedure. You will want to speak with opposing counsel to see what they may agree to in regard to the child's interview. Will they agree that no one be present? Will they agree that they do not interrogate the child? Will counsel agree to submit questions to the judge, in advance, so that the court can make an educated assessment as to what issues are important to both parties before asking the child questions? Must you, at least, be present when the judge questions your child client, even if the other attorneys are excluded?

(ii) *Case Study*

You represent a fifteen-year-old boy. During one of your meetings with him, he has vividly described his father's behavior and how it makes him feel, and what result he believes should come of the custody litigation. After talking to quite a few collateral witnesses and both parents, and reviewing all the documents available to you, you believe that this fifteen-year-old child is mature and has information that cannot be obtained through other admissible evidence, is relevant, and is important to the court's overall decision. The trial is approaching, and you are torn between your need to keep the child removed from litigation and getting the information to the court. What do you do?

I would start by talking to the child client. In this situation, it may be irrelevant whether I represent his best interests or his express position. Talk to your client about the information he shared with you and how you believe a judge would want to know that information. Talk to him about court rules and how you cannot tell the judge that information, nor can anyone else except for the child, who has that information. Talk to him about whether he might be willing to go to court and speak with a judge. The child may have a lot of questions at this point. What will it look like? Will other lawyers question me? Will I be sitting in a courtroom? Will I miss my school day? Who else will be in the courtroom? What will my mom and dad do? Will they see me?

The truth is that you may not know all of the answers to these questions. If the parents have lawyers, approach them. Tell them you believe it is very important that your child client speak with the judge, but that you want to do so in the least confrontational way, with the goal of protecting the child as best you can. In most cases, the lawyers will work with you to create a process to permit the child to speak with the judge in the least detrimental way. What will the child's participation look like? When I last contemplated having a child client testify, I asked both parents' counsel if the parents would agree to join in a motion requesting the court hear from the child. However, it would be done in chambers, with only the lawyers present. The lawyers would submit written questions, in advance, to the judge, with the judge having final authority to select and ask the questions. I was fortunate that the counsel in this case were extremely sensitive to the situation. I knew counsel and believed them to be reasonable individuals who would also work to protect the child. I did, however, feel strongly that the child not be confronted by either parent.

It is necessary to have a game plan and to prepare the child client. The child client must know exactly what he or she may see and feel. It may actually benefit the child to go to the courthouse with you a few days in advance, walk around, see the inside of a courtroom, and gain a small sense of familiarity before going to court on the day of trial.

I work with both parents to ensure that the day and time the child is heard is the least disruptive to his or her schedule. When I represent a child, I hate disrupting their routine. I do not like the child to miss school or activities. This may mean that I have to see the child on evenings and weekends, particularly for an overscheduled child. If the court is willing to sit late one day, that may work best for a child, particularly if the child's dismissal time is closer to 4 p.m. and the court ends at 5 p.m. The courthouse may be quieter at an off-peak time. However, the child may simply need to miss school; thus, I hopefully already established a solid relationship with the school in advance, so I can speak with the principal or guidance counselor about what will happen. I also like to give someone at the school advance notice of the situation, so the child's primary safety network is looking out for the child to ensure he or she is showing no signs of stress that could be impairing or debilitating. The goal is to minimize the child's direct involvement in the litigation process, while respecting the child's need to have his or her voice heard in a process that affects the child more than anyone else in the family.

d. Preparing a Child Who Will Testify

Each child is different from the next. Each child therefore needs different preparation for any court testimony or judicial interview. A child may be very anxious to testify, even if he or she wanted to be a direct participant in the process. Therefore, the best preparation is to help the child envision what the process may look like. This visualization requires preparatory work even before having a discussion with the child because it requires the child's attorney to know the judge's requirements, process, and how opposing counsel and the child's parents will be involved in the child's interview or testimony. It may require you to know the precise judge in front of whom you will appear—something that some courts cannot predict until the day of trial.

The child is going to want to know if you will be present during their participation. The child may also want to know what questions people will ask of him or her. The child may want to know how they should answer. There may be a line where you prepare the child so much that the child is now living, breathing, and eating this court hearing, distracted from schoolwork and social activities. The child, if he or she feels they know precisely what will be asked of him or her, may rehearse answers to questions, may discuss these questions and how to answer them with a parent, or may act panicked if your questions are different from their expectations. You must address the impact the child's testimony may have on a child who has to leave the courthouse with a parent who may be unhappy with what the child has said. You have to assess whether your child client's words will be credible or coached, and you may be put in a position where you have to discredit your own child client's testimony.

Your child client may be more than the subject of his or her parents' court case. In some states, the child has legal standing to pursue some type of custodial arrangement on his or her own behalf. In that case, your child client may not only testify; the child may need to be prepared to more fully participate in the case in other ways as well. You will need to present admissible evidence on behalf of your child client. Ensure that the child fully understands the breadth of his or her involvement, what evidence can or cannot be presented, and the rules about what can and cannot be said in testimony.

If the child will be directly involved in the litigation, yet another question arises: Is the child subject to discovery? How do you, as the child's attorney, protect the his or her interests if something the child said at an earlier stage in the case is reflected differently in the stress of a courtroom environment? Are we mandating a child take a position about a parenting plan, and what happens if that position changes? A child tends to be self-focused. He or she may be focused on a moment in time and not a continuum or the future. The child may reflect things inartfully for court purposes. The child client may say one thing and mean something different, use different words to reflect things, or talk about his or her own life as if it was the life of a friend. Children may mix their situation with stories they have heard, television shows they have watched, or things they want to happen. They may reflect things as being the present circumstances when, in fact, this is not the reality. Should any child who testifies do so through, or with the guidance, of a mental health professional? Would a child's testimony be rendered useless to a judge without additional preparatory work to educate the judge about this particular child's deficits, abilities, maturity, etc.? Should the child be the last to testify, regardless of what order the case is presented, so the judge has sufficient background information to weigh the child's statements?

e. Preparing a Child for an In Camera Interview

An in camera interview may be less intimidating for your child client. It may also permit more flexibility for a judge and child in their interactions. It is also a bit less predictable than a traditional witness testimony, so it may be more difficult for you to prepare your child client for what he or she should expect.

Again, your child client may inquire about what the judge will ask. It is important, if you can, to help the child visualize the setting in which the judge will talk to him or her. This may help calm fears. If the child has a security blanket, a favorite book, or a teddy bear, it may be helpful for the child to bring that item along for the interview.

Whenever your child client is speaking with a judge, you will need to coordinate with his or her parents, particularly the parent who has the child on the morning of the court appearance. That parent will be responsible for transporting the child to the courthouse. That parent may need to bring the child at the same time the parent comes to the courthouse. If your courthouse has no daycare facility, you should speak with the parent about a third person's availability to sit with the child outside of the courtroom, and possibly transport the child to and from the courthouse. You should coordinate with the parents and judge to minimize the impact on the child's school day and extracurricular activities. This child's parents' dispute is already disruptive to the child, so you should do whatever you can to minimize further disruptions.

You will sit in the courtroom during the trial as your child client's advocate and not with the child outside the courtroom, so you need to put things in place in advance to ensure the child is appropriately supervised. You should also consider that there may be people who you do not want having access to the child client immediately before he or she testifies or meets the judge; that person may create additional tension or fear for the child. You need to schedule time with your child client in advance of the trial to prepare him or her, then be ready for the child's arrival in court if you want to speak further.

f. Courtroom Accommodations for the Child's Attorney

Courtrooms are not designed to accommodate a third lawyer in most jurisdictions. As a child's attorney, my usual spot in the courtroom is the jury box. In one courtroom, I was asked to sit at one of the counsel's tables. I moved as far to one side as I possibly could because it felt awkward and invasive; furthermore, I did not want a visual that I was siding with that parent. Regardless, I have had to do without comfortable chairs or a table on which to write or set exhibits. I am often set back beyond the judge's usual line of vision so that I have to stand, if not also step a few feet forward, to ensure I make my presence known. Many judges have become accustomed to only addressing the plaintiff and defendant, so they will often forget to turn to the child's attorney out of habit. Be organized. Use expanding file folders, a laptop, or whatever is easiest for you to access exhibits and other documents. I prefer exhibits and documents to be scanned. It is easier for me to access everything on a laptop, including my notes, witness questions, opening, and closing, rather than trying to thumb through binders that may be sitting on the floor or another chair in the jury box.

(i) *Courtroom Accommodations for the Child*

A courtroom is even less accommodating to a child than to that child's attorney. The best way to prepare for a child's participation in court is to talk to the judge's law clerk; be transparent and include both parents' lawyers when doing so. Ask the judge to exclude other people, particularly those not affiliated with your case, from the courtroom. Discuss, in advance, whether the child's discussion with the judge will be recorded, whether the judge will allow counsel to submit questions in advance or question the child directly, and whether the parents are permitted to be in the courtroom (or just their lawyers, or no one). Discuss with everyone whether you are permitted to be in the courtroom with the judge and child, even if no other lawyer is permitted in the room. A lot of this preorganization will come easier if you have a good relationship with the parents' counsel.

g. Third-Party Access

Each jurisdiction has its own third-party access/custody laws in place. The Uniform Law Commission is in the process of drafting a uniform act to address the variations in custody and visitation laws among states when it comes to third parties who are not parents and their rights to children.[2] Third-party custody cases will often include a child's attorney. Remember that you are an attorney for the child, not a social worker doing a home study or a psychologist doing an evaluation of the child's attachment to a third party. Abide by the laws in your jurisdiction. Structure your position in a way that is supported by the laws and how the facts fit the law.

Depending on the third parties, you may have significant hurdles, as discussed in other parts of this book: the child's psychological attachment to the person, an assessment of the party's financial contributions to the child (if that is part of the legal analysis under your law), multiple jurisdictions (particularly if you live in a metro area such as Washington, D.C., where family can easily live in Maryland, the District of Columbia, or Virginia),

---

2. *See* the Drafting Committee's website, including its memos and drafts, at: http://www .uniformlaws.org/Committee.aspx?title=Nonparental%20Child%20Custody%20and%20 Visitation%20Act (last accessed 7/2/17).

cultural issues, gender issues, and constitutional legal issues (related to the biological parent's rights).

You must also recognize that today's families do not always include a traditional mother, father, and child. Keep apprised of the law in your jurisdiction related to surrogates, adoptive parents, stepparents, grandparents, and others who have emotional connections to the child client. Some may have standing to pursue access to the child. Some may have no standing. Some may have standing, but not want to pursue access. As the child's attorney, you may be responsible for bringing these connections to the court's attention. For example, will one caretaker foster extended relationships more than the other caretaker? Stay up to date on child psychology and how to determine a child's psychological attachment to a particular individual, and how you, as the child's attorney, can bring that information before a court.

Practically speaking, having third parties involved may or may not make seeing your child client or gathering information harder. This may be particularly true if there is no clear order in place for you to gather information from the third parties or if the third party does not yet have any custody rights to the child and therefore cannot request documents for you from others (schools, doctors, etc.).

h. Whether to State a Child's Preferences

Know your jurisdiction's law, procedures, rules, and child representation guidelines before disclosing a child's preference. In one of my two jurisdictions, I am obligated to state my child client's position if I disagree with that position, even if I am appointed to represent his best interests and even if the information the child discloses to me is otherwise confidential. In a situation like this, you must advise the child client that this will happen. When stating a child client's position (whether or not it ultimately has any bearing on your position or the final custody order), it may have ramifications for the child in his or her daily interactions with his or her parents.

If you say in court that "Johnny wants to live with his father," then one or both parents (or others) may question Johnny about your statement. Johnny needs to know you are required (*if* you are required) to disclose his position. Forewarn Johnny's therapist (if any) that you must provide this information to the court. The therapist may be a resource for Johnny after the court issues a final custody order and your role as child's attorney ends.

If you are not required to disclose your child client's position in court and your role is to represent his or her best interests, not his or her wishes, then you need to be mindful of your ethical obligations to the child as client and hold the child's confidences. Furthermore, remember to distinguish an obligation to disclose your child client's position in court with disclosure of your child client's statements in settlement negotiations. Be cautious when speaking with counsel or the parents. If you describe things too loosely or are not careful about how you speak, things may get twisted and may land back on the shoulders of your child client, which could affect your relationship with him or her.

(i) *Advocating for a Child's Best Interests*

If you are advocating for a child's best interests, the child's desires may be irrelevant. Presumably, in your role as the child's attorney, you considered what the child told you he or she wants. Be certain to follow your jurisdiction's guidelines. Put forth sufficient evidence to support your position in the child's best interests and why that position differs from the child's position. This may include evidence or testimony showing a parent persuaded the child or influenced the child to make certain statements. It could involve psychologist testimony or evaluations. You need a good reason as to why your position differs from the child's desired or stated position.

(ii) *Advocating for a Child's Position*

If you are representing a child's stated position, be certain you clearly understand their position. A child may have difficulty articulating a position—their language and communication skills are still developing. They may have different views of time and place. They may say something one day and something different the next. The child is not necessarily immature and their position should hold no less weight for you or the court. You simply need to speak with the child and conduct an independent investigation—sufficient enough to comprehend his or her position so you can articulate it clearly to a judge. You will want to present all of the necessary details for a judge to issue a comprehensive court order: precise schedules, transportation, schools, medical issues, preferred therapists, holidays, vacations, and extracurricular activities. All of this must be substantiated with evidence.

(iii) *Case Study*

You represent a fifteen-year-old boy. By all reports, he is extremely intelligent and mature. When you speak with him, he clearly voices a very articulate opinion. After questioning him, you are satisfied that he is mature enough to voice this opinion to a court. You take the position that his opinion should be implemented. When you articulate his opinion to the lawyers, the client's mother begins questioning the child. The child apparently tells her something different than what he told you, so now the mother refuses to respect your position.

First, you must be completely clear on your role in representing this child. Do you represent the child's best interests or the child's stated wishes? In this case study, you would likely advocate for the same result in either situation, regardless of your appointed role. When you give the parents or their lawyers your position (which happens to also be your child client's position), you must be very careful on how you represent that position so you are not disclosing the child's confidences and not putting the burden on the child. Regardless, even if you convince everyone this is *your* position, not the child's, you cannot control the parents, questioning the child and possibly receiving a different story.

In this case study, speak with the mother's lawyer. Try to understand the mother's conversation with your child client. Do your best to not be noticeably agitated on your call with the lawyer. Ask to schedule another appointment with your child client. Be aware that the child may be less candid with you now, out of fear that he may be questioned yet again by his mother. If you are fortunate, the child probably knows his mother is someone who would intervene, so he dismissed it. Listen to the child, and see if his recitation of the facts and his position remain clear and confident. Is he affirming the position you adopted as your own, or is he recanting and taking the mother's position? After speaking with your child client, act accordingly. Did you confirm the mother's intervention? Does her behavior cause you to rethink the position you took for your child client?

i. Closing Arguments

My closing argument is perhaps the most important part of my presentation in court. When I give an opening argument, I rarely state my position on behalf of my child client. I do not want to supplant my judgment for that of the court, and I want the court to see the evidence and draw its own conclusion. Some judges may not fully grasp that I am not an evaluator, particularly in jurisdictions that only just recently began prohibiting child's attorneys from writing reports or testifying.

At times, new information is presented at trial that affects the position I plan to take on behalf of my child client. Before trial, the parents and their lawyers know my thoughts on the case, including the position I am leaning toward, if I am taking one. However, if we are forced to a trial, I look at the information with fresh eyes.

In your closing argument, the judge typically wants you to "tell" him or her "what to do." If you practice in a jurisdiction where you are obligated to state your client's position, use your closing argument to do that. Summarize the evidence and state any positions you have. You may not have a concrete position. Even after trial, you may still feel as if you have insufficient information. During the trial, issues may have conflated or certain witnesses may have seemed less credible than anticipated. You are not the judge. You are not a custody evaluator. If you have no position, then very clearly lay out the evidence focusing on your client. Go through the same legal analysis the judge will ultimately need to do. If you do this, the judge should have the tools he or she needs to resolve this family dispute for your client.

Be prepared for the judge to ask you questions during your closing. A judge may try to box you into a concrete, detailed position. Although you will organically reach a conclusion in most cases, sometimes you will not be able to reach a concrete position. You may have thoughts or even gut feelings. You may see certain evidence that you feel is more relevant to your client than other evidence. Your job is to aid the judge in focusing on your client, either that child's stated wishes (and why those wishes should be respected) or on that child's best interests. I have had judges try to shame me into making their decision for them. I, myself, have felt shame for not taking a concrete position at times, particularly if I am being paid as a third attorney. However, you need to stand your ground. You are not a judge. You are not a custody evaluator. You have a job. Do it, even if it may not make everyone entirely happy.

The reality is that representing children can be fairly lonely. You sit in court alone. You are typically away from the other lawyers, often in the jury box. The judge may forget to let you take your turn. You show up to court right before trial, with the other lawyers and their clients either propositioning you or avoiding you entirely. By the time you get to trial, you have likely said enough to cause at least one side, if not both, to be upset with you.

j. Proposed Custody Order

I practice in two different jurisdictions. In one, judges will often ask for proposed custody orders (including full findings of fact, conclusions of law, and final proposed judgment). In the other jurisdiction, this is rare.

If you are representing a child, there may be significant issues the court must address above and beyond an access schedule. The court may need to address special protective measures related to the child's travel, relocation, a parent's substance use/abuse, parenting classes, therapy, parenting coordination, and future evaluations, among others issues. It may be helpful to the court that you propose a comprehensive custody order (or parenting plan) that supports your position. This also gives you a second chance to summarize the position you stated in your closing. A proposed order allows you to clearly articulate a schedule for the child, including holidays, times, and exchange locations.

Judges have a huge undertaking and do their very best to address all necessary issues with a comprehensive order. However, it is easy to miss a point that may be small, yet consequential to your child client. If and when you propose a custody order, be certain that the position you take in that proposed order is supported by evidence presented at trial.

k. Evidentiary Issues

(i) *Authenticating Records*

Remember that you are an attorney. If you plan on presenting documentary evidence to a judge at trial, you must authenticate it. Issue discovery (requests for admissions) to request authentication or stipulations to certain documents. Request business records certifications, even if the records are voluntarily turned over to you from a provider. Follow proper procedure for asking a witness to authenticate a document in court, whether it is an e-mail or bank record.

(ii) *Hearsay Issues*

In nearly all custody trials, at least one witness will say, "Little Johnny said … ," then relay a child's statements to that person. Is this hearsay? Yes. Should it come in? It depends. Does it fall into one of the hearsay exceptions? Is it a present-sense impression (a statement describing or explaining an event, made immediately after or while the declarant perceived it)? Is it an excited utterance (a statement relating to a startling event, made while under the stress or excitement causing the statement)? Was the statement made for medical diagnosis or treatment (made for and pertinent to diagnosis or treatment and describes medical history, past or present symptoms, their inception, or their general cause)? Is it not being offered for the truth of the matter asserted in the statement? Is the statement said to a forensic expert and used in rendering an opinion? Be creative if you would like certain statements to be admitted at trial.

§5.02 PARTICIPATING AS AN EXPERT WITNESS

The ABA and the AAML clarified the role of a child's attorney to limit the attorney to only that of an attorney. You are not a witness. The standards attempt to deconflate the role of attorney from that of a guardian *ad litem*, which is now more synonymous with a professional who is appointed to testify about the child's best interests. Although the child's attorney may take on the role of a best interest attorney, the role of child's attorney is always as an advocate, not a professional expert. There may be some jurisdictions that still require a child's attorney to serve in a quasi-expert role, prepare a report, and make clear recommendations, almost as if serving as an evaluator. If you serve in this role, then you need to be fully cognizant of your limitations and your liabilities. You need to exercise discretion and best practices in preparing a written report (if one is required), what credentials are required of you to qualify as an expert (and an expert on "what"), and how you should make a clear recommendation that is, after all, founded in law and admissible evidence.

a. Best Practices in Preparing a Report

If you prepare a report for a judge, be certain that the judge clearly articulates what he or she expects as part of that report. The report should be factual and based on admissible evidence. As a rule of thumb, if it goes in a report, there should exist some piece of evidence at trial to substantiate it. The report may also require a legal analysis, akin to a brief. The report may take the form of a pretrial statement, outlining the jurisdiction's best interest factors; for each factor, it can outline the evidence that will be presented at trial to support it, as well as an argument for or against a particular outcome. If your report is that of an expert witness, be certain to follow proper protocol for your profession and jurisdiction.

If your report is more than a summary of your recommendation and is, instead, an expert report, it will need to provide a written summary opinion discussing the testimonial subject matter, the facts and opinion, the basis for your opinion, reports, lists of publications authored by you, and a record of your previous testimony. You will have been subject to discovery before trial and should have disclosed summaries of your opinion, your qualifications, any publications, your compensation, and other requested information.

b. Qualifying as an Expert

Attorneys are not experts. Furthermore, ethical rules exist against testifying, as well as certain conflicts of interests in doing so. If you are expected to testify as an expert, you must meet qualifications to provide your expert opinion to a judge. Your opinion should be based on facts or data you have actually seen, heard, or had communicated to you at or before the hearing in court. You may be less concerned about the admissibility of the facts or evidence upon which you rely. Typically, experts are trained in a concentrated area of practice and apply known techniques to reach their conclusion. You need to be qualified through knowledge, skill, practical experience, training, education, or a combination of these factors. You must know the methodology and procedures employed and have a sound basis for your opinion.

c. Making a Clear Recommendation

As an expert, you can express an opinion on an ultimate issue of fact, but not the mental state of a person. As an attorney, you would be incapable of providing an opinion on your child client's maturity or mental state. However, you could provide an opinion on the ultimate issue in the case—where the child should reside, which parent should make a legal custody decision on his or her behalf, and what other measures need to be employed to protect the child.

§5.03 SIMULTANEOUS PROCEEDINGS

Other cases may directly affect your child client simultaneous to your custody case, such as abuse or neglect proceedings, domestic violence protective order cases, or a Hague Abduction return petition. Do you have an obligation to also participate in those simultaneous proceedings? This will directly relate to your jurisdiction's rules. Do you have standing to petition the court in another case where you are not the child's attorney, either on behalf of your child client or independently? Do you have the authority or obligation to bring the other case to your custody judge's attention and ask that the judges in the two proceedings communicate, and, if able, consolidate efforts? Should you request, if possible, that the same judge be assigned to both matters, if within the same court?

Be certain to review your court order of appointment. You are limited in what you are permitted to do, and you must remain within the bounds of your appointment. If your jurisdiction permits, authorizes, or mandates your participation or intervention in other proceedings, be very clear in what your role and limitations will be. Your work in another case, despite your best efforts, may create an ethical dilemma where you may be mandated to disclose otherwise confidential information, pursue relief that your client may not want, or testify when you may otherwise be prohibited from doing so. The simultaneous proceeding may mandate the child's participation even if your position, acting on the child's best interests, is that their participation is not in the child's interests. You may find it difficult to execute your duties under the appointment order if thrust into another proceeding. However, if the simultaneous proceeding will yield an outcome that could directly affect your custody case, it cannot be ignored. When in doubt, file an appropriate notice or motion with the court in your custody case so that your judge is aware of the simultaneous case.

§5.04 SEALING OR SHIELDING A CASE

Each jurisdiction has its own rules and procedures for when it is appropriate to seal a case file from public inspection or shield certain information in the file. It may be important for your child client to limit other's ability to review the court file. In one of my jurisdictions, all docket entries are listed publicly online. Therefore, if there is an order for my child client to engage in therapy, that child's future college or employers will see that entry and know my client has some level of emotional or mental health issues that are being treated.

In most jurisdictions, if you go to the courthouse, you can access the court file, review it, and even photocopy parts of it. Although it is less likely that a college or employer will go to that length, there are still nosy neighbors, the parents of your children's school friends, or possibly even strangers who can access, at times, very extensive orders related to your child client's health and well-being—including what days, times, and locations the child can be found and with whom. It provides a treasure trove of information for people who may potentially wish harm on your child client, such as if your child client has a stalker or their parent is a district attorney who prosecutes criminals.

Although jurisdictions should have certain privacy rules in place to limit disclosure of identifying information such as full names or birth dates, some lawyers may forget the rules. Alternatively, there may be a need in certain circumstances to include all of those details directly in a court order (e.g., if law enforcement will pick up the child from an abducting parent). Do not expect the parents' lawyers to request the court to either shield or seal parts of the case file. You should take this additional step, before the conclusion of litigation, to ensure that your child client's privacy and safety are protected.

INTERNATIONAL CASES

6

§6.01 THE ROLE OF THE CHILD'S VOICE IN INTERNATIONAL CUSTODY CASES

a. Introduction[1]

Article 12(1) of the United Nations Convention on the Rights of the Child (UNCRC) states, "States Parties shall assure to the child who is capable of forming his or her own views the right to express those views freely in all matters affecting the child, the views of the child being given due weight in accordance with the age and maturity of the child." As of this book's publication, the United States is the only country that has not become a treaty party to this international human rights instrument.

I mention the UNCRC not to cast aspersions on the United States. One may argue that the United States far exceeds the mandate in the UNCRC to protect children, or at least goes beyond many countries that are States Parties. I bring the UNCRC to the reader's attention because it is the backdrop of other countries' views of

---

1. Judge Peter Boshier, the Principal Family Court Judge of New Zealand, penned an article for the Association for Family and Conciliation Courts nearly ten years ago advocating for counsel (or another appropriate advocate) to be appointed for children in every child custody case. *See* http://www.afccnet.org/Portals/0/PublicDocuments/ProfessionalResources/judgeboshier-WITHendnotes-web.pdf?ver=2013-08-21-072408-000 (last accessed 1/14/17). In another example, the Constitution of the Republic of South Africa (1996) provides every child the right to "have a legal practitioner assigned to the child by the state, and at state expense, in civil proceedings affecting the child, if substantial injustice would otherwise result" (Ch. 2, Sec. 28(1)(h)).

the United States and the manner in which our children (and their children if their children are so subjected to our family courts) are given a right to express their own views in a custody proceeding.

This chapter is also not meant to debate the merits of the many methods by which a child's voice may be heard in child custody proceedings—custody evaluations, child specialists, mental health professionals, teachers, parents, or the children themselves, to name a few ways. This chapter aims to give the reader an understanding of how a child's attorney can be incorporated in an international case, as well as the difficulties and benefits in doing so. If another country believes the child's voice must be heard and given weight based on the child's age and maturity (because that country's laws mandate it), then a U.S. family court should consider how this will affect an international custody arrangement involving the United States and that other country.

Note that I refer to "international" cases in this chapter. This reference is meant to include custody cases with international elements, not custody cases in foreign courts.

b. Hague Convention of 19 October 1996 on Jurisdiction, Applicable Law, Recognition, Enforcement and Co-operation in Respect of Parental Responsibility and Measures for the Protection of Children ("1996 Convention")

Although many practitioners may be familiar with "the Hague Convention" (i.e., the 1980 Hague Convention on Child Abduction), a number of Hague Conventions affect children and families. The 1996 Convention was signed by the United States on October 22, 2010.[2] The Uniform Law Commission reconvened its drafting committee for the Uniform Child Custody Jurisdiction and Enforcement Act (UCCJEA) to add amendments to the UCCJEA so that it comports with the United States' obligations under the 1996 Convention. As of this book's publication, the U.S. government is advancing this treaty through the ratification process; it is not yet law in the United States.

The 1996 Convention is important for a number of reasons—one of the most essential being to "provide for the recognition and enforcement of … measures of protection."[3] For our purposes, in this book, measures

---

2. *See* the Hague Conference's Status Table for the 1996 Convention at https://www .hcch.net/en/instruments/conventions/status-table/?cid=70 (last accessed 1/14/17).

3. *See* Article 1(1)(d) of the 1996 Convention at https://www.hcch.net/en/instruments/conventions/full-text/?cid=70 (last accessed 1/14/17).

of protection equate to custody orders. This treaty will more readily enable U.S. custody orders to be recognized by other countries that are treaty partners with the United States under this convention.

Family practitioners need to be cognizant of a specific provision in the 1996 Convention that relates specifically to this book, which is that a foreign treaty partner may nonetheless refuse to recognize a U.S. custody order if that custody order was made "without the child having been provided the opportunity to be heard, in violation of fundamental principles of procedure of the requested State."[4] This language should raise a red flag to a practitioner who is handling an international custody case and alert that practitioner to the importance of ensuring the child's voice is heard in the U.S. custody proceedings, in a manner that comports with the other country's methods of hearing a child.

During the Hague Conference's Sixth Special Commission meeting on the Practical Operation of the 1980 Convention and the 1996 Convention, delegates discussed the role of the child's voice in international custody and abduction cases. The delegates reached two conclusions that were memorialized in an official Hague Conference document at the end of the first of two separate meeting dates, specifically:

> 50. The Special Commission welcomes the overwhelming support for giving children, in accordance with their age and maturity, an opportunity to be heard in return proceedings under the 1980 Convention independently of whether an Article 13(2) defense has been raised. The Special Commission notes that States follow different approaches in their national law as to the way in which the child's views may be obtained and introduced into the proceedings. At the same time the Special Commission emphasises the importance of ensuring that the person who interviews the child, be it the judge, an independent expert or any other person, should have appropriate training for this task where at all possible. The Special Commission recognises the need for the child to be informed of the ongoing process and possible consequences in an appropriate way considering the child's age and maturity.

---

4. *See* Article 23(2)(b) of the 1996 Convention at https://www.hcch.net/en/instruments/conventions/full-text/?cid=70 (last accessed 1/14/17).

51. The Special Commission notes that an increasing number of
States provide for the possibility of separate legal representation of
a child in abduction cases.[5]

The language of the Hague Conference left open the possibility for children's voices to be heard through a variety of mechanisms. U.S. practitioners
are familiar with many of those mechanisms, some of which may be valuable and warranted in some cases, but inappropriate and harmful to the child
in others.[6] Depending on where a person practices in the United States, some
mechanisms for hearing a child's voice may be unavailable or, if available,
might be cost-prohibitive for some families. Judges and lawyers weigh their
options on a daily basis as to how to ensure a child's voice is heard, when
appropriate and in the child's best interests, in a way that is effective, helpful,
and designed to ensure a comprehensive and fair result for the child.

This author advocates that a child's attorney is perhaps one of the most
appropriate ways to incorporate a child's voice into custody proceedings,
provided that the child's attorney is trained. That attorney can not only assess
the child's maturity, advocate for a good result, and ensure the child's voice
is heard in an appropriate and healthy way, but also can ensure that the child
is informed of the legal process and possible outcomes. A child's attorney
can work with other professionals, such as mental health experts, to provide
for a comprehensive outcome for the child.

c. Direct Involvement of Children

If you work with an international family, you must educate yourself on the
laws of the other country, specifically the laws relating to a child's participation in legal proceedings. Even though your case is pending in a U.S. court,
your goal should be to take whatever steps are necessary in your proceeding

---

5. *See* the Hague Conference's Sixth Special Commission Meeting—Part I Conclusions and
Recommendations, numbers 50 and 51, at https://assets.hcch.net/upload/wop/concl28sc6_e
.pdf (last accessed 1/14/17).

6. The Hague Conference's Practical Handbook on the 1996 Convention specifically states,
at paragraph 10.6, page 105, "The Convention does not seek to amend national procedural
rules regarding hearing children and this provision [in Article 23(2)(b)] operates so as to allow
a requested Contracting State to ensure that its fundamental principles in this regard will not
be compromised when recognizing a decision from another Contracting State. The provision
is influenced by Article 12 of the UNCRC, which sets out the right of the child to be heard
in proceedings that concern him or her. However, it is important to emphasise that it is only
where the failure to hear the child is contrary to the fundamental principles of the requested
Contracting State that this may justify a refusal of recognition." *See* https://assets.hcch.net/
docs/eca03d40-29c6-4cc4-ae52-edad337b6b86.pdf (last accessed 1/14/17).

to ensure your custody order will be enforceable in the other country having connections to this family. If the other country has law mandating a child's voice be heard in a custody case, you need to understand that law and know the ways that the other country permits the child's voice to be heard. In some foreign countries, lawyers are appointed for the child. In others, a social worker will conduct an evaluation. However, in quite a few, particularly because the United Nations Convention on the Rights of the Child is law in all countries but the United States, a child will (and must) be heard directly by a court. You need to understand how another country's mandate to hear a child directly by the judge will affect your court case. For example, if the foreign country mandates that a judge must interview the child and your U.S. judge does not interview your child client, your U.S. custody order may be unenforceable in the foreign country. It also may be subject to being entirely modified by the foreign court should the foreign parent seek to open a case in that country.

U.S. judges are typically averse to hearing directly from a child. With U.S. judges being appointed, elected, and shifting between civil, criminal, and family dockets during their careers, a U.S. judge may have little experience interviewing a child. For some children, being brought before a judge in a courtroom or in chambers may be particularly traumatic and may even cause the primary custodial parent to influence the child's statements to the judge. However, if you have an international family and your child client needs this custody order enforced in the foreign country, you must educate yourself about foreign law.

The Hague Conference on Private International Law, at its Seventh Special Commission meeting in October 2017, concluded that a court "should incorporate into the order for measures a record of the way the child was heard, or if a decision is made not to hear the child, an indication that consideration was given to doing so and the reasons for the decision not to hear the child."[7]

§6.02 PRACTICAL ISSUES: HOW TO REPRESENT A CHILD WHEN THAT CHILD IS OVERSEAS

a. Traveling and Culture Judgments

It is atypical for a child's attorney to be afforded the resources to travel to another location to meet with his or her child client. This is even more

---

7. *See* Conclusions and Recommendations of the 7th Special Commission, para. 50, at https://assets.hcch.net/docs/edce6628-3a76-4be8-a092-437837a49bef.pdf (last accessed 12/20/17).

prevalent in cases where the travel involves the cost of the attorney traveling overseas, obtaining visas, and maneuvering in other cultures. If the attorney believes it is absolutely necessary to see the child in the child's overseas environment, however, the attorney should request sufficient funds from the court (through the parents) to permit this travel, justifying why the travel is needed, particularly when the lawyer cannot testify as a witness to what he or she observes.

If the child is unable to travel to his or her attorney and the attorney believes it necessary to meet with the child client in person, then travel may be necessary. If the attorney needs to observe the child client within a particular culture, setting, home environment, school, or other surroundings, then the travel is important. The attorney must use his or her judgment as to whether the benefit of seeing the child in this other country outweighs the cost to the family. Seeing a child within this other culture may be significant for the attorney—it may help the attorney frame his or her investigation, may provide insight that cannot be had through a conversation, and may help the attorney move outside of his or her implicitly biased American stereotypes. If the attorney visits the child or his or her parent's environment in the United States, then a visit overseas may show a balance in the attorney's investigation. Alternatively, a request for compensation to travel overseas may be seen as a luxury—frivolous or wasteful by the attorney. However, the attorney should not underestimate the value of observing the child client in this foreign environment, particularly if the issues before the court are whether the child should be living in or visiting this environment.

b. Comparative Research on Countries

A child's attorney may be obligated to represent the child's actual wishes or may represent the child's best interests. Regardless, it is important to understand everything in its own cultural context. Things that may be considered dangerous, unlawful, or neglectful in the United States (e.g., letting a young child ride the subway alone to school at a young age, leaving a child alone in a stroller in the cold outside of a restaurant) may be common in another country. A child's attorney needs to independently research both environments in which a child may be living or visiting. You need to assess the context in which a parent makes certain decisions. Is a child better off living with one parent who lives in a house that has a panic room and requires a security escort to school each day, or with a parent who lives in an affluent suburb across the street from a top-notch elementary school? When one parent paints a very bleak picture of the other parent's living situation, the child's attorney will need to research the situation further.

The child's attorney should not assume that he or she knows or understands another country, its culture, or its customs without further research. A child's attorney is not a parent's lawyer who must advocate that the other parent lives in the bowels of hell. Every child is different, and some may thrive better in certain situations than in others. A child's attorney may also need to assess the different countries' social welfare systems, health care, and education, among other subjects. Parent A may live in a country with very poor public schools, but there may be private school options. Parent B may live in a country where protests are a daily occurrence, but in a gated community on the outskirts of town, away from the protests. A child's attorney needs to look at a variety of factors about a country.

The child's attorney should first look to easily accessible resources, such as the U.S. Department of State's website. Are there travel bulletins for a particular country or region? Is the country listed on the Department of State's yearly report as being noncompliant with laws and treaties that relate to child custody and abduction?[8] Should you consult with a risk assessment professional, who can talk to you about the living situation in the neighborhood where the child would be living or going to school in the other country? For instance, if the country has a high crime rate, would the parent be exposing the child to danger, or is the neighborhood that the parent chose safe? Is the neighborhood policed routinely, does the house have a panic room, is the child escorted to school, are there U.S. embassies or consulates to serve Americans nearby, and how does this compare to where the child may reside in the United States?

It is not enough to gather information about the country, but the child's attorney must also ask how that information affects this child. Will the child be living with a parent in Country C working in a job that is dangerous (e.g., a foreign aid worker, military, high-level official who needs security)? Will the child be living with a parent who works long hours or travels a lot for work? Will the child be in the care of a nanny or live-in companion (which may be more common in some countries than in others)? Does a particular country have better resources, tutoring, or

---

8. The U.S. Department of State compiles statistics each year and produces a report on whether countries comply with legal obligations to return children taken to that country or retained in that country. You can see the report at https://travel.state.gov/content/childabduction/en/legal/compliance.html (last accessed 1/14/17).

assistance for any developmental disabilities a child may have? Does a particular country have better social services or better health care, such as free care for a child who may have a significant health issue? Does a particular country recognize the parent–child relationship of your client, or will your child client risk being put into foster care because the child was adopted or is the child of a same-sex couple that is not recognized in the other country? Would the child be enlisted into military service at a specific age? Would the country mandate certain cultural, religious, or social obligations on your child client because of the child's gender or age, or the gender, marital status, or religion of their primary caretaker parent? Does a child have a health concern that would be more prominent or less treatable in one country over the other?

A child's attorney must also ask how a particular country may affect the words a child uses when talking to you. Does the child strongly object to living in Country B because the Internet is not reliable and he or she cannot play his or her video game console? If the child is scared or nervous about living in Country A, is it because of the potential for residing with a particular parent, or is there something about the country causing the child stress? How are the child's social networks and relationships in different countries? For example, will the child be able to participate in extracurricular activities and sports in one country but not another due to a lack of availability, gender, living conditions, or resources? Will a child's needs be fostered better by the living conditions in one country over another? Will the child have materially better opportunities in one country over another? Are the parent's opportunities better in another country than in the one where you sit, providing better stability? Will a multicultural child be able to explore all of his or her cultures in one country better than in another?

A country's details should also only be one factor among a variety affecting the ultimate resolution of any contested custody case. A child could have a significantly different experience while living in one country with Parent A than with Parent B, given each parent's strengths and weaknesses.

The child's attorney may also need to consult with an attorney in the other country. If a child may live in or travel to another country, it is important to know that the U.S. custody order you obtain will be recognized and enforced in that other country. You may also want to research the immigration law of the other country to know how a child may enter or leave a country, with whom, on what permissions, and under what circumstances. A parent's immigration status within the United States may also play a role in whether that parent may need to leave this country, and whether they have any legal right to return for access to the child.

How do you obtain all of this information? Ideally, you will have the opportunity to travel to both homes where the child will reside and visit. However, realistically, this will not happen. Very few families have the financial resources to provide you the opportunity to travel. Furthermore, given your own implicit cultural biases, are you the appropriate person to conduct a home study, particularly if you are not a witness in the trial? Are there other ways of obtaining admissible evidence about the other home? Can you obtain videos or photos? Can you contract with a social services agency to do a home study in the other country? Can that social worker then testify by video or Skype? It may be particularly difficult if you cannot travel to the home in the other country yourself. However, at the very least, you should make every attempt to meet the parent who lives in that other country in person. As part of your independent investigation, it may be extremely important for you to see your child client interact with this parent—not because you can testify to what you observe, but because it will provide background information that will help you communicate with the child and weigh the child's maturity, credibility, and statements. It will provide data points to give you direction in your investigation to represent your child client.

c. Talking to the Child Electronically

Many parents believe that video chats (e.g., FaceTime, Skype) with their child are a poor replacement for in-person time. They may be correct. However, if a parent lives in a different country (or even a different state) than their child, the parent is going to need to supplement their in-person time; furthermore, the parent may need to reach out to the child at an inconvenient time (e.g., waking up in the middle of the night, stepping out of work, etc.). For a child to maintain a strong bond with a parent, the child needs contact with that parent. Children are routinely on their devices, so this type of contact may feel more normal to the child than to the parent. The parent must work hard to engage the child, who may be looking at other applications on his or her phone. If the child is young, the parent will need help from an adult on the child's side of any call. When you represent a child, you should speak to your child client about this type of access: Will they actually engage? When is a good time for the child to chat with his or her parent?

If your child client resides in another jurisdiction, electronic access can be a useful tool for you to speak with your child client. The child, depending on age and ability, may be quite comfortable or familiar with using technology to communicate. However, you will want to take steps to assure yourself that the child client's parent is not observing your communication with the child or recording it on the electronic device.

d. Requesting the Child Travel to the United States

If your child client already resides in the foreign country but, for jurisdictional reasons, the custody matter is commenced in the United States, you need access to the child, as well as all data that tell the child's story, such as medical and school records. Your U.S. court order appointing you to represent the child may mean very little to a foreign school or doctor. You will have little to no power to enforce your appointment order on people in a different country to seek their cooperation and compliance with your requests for information. You will be beholden to the foreign parent's cooperation to get information by having that parent introduce you to appropriate caretakers, professionals, and educators and requesting that these third parties cooperate with you.

You will also need access to your child client. If the child is physically present in a foreign country, how do you adequately represent the child? You need to speak to your client, but doing so telephonically or over Skype/videoconference has limitations. It can be awkward, you may have difficulty reading your child client's nonverbal cues, and you are at risk of being monitored by the child's parent or other third parties. When a person speaks to you electronically, it is easier for their attention to be pulled in other directions and their focus to stray away from you. You will need to ask to meet with the child in person, recognizing the cost, difficulty in scheduling, and the circumstances of seeing your child client outside of his or her home community, jetlagged, and likely confused about why he or she needs to be inconvenienced to meet with you.

This introduces an opportunity to ask that, instead of a plane ticket for the child to travel to the United States, it may be appropriate to pay for one for you to travel to the other country and see the child in his or her environment. However, this also has its limitations. Depending on the U.S. parent's prayer for relief, you may have even more reason to observe the child with that parent. For example, did the U.S. parent ask for a complete change in custody? If so, you would want to see if the child seems comfortable with that parent and in the United States, where the child would live if the court agrees and switches custody.

The short answer is that each case is different. You must make a judgment call when representing your child client. I have gone through cases without seeing the other parent's home, located out of state or out of the United States. In some circumstances, there was no money for me to travel. In other cases, I had gathered sufficient information about the child and his or her interactions with the distant parent. Based on that parent's prayer for relief, it seemed frivolous for me to go to that parent's home and spend their money. I had every reason to believe that any trip would not change the position I formed.

It may be important or necessary to take the extra step of seeing the child in person (either them traveling to you or you traveling to them) for another reason. If you are taking a position on behalf of a child, you need to have a truly sound foundation for your position. It is much easier to negotiate a settlement if you have exhausted every possible source of information before forming a position on behalf of your client. It is harder to argue with you if you have talked to every single collateral with whom you have been asked to speak. Without information, how do you know you are taking the right position? If you are not even sure, how does a parent know you are taking the right position, and how would a court know?

§6.03 FOREIGN CUSTODY ORDERS IN THE UNITED STATES

a. UCCJEA Application to Foreign Custody Orders in the United States[9]

The Uniform Child Custody Jurisdiction and Enforcement Act (UCCJEA), in Section 105, mandates a state treat a foreign jurisdiction as if it were a state of the United States for the purposes of jurisdiction to issue an initial custody determination and jurisdiction to modify a custody determination. The UCCJEA also mandates that a state recognize and enforce a foreign custody determination, provided it was rendered under factual circumstances in substantial conformity with the jurisdictional standards of the UCCJEA. The very narrow exception to applying the UCCJEA to foreign custody orders is if "the child custody law of a foreign country violates fundamental principles of human rights."[10] The UCCJEA commentary clarifies that a court

---

9. *See* http://www.uniformlaws.org/Act.aspx?title=Child%20Custody%20Jurisdiction%20 and%20Enforcement%20Act for the UCCJEA (last accessed 2/8/18).

10. *See* Section 105 of the UCCJEA.

should scrutinize the child custody law of that foreign country and not other aspects of that country's legal system and that this standard is invoked in only the most "egregious" of cases.

The UCCJEA's application to foreign custody orders means that one may take a foreign custody order, register it in the U.S. jurisdiction, and ask that it be enforced, but for very narrow exceptions. The converse is not necessarily true. Particularly because the United States is not yet a treaty party to the 1996 Convention, there is no guarantee that a U.S. custody order will be recognized and enforced in a particular foreign jurisdiction.[11]

The UCCJEA's provisions requiring a U.S. judge to initiate direct judicial contact with their foreign counterpart may be impractical in an international case. It may be incumbent upon you, particularly if the other counsel in your case is ignorant to a foreign court's practice and laws, to bring to the attention of your judge the processes available to reach out to a foreign judge. In civil code countries, if the code does not expressly permit direct judicial communication, it is considered prohibited. If your judge reaches out to his or her foreign counterpart and receives no response, the judge should *not assume* that silence is acceptance or a declining of jurisdiction. The Hague Conference on Private International Law has created a network of judges in many countries who are valued members of the bench with expert knowledge of international and cross-jurisdictional family matters. If your judge needs to contact his or her foreign counterpart, that judge should initiate contact through this network. The U.S. judges who are members of this network operate through the U.S. Department of State. The U.S. Department of State can help to coordinate communication through this network if you send an e-mail to JudgesNetwork@state.gov.

You may need to consult a foreign lawyer or legal expert if a foreign custody order is being registered and enforced in the United States. Not all countries use the same verbiage (not all states do either) when speaking about custodial rights. Orders may be unclear or vague. The orders, particularly when dealing with a mobile family, may be inapplicable. The UCCJEA has the concept of "continuing, exclusive jurisdiction," which many other countries do not have. Although oversimplified, this concept gives the jurisdiction that issued the custody determination the authority to continue modifying the order under certain circumstances related to the relationship between a

---

11. *See* Section 305 for information on how to register a foreign custody order in your U.S. jurisdiction.

parent or child and the issuing state. Other countries may permit the child's new habitual residence, after the child moves, to assume authority to modify the custody determination. This may lead to a conflict where your U.S. state may decline to modify the custody order until the foreign jurisdiction gives a positive indication that it no longer has authority or declines authority to modify the order. This can be an extremely complicated topic, so you need to educate yourself about the foreign jurisdiction and its interplay with the U.S. court, and involve foreign counsel in the case. When in doubt, consult with an international family lawyer who can help you parse through the conflicts of laws issues.

§6.04 CHILD ABDUCTION

a. Child Abduction Risk Factors

Any lawyer representing a parent or child in a custody case needs to assume, unless advised differently, that their U.S. custody order may be unenforceable in another country. It is important that a child's attorney seek advice from foreign counsel during litigation or negotiation to assess any order's enforceability in the other country implicated in the case and whether there needs to be any unique language incorporated into the U.S. custody order by a judge (or negotiated settlement by counsel) to help ensure enforceability.

There may come a situation where you believe one of your client's parents may abscond with the child or travel to another country for a trip and refuse to return. You need to be particularly concerned about this when the child may mention or hint at travel. You should make inquiries of the parents and collaterals to delve deeper into this issue. When you are doing your independent investigation, there are certain things that may indicate a parent is more likely to take his or her child and not return. One of the most comprehensive lists of these child abduction risk factors is found in the Uniform Child Abduction Prevention Act (UCAPA).[12] UCAPA is not the law in most U.S. states as of the publication of this book. However, the act itself serves as an excellent resource to help practitioners pinpoint risky behaviors that may lead to a child's abduction.

Section 7 of UCAPA includes risk factors relating directly to a parent's behavior, as well as risk factors relating to the country to where a parent may

---

12. You can find UCAPA at http://www.uniformlaws.org/Act.aspx?title=Child%20Abduction%20Prevention (last accessed 1/14/17).

take a child. It is incumbent upon counsel to investigate these risk factors and ask questions in any international case, whether or not the family is entirely situated in the United States or is already expanded across borders. UCAPA's risk factors are not entirely unique to international families, and most can apply in domestic cases.

A child's attorney should not assume that either parent's lawyer has already asked the pertinent questions and done their due diligence in investigating the potential for a child abduction. The child's attorney is not always simply the mouthpiece for the child, but the lawyer who is to act in advocating for a position that is best for a child, which presumably means advocating for enforceable terms in a valid court order protecting the child now and in the future, including against unlawful movement from one country to another that could traumatize, alienate, or otherwise stress your child client.

A child's attorney should look into the following factors that relate to both parents, as well as the parents' family and friends:

- Has anyone previously abducted or attempted to abduct the child?
- Has anyone threatened to abduct the child (or made statements about taking the child)?
- Has anyone recently engaged in activities that may indicate an abduction is being planned, such as leaving a job, selling a home, terminating a lease, closing financial accounts, hiding or destroying important documents, applying for passports or visas, or obtaining birth certificates or school or medical records?
- Has anyone engaged in behavior that could be seen as domestic violence, stalking, child abuse, or neglect?
- Has anyone refused to follow a child custody determination?
- Does a parent lack familial, financial, emotional, or cultural ties to the United States?
- Does the parent have familial, financial, emotional, or cultural ties to another country?
- Is anyone in the family undergoing a change in his or her immigration status that would affect that parent's ability to travel or live in any particular country, including the United States?
- Has a parent been denied an application for U.S. citizenship, a visa, or other travel permission into the United States?
- Has a person forged or misrepresented information on a government application or form, including to obtain travel documents, a

social security card, a driver's license, or other government-issued identification?

- Has a person used multiple names?

A child's attorney should also research the countries that are implicated in their particular custody case, specifically the following:

- Does the other country have legal mechanisms, such as the 1980 Hague Child Abduction Convention, extradition laws, or other internal or bilateral arrangements, that provide for the safe and expedient return of the child to the United States if abducted?
- Would the other country enforce our U.S. custody order if required?
- Even if laws exist, would the country have the mechanisms to enforce any of its own court orders to ensure the return of the child?
- Does the other country abide by its legal obligations to ensure the return of an abducted child?
- Is the other country one that might pose a risk to the child's physical or emotional health for any number of reasons, including human rights violations against children or certain genders or religions?
- Does the other country have laws that actually protect abductors, such as enabling the abducting parent to prevent the child from having contact with the left-behind parent, restricting the left-behind parent from traveling to that country, or restricting the child's ability to leave the country?
- Is the country on a U.S. list of state sponsors of terrorism?
- Does the United States have a diplomatic presence in the country?
- Is the other country engaged in active military action or war, civil unrest, or political protests to which the child may be exposed?

A child's attorney should not become overly pessimistic about a parent's potential travel or relocation based on one or two or even ten of the above risk factors being present. Every family and every situation is different. Every child is different. A fifteen-year-old child may be more adept at calling the police or getting on a plane himself than a five-year-old child, if being abducted.

b. Child Abduction Prevention

UCAPA's other prominent feature is a list of prevention measures that a judge can incorporate into a U.S. custody order (or stand-alone prevention order) or that counsel can incorporate into a settlement agreement between the parties that may later be incorporated into a custody order.

Clearly, if the child's attorney believes there is a risk a parent may abduct his or her child, then the child's attorney needs to assess what, if any, things should be negotiated or incorporated in a court order to protect the child client. A court can order a wide range of things, from very restrictive to relatively benign. It may be incumbent on the child's attorney to suggest certain prevention measures to protect the child client.

On the continuum of prevention measures, a court may order the following:

- Supervised access
- Prohibiting the child from traveling outside of certain geographic areas without a court order or written permission from the other parent
- Requiring a parent to register the U.S. custody order in the other country before the child travels to that other country
- Requiring a parent to mirror the U.S. custody order in the other country before the child travels to that other country
- Requiring a parent to relinquish his or her passport and travel documents before having access to the child, and only receive the documents back when access is complete
- Requiring a traveling parent to provide certain information about any trip, such as itineraries, addresses, phone numbers, and copies of travel documents
- Prohibiting a parent from removing the child from school, child care, or other location
- Directing what parent or third party holds the child's passports and travel documents
- Prohibiting anyone from applying for new or renewal passports, visas, or other travel documents or permissions for the minor child
- Including the child in the U.S. Passport Issuance Alert Program[13]
- Registering the child, or providing other documentation, to the U.S. embassy or consulate in the other country

---

13. The U.S. Passport Issuance Alert Program can be found at https://travel.state.gov/content/childabduction/en/preventing/passport-issuance-alert-program.html (last accessed 1/14/17). Parents may enroll their children in this program, which will trigger an alert that is sent to the enrolling parent if anyone should apply for a new, renewal, or duplicate U.S. passport for the child.

- Requiring the parent to post a bond or other security to deter an abduction and to be used to recover the child if abducted

Above all, as the attorney for the child, you need to ensure that any agreement or court order is clear, concise, and drafted with the understanding that a foreign judge may be interpreting its terms.

c. Hague Convention of 25 October 1980 on the Civil Aspects of International Child Abduction ("1980 Convention")[14]

Although a child's attorney is more readily appointed in custody cases in the United States, counsel may also be appointed for a child in a separate and distinct proceeding—a Hague Abduction return proceeding. A Hague return proceeding is *not* a custody case. There is no analysis of the best interests of a child. The 1980 Convention is a simple straightforward action that has only one of two results—returning a child to the child's habitual residence or not returning the child. There is no analysis as to whether it is in a child's best interest to return the child.

The treaty was premised on it being best for a child to return the child, resume the status quo, and let the child's habitual residence resolve further issues related to the child's care and well-being. The treaty does not resolve what country has jurisdiction to establish, modify, or enforce a custody order. The treaty only aims to return a family's situation to the status quo as expeditiously as possible so the family can then resolve their custodial dispute. The 1980 Convention envisions a full resolution be reached within six weeks. Often, the cases are brought in U.S. federal courts, which have concurrent jurisdiction with state courts under the federal implementing legislation for the treaty.[15]

(i) *Petitioner's Request to Return His or Her Child*

When a person's child is removed from his or her habitual residence or retained outside of his or her habitual residence, it is wrongful under the 1980 Convention. This warrants the prompt return of the child, if the removal or retention breaches the left-behind parent's rights of custody to the child that

---

14. For a thorough review of the 1980 Hague Convention, please *see* Jeremy Morley, THE HAGUE ABDUCTION CONVENTION: PRACTICAL ISSUES AND PROCEDURES FOR FAMILY LAWYERS (2d ed. 2017) , published by the ABA.

15. The 1980 Convention is implemented in the United States through the International Child Abduction Remedies Act (ICARA), 42 U.S.C. § 11601, et. seq. Section 11603 states that state courts and federal courts have concurrent jurisdiction. ICARA also provides for burdens of proof, provisional remedies, and a fee-shifting statute, among other things.

they were actually exercising at the time of removal or retention.[16] Therefore, to have a court order for his or her child to be returned, a left-behind parent only needs to prove that the child was removed from or retained outside of the child's habitual residence (a term that, as of this publication, has differences in definition among the U.S. circuits), that the left-behind parent had rights of custody (pursuant to a court order, agreement, or by operation of the law of the habitual residence), and that the left-behind parent was actually exercising those rights of custody at the time of the removal or retention.

Again, the 1980 Convention is not a law that determines custody jurisdiction, nor is it a law that determines a final custody result in a child's best interests. It is merely a treaty designed to return things to the status quo so that the child has stability while his or her parents are in the process of resolving the underlying custody matter in the appropriate venue. The treaty also serves to stay any custody case that the taking parent may have commenced until the court reaches a resolution on the Hague return petition.

(ii) *Respondent's Argument Against Returning His or Her Child*

Although it seems that having your child returned using the 1980 Convention is fairly formulaic, the "taking parent" can make a few arguments in an effort to convince a judge that a child should not be returned to his or her habitual residence, challenging the left-behind parent's case. Even if successful, Article 18 of the 1980 Convention specifically states that the treaty does not limit the power of a judicial or administrative authority to order the return of the child at any time.

The arguments a taking parent can make include the following:

   a)   Under Article 12, if one year has passed since the wrongful removal or retention, the taking parent can argue the child is now settled in his or her new environment.
   b)   Under Article 13(a), the left-behind parent consented or acquiesced to the child's removal or retention.
   c)   Under Article 13(b), there is a grave risk that the child's return would expose him or her to physical or psychological harm or otherwise place the child in an intolerable situation.
   d)   Under Article 13, the child reached an age and degree of maturity at which it is appropriate to take into account the child's views, and the child objects to being returned.

---

16. *See* Article 3 of the 1980 Convention.

e) Under Article 20, a return of the child would not be permitted by the fundamental principles of the requested state relating to the protection of human rights and fundamental freedoms.

All of the potential arguments a taking parent can make are construed very narrowly, and some have extremely high burdens of proof.

A child's attorney can play an integral role in a 1980 Convention case, but the role needs to be very narrowly tailored to this specific type of case and may not always be appropriate—particularly if the appointment of a child's attorney causes delay in resolving the matter quickly, as the 1980 Convention intended. A child's attorney can speak with the child, obtain the child's views, help the court assess the child's maturity, and gather evidence as to whether there has been a grave risk, whether the child's habitual residence may have shifted, or whether the child is now settled in the new environment. A child's attorney cannot supplant his or her judgment for that of the court and cannot make arguments outside of the treaty. A child's attorney can also work with both parents and the child to try to secure a voluntary return of the child (see Article 7 and 10), a voluntary dismissal of the Hague return petition, and a fuller settlement arrangement, as well as help parents who likely have not communicated with one another to see matters from a different perspective. A child's attorney can also be helpful in securing some interim access or other arrangements for the left-behind parent to see the child pending a final resolution and can argue for certain measures to be put in place to protect the child during the lawsuit.

(iii) *Requests for Access*

The 1980 Convention also permits a parent to request access to his or her child. Ultimately, such a request, when addressed by a court in the United States, would take the form of a custody trial that looks at a child's best interests to determine what type of schedule the child would have with the left-behind parent.

d. What Special Considerations Are There When the Child Has Been Previously Abducted?

A child who has been away from one parent for an extended period of time may have difficulty readjusting to spending time with the left-behind parent. In the most egregious of cases, the parent who abducted the child may have told the child negative (and perhaps untrue) things about the left-behind parent, including that the parent died, did not want the child, or was abusive.

An abducting parent may try to change the child's identity, move to a country where the child has no friends and does not speak the language, or isolate the child. Some abducting parents may move the child from location to location or hide the child, causing the child to feel unsettled. The end result is that the child may experience stress and significant anxiety if they are returned to their former home environment or the left-behind parent. The child may need some type of intensive therapy to reunify the child with their past environment, life, and relatives. They may resist. This may be extremely painful to the left-behind parent, who may have little patience after having lost time. The left-behind parent may want things to simply "go back to normal."

When working with a child who has been abducted, you need to be extremely careful. You need to speak with the child's therapist and other professionals. You need to be very cautious with the child. You need to understand that certain questions, words, sounds, perfumes, music, or other things may trigger memories, which could negatively affect your child client. You may need to let the child tell you their story in their own words and in their own time. You may want to consider working with a mental health professional to hear the child's story. If the child lost a gap of time in their life or if they came to believe they were someone completely different because of a change in identity, name, language, haircut, and clothes, they may not even understand who they were. They may have been too young to understand their situation and may even relate back to the abduction as if it were a movie and not actually their life.

Working with a trained professional will help this child put a story to their life and address the new stresses, which are natural in a situation of reuniting with a lost parent and an old environment that is now new to the child. The professional can help you understand your limitations in communicating with the child and present options for how you can appropriately and sensitively approach the child. The therapist can suggest appropriate paths forward for the child. If the taking parent is still present in the child's life in some way, reaches out to the child, or is seeking access to the child, a mental health professional can be a significant resource on how this is best achieved when (or perhaps whether) it is practical, feasible, or healthy for the child.

In many cases brought under the 1980 Convention, the taking parent may claim that they did so because the child or the taking parent was subject to domestic violence or abuse. If the child was, in fact, harmed or exposed to the harm of their taking parent, they may have a different type of trauma. Children who experience such trauma may have significant difficulty communicating. Advocate for professionals to help the child. The National Center for Missing and Exploited Children has excellent resources available to families in which children may need therapy related to the family's circumstances and their unilateral relocation by one parent.[17]

§6.05 CULTURE AND LANGUAGE SKILLS

a. Understanding Your Own Cultural Biases

You have implicit biases. You are a unique person with unique experiences; because of that, you may misinterpret, misunderstand, or entirely miss something the child communicates to you (verbally or nonverbally). This is not bad—it simply happens. You need to be cognizant that it will happen. You are not immune, and you should not believe you are some all-knowing, all-understanding, sensitive person who will pick up on everything, understand everything, and empathize with everything. A child, by virtue of age and experience, will be different than you. However, you need to understand how gender, nationality, race, geographic upbringing, language, and your own relationships, education, and communication patterns and styles affect your ability to communicate and understand the child, his or her parents, and collateral witnesses, among others. There is no magic bullet. Simply be aware of yourself. Before jumping to a conclusion, take a deeper look at how you are interpreting things. Is there something in your background leading you to interpret a piece of information in a specific way?

Some things can be overt. For example, suppose that a mother tells you she co-sleeps with her eight-year-old son. I may automatically cringe in fear and concern. However, that may be my American way of understanding the situation. What if the mother is Japanese, and you researched and learned that it was common and typical for this to occur in Japanese society? There may, however, be more nuanced situations. Perhaps you are talking to a father and you ask him a very specific, pointed question. He does not answer your question directly, but instead tells you a story. To you, he may sound like he is talking in circles, wasting your time, being evasive, or perhaps even lying. What if this man is from a culture where the cultural communication style involves storytelling to demonstrate an answer? The storyteller expects, at the end of the story, that he has laid the foundation to lead you directly to

---

17. You can access the National Center for Missing and Exploited Children's resources at http://www.ncmec.org (last accessed 2/8/18).

his answer. The American lawyer in you may be appalled that your cross-examination did not "work," and you may become frustrated with the father. However, it may be you, not him. Simply be aware.

b. Understanding How Culture Affects a Child's Communication[18]

A significant amount of psychology is involved in a child's communication.[19] However, there may be an equal amount of culture involved. Do the child's cultural communication patterns focus on relationship building, or direct and blunt answers? Does the communication style value storytelling and circular discussions, or is it more linear and chronological? Does the child talk about his or her life as if the child is a cast member or character in a book? Does the child recite back information by rote memorization, or must the child be actively engaged in some type of activity to reflect back on something?

Does the child focus on one activity or event at a time, or does the child conflate a lot of stories, activities, and reflections of past events into one large story? Does the child interrupt you, or does he or she value taking turns? Does the child need to sit close to you or farther away? Some of my child clients virtually climb on me when talking to me. A child's averting his or her eyes while talking to you does not necessarily indicate lying.

Does the room's arrangement affect the child's communication and comfort? Volume, pitch, rhythm, tempo, resonance, and tone may all be affected by culture. If a parent seems angry or aggressive, is that an accurate assumption? If they are passive or quiet, should you assume the child has been harmed? Not necessarily. "Yes" may not always mean *yes* in some cultures; rather, it may simply mean, "I hear you."

c. How to Present Information About a Child's Culture to a Court

Even if your jurisdiction does not incorporate the child's culture into the laundry list of "best interest" factors in a custody case, a child in a multicultural or multinational family needs this discussion to be had in court for a complete assessment of what is best for this child. A judge, who may be ignorant to certain cultural practices, may pass judgment. It is incumbent

---

18. *See* Melissa A. Kucinski, *Culture in International Parental Kidnapping Mediations*, 9 PEPP. DISP. RESOL. L.J. 3 (2009).

19. For a further discussion on child psychology and appropriate communication with children that you represent, *see Representing Children in Dependency and Family Court: Beyond the Law*, by Rebecca M. Stahl and Philip M. Stahl, publishing in 2018

upon the lawyers to produce evidence, elicit testimony, and incorporate the child's cultural background and needs into any position the child's attorney takes on his or her client's behalf. Does the child's culture value extended family or simply the nuclear family? How are boys versus girls treated in the child's culture? Is certain conduct that may be (very literally) foreign necessary to explain to a judge, such as certain discipline? Does the child's culture value the larger community's involvement in child rearing (and by extension, the judge should consider the child's geographic proximity to that community)? How will each parent foster the child's multicultural background and upbringing?

§6.06 RELOCATION

When a parent wants to relocate a child, you have a difficult case. When that relocation is taking the child to a different country, you have one of the most difficult cases. Not only is the case about what parent may be best for the child, but also what cultural upbringing and country may be best for the child. A court will be looking at customs, laws, and systems that are foreign and may be significantly different from those one may expect in the United States. When you represent a multicultural child or a family that will ultimately have parents living in two very different places, you need to do your homework on behalf of this child. His or her experience in the other country may have been significant, it may have been limited to summer vacations or periodic visits, or the child may have never stepped foot in the other country.

You cannot count on the child informing you about the country or having strong or mature views about what it may be like to live in another country. Although any relocation means leaving certain comforts (the child's school, friends, neighborhood, and network), relocating to another country may mean so much more than building a new locus of life. It may mean experiencing very different ways of living, structure, tempo, communication, gender views, religious integration, and cultural norms. Your child client may be overwhelmed and frightened or very excited, but neither reaction gives you a solid sense of the child's views about this new adventure. Most U.S. jurisdiction's relocation laws (or lack of relocation laws) may leave you scrambling to determine how best to present a case and assess what position you will take on behalf of your client. Where do you find direction?

a. Washington Declaration

In 2010, judges from across the globe gathered in Washington, D.C., to discuss the issue of international child relocation. From that meeting, the judges agreed on several core principles, which were incorporated into a document called the Washington Declaration and published by the International Centre for Missing and Exploited Children and the Hague Conference on Private International Law.[20] Among other issues the judges explored, they agreed on thirteen factors that decision-makers should consider when resolving an international relocation case. Among those factors, the judges highlighted the child having contact with both parents, whether a relocation was practical, the child's views, the underlying reasons behind the relocation, past family abuse, any existing custody and access determinations, extended family and community, facilitating the child's relationship with both parents after a relocation, whether postrelocation contact was realistic given the cost and distance and burden to the child, the enforceability of any arrangement, and the mobility of family members. Although a child's attorney may avoid any discussion or resolution of family finances or child support, international relocation cases often necessitate some discourse on how the family will financially sustain an international lifestyle. Discussions also require an analysis of school calendars, the length of flights between locations, flights through possible dangerous airports or countries, security concerns, and any other practical daily factor that will affect the child routinely.

b. What Additional Considerations Should the Child's Attorney Bring to Light

Other sections discussed the importance of exploring obvious differences between living in the United States and in another country, specifically language and culture. A child's attorney should, however, thoroughly compare and contrast the child's two homes. Where would the child live, go to school, and engage in activities? Would the child need to learn a new language, take special lessons, or be in a community where all his or her contemporaries could exclude him or her due to cultural or language differences? Would the child be attending private school or public school? Are there any differences in the child's school calendar? Would there be expatriates in the child's community that would share the child's same challenges in a new environment?

---

20. You can find a link to the Washington Declaration at https://www.hcch.net/en/news-archive/details/?varevent=188 (last accessed 1/15/17).

Does the child have family or friends in either country? Would the child need to be set back in school if moving to a new country? Should the child's attorney travel to the other country and conduct a home visit to see the child in the other environment? The child may sit in the United States and speak with his or her counsel, sharing his or her views about the other country. However, those views may vary dramatically once the child is in the other country or if they are present in the other country when talking with their counsel.

The child's attorney may also need to investigate the foreign country's laws. Is the child legally allowed to live in the other country? Would the child be conscripted into military service at a specific age? Does the other country limit persons of certain genders? If the child's parents are of the same gender, would the child be subject to certain limitations or lack certain rights? If the child's parents were unmarried, would that create legal issues for the child? Would the other country respect the U.S. custody order? Does the country have treaties or agreements in place with the United States? What are both countries' rules for passport issuance, travel permissions, and any registration of both parents on paperwork in both countries to establish paternity or legal parental rights?

c. Assessing Whether the Child Understands the Impact of Relocating to a Different Country

Any person, including an adult, would be excited and stressed about moving to a new country. The difficulty you will have is determining whether your child client truly understands the impact of the relocation. The child may not fully comprehend the (sometimes significant) differences in school systems and language barriers. Children in other countries may behave quite differently due to their upbringings and cultural expectations. Does your child client know that he or she may have to take the subway to school? That he or she may have to attend school all summer? That he or she may not be able to participate in afterschool sports? That stores may not be open past 6 p.m.? That movies may have subtitles? That social activities and norms may be significantly different?

In some situations, the differences will be even more dramatic. The child may have already lived in that foreign country. They may have visited the country or spent significant time in the country, so they may know precisely what a move will entail. If they are only familiar with their small American enclave, however, the change could be dramatic and could affect the child's personality and mental and emotional health. Is your child client someone who is adaptive and thrives on change? Could change significantly set the child back? How does the child define stability—is it the parent with whom they live or the environment where they reside? In some situations, stability and certainty come from a specific school, neighbor, relative, or friend even more than the child's home life. You must fully understand what the child's daily life would look like in that other country so that you can have a meaningful dialogue with your child client and fully represent that child's best interests (or weigh whether their position is founded in reality and made with a mature understanding of their circumstances).

d. Language Skills

Multicultural families may already be raising their children to be fluent in more than one language. There are excellent schools in the United States that teach their core academic courses in a language other than English and foster foreign cultural customs and norms. Does the other country in your child client's life have similar institutions? Many parents, you will find, prioritize language skills above all else when talking about their child's multicultural background. This could be because foreign language skills enable the child to communicate with family and friends in a foreign country and more easily assimilate into that culture when returning for a trip or relocation. You should investigate what is available to a child in each environment. In addition, gauge each parent's willingness to foster or support a child's foreign language skills. Furthermore, you should understand the child's perspective. Although you may see value in being bilingual in our shrinking globe, a child may not see the same value.

e. Cultural Customs Incorporated into Daily Life

Although it is an important aspect of sharing culture, language is not the singular element comprising one's culture. If a parent encourages a child to be bilingual, that may be very different from sharing customs with the child, teaching the child stories of the other culture, and even traveling to that cultural environment. I represented a young boy in the past, who had one parent insisting that the child must attend "Japanese school" to continue learning about his Japanese heritage. The other parent disagreed adamantly, expressing concern that this Japanese school was merely teaching advanced math, science, and reading in the Japanese language but did little to teach the child about Japanese customs and culture.

However, customs and culture may never be able to be learned by sitting in a classroom. Typically, you need to experience the environment.

You may not need to be in the foreign country to do so. Does either country have communities, churches, or youth groups that foster the child's multi-cultural heritage? When in the United States, depending on where you live, it may be easy to work with a child to ensure that the child understands his less dominant culture. However, what happens if the child lives in the foreign country and the American part of the child's identity becomes less dominant? Are there American expatriate groups in the foreign country or events at the U.S. embassy? Can the child celebrate the Fourth of July and U.S. Thanksgiving with their American parent? Is this even important for this family and this child?

f. Young Children and Distance Parenting

Young children with parents who live significant distances from one another have special needs. A typical parenting plan for a young child that involves the child seeing the non–primary caretaker parent for frequent small chunks of time is impractical. Because of the cost of travel and the significant amount of time it will take to travel from one to another country, acclimate to a different time zone, and adjust from jet lag, it may be best for you to assess how the child will do with larger chunks of time away from his or her primary caretaker parent. This may include sleeping in a different home, being bottle fed instead of nursed, sitting on an airplane, and having sleep patterns adjusted, among others.

§6.07 DISTANCE ACCESS

a. Time Zone Issues

Whenever you represent a child who resides in a different time zone, you need to be flexible in communicating with that child. Even if the child is in your time zone, try to minimize disruptions to the child's routine as little as possible when meeting with the child and observing the child with others. This may mean meeting with a child on evenings or weekends. I often like to see a child at their home right after school because it gives me a good sense of their routine (e.g., snack, homework, how the parent interacts with them) but does not interfere with dinner. This becomes more complicated if the child is scheduled for activities immediately after school. If a child is in Australia, you may need to get up in the middle of the night to communicate with the child electronically. If you are working with a child needing immediate attention, the child will need to understand that if he or she reaches out to you, you may be asleep; thus, it may take some time to coordinate a response.

b. Technology

Children are typically more adept at using technology than adults. Your child client may wish to communicate with you using technology, whether they live near you or at a distance. I established an office line using Google Voice, which permits text messages to be forwarded to my e-mail account. Whether it is familiarizing yourself with the current popular toy or movie, or ensuring you know how to text or use social media, you need to be at your child client's level and ensure you can build a rapport and communicate. Technology helps if the child is living at a distance and you need access to the child. It also helps if you are working with a family to ensure a resolution, either through negotiation or court, and one parent is naturally going to be absent from where the child ultimately resides. You should familiarize yourself with tools for parents to enable them to communicate from a distance, and to ensure healthy and appropriate access between parent and child.

c. Traveling Parent Issues

If you work with a family that resides in two different and distant locations, you need to work with a parent who has to travel to spend time with their child. Children can travel, but there are necessarily additional burdens when that happens—cranky, jetlagged children; adults accompanying younger children on flights; costs for two tickets; working within the school's schedule; and whether the child is of an age where it is appropriate to travel on flights of specific lengths or on trips with multiple legs.

Adults, particularly those who live an international lifestyle, are better suited for travel. However, it may be important for a child to travel (when the child is healthy and the travel is arranged carefully) so that the child can experience their dual cultural background, see extended family, and see their other "home." It may be impossible for children to travel if a court has determined traveling is not in the child's best interest, including if the parent who wishes the child to travel may not return the child at the end of the trip.

The parents will need to discuss the frequency of trips, the cost of trips, the duration of each visit to the child's location, and age-appropriate parenting arrangements for those visits. It is also important to recognize that the child may have not seen the parent for significant chunks of time and may need periods of reintroduction; the child also may experience anxiety. Each child is different. For a child who begins down this path at a young age, periodic visits to another country will become commonplace and normal. For others, the child's life turns upside down. This is again a time when you should consult a mental health professional, or consider working with the family to engage professional help to ensure the child is adapting to this different type of access. When a parent is traveling, the two biggest issues are cost and time away from work. This is a reality that must be addressed, particularly if you determine it is important for your child client to have meaningful and frequent access to this parent who lives in another country.

§6.08 CONCLUSION

It is my genuine hope that this book is a good reference manual and practical handbook for serving your child clients. Working with a child client is significantly different than working with an adult client. Not only is your role different, but also your approach, your mandate, your obligations, and the status you hold in the eyes of the court, the parents, counsel, and the child. You are not just a lawyer but also an educator, a communicator, an investigator, a negotiator, an intermediary, and an interpreter. We do not take the client's words as they are—we dive deeper. We ask the difficult questions. We then help the parents, their lawyers, the child, and, specifically, the judge to focus on the relevant issues where they may otherwise get lost in the forest. We provide a much-needed buffer between the child and the litigation. We pursue settlement and creative solutions for the child.

   More complicated is the fact that we are not mental health professionals. Although many child attorney trainings require a review of psychological literature and child-focused parenting plans, we will often need to engage others to help us in our journey in representing our child client. You will work with children of varying ages, maturities, cultures, communication skills, educational levels, states of health, and social networks. You must recognize your biases and your limitations. You will need to protect the child's health and understand the child at the child's level and capabilities, but also protect yourself. These cases are exhausting both in time and in emotional impact. You must also protect yourself legally: Your malpractice coverage should be sufficient for this type of role, you want to ensure a solid clear court appointment order, and you should know the rules of whether you have any quasi-or full immunity. You should know what is expected of you when testifying, writing reports, and presenting evidence. You also will want to monitor the reactions of all involved, especially if one or more of the people in your high. conflict case may be a danger to you or your child client.

I wish you the best of luck. I have found that working with children has been the highlight of my career.

APPENDIX

1

Appendix 1 is comprised of three charts used by the Uniform Law Commission Drafting Committee for the Model Law for the Representation of Children in Abuse, Neglect, and Custody Proceedings Act. The three charts were created by the ULC Drafting Committee in 2004–2005.

Helpful Regulations

STATE	DEFINITIONS	DUTIES	FEES	IMMUNITY	QUALIFICATIONS	OTHER
Alabama			GAL: Ala. Code §26-17-17(c)			
Alaska			Atty: AS 25.24.310(b) GAL:AS 25.24.310(c)			
Arizona						
Arkansas		Atty. ad Litem: ACA §9-27-316(f)(2)–(5), Sup. Ct. Admin. Order 15 §§2, 5 CASA: ACA §9-27-316(g)(3)–(5)	Atty. ad Litem: A.C.A. §§9-13-101(d)(4)-(7), 9-13-106(d)-(g)	CASA: ACA §9-27-316(g)(6)	Atty.: Sup. Ct. Admin. Order 15 §4 Atty. ad Litem: Sup. Ct. Admin. Order 15 §1 CASA: ACA §9-27-316(g)(2)	
California		Atty.: West's Ann. Cal. Fam. Code §§ 3151, 3151.5	Atty.: West's Ann. Cal. Fam. Code §7863 GAL: West's Ann. Cal. Fam. Code §3153			
Colorado		Atty.: C.R.S.A. §14-10-116(2)(a) CASA: C.R.S.A. §§ 14-10-116(2)(b), 19-1-208 to 19-1-211 GAL: C.R.S.A. §19-1-111(3)–(6)	Atty./CASA: C.R.S.A. §14-10-116(3)	CASA: C.R.S.A. §19-1-212 (see §13-21-115.5 (4)(a)	CASA: C.R.S.A. §§ 19-1-204, 19-1-205	CASA: C.R.S.A. §§19-1-206 (appoint), 19-1-207 (restrict.)

STATE	DEFINITIONS	DUTIES	FEES	IMMUNITY	QUALIFICATIONS	OTHER
Connecticut		Atty./GAL: C.G.S.A. §46b-129a(2)	Atty.: C.G.S.A. §46b-62; Atty./GAL: C.G.S.A. §46b-129a(2)			
Delaware		GAL: 29 Del. C. §§ 9002A(12), 9007A(c)				
D.C.						
Florida	GAL: F.S.A. §39.820	GAL: F.S.A. §§ 39.822(3), 61.403	F.S.A. §39.822(2)	GAL: F.S.A. §§ 39.822(1), 61.405	GAL: F.S.A. §§ 39.821, 61.402	
Georgia				GAL: 2003 GA HB 264(SN)		
Hawaii						
Idaho		Atty.: I.C. §16-1618(b); GAL: I.C. §§16-1631-1632	Atty.: I.C. §16-1618(c)	GAL: I.C. §16-1633		
Illinois		CASA: 705 ILCS 405/2-17.1(1)-(2); Misc.: 750 ILCS 5/506(a), 19th Judicial Cir. Ct. Rule 11.04, 16th Judicial Circuit Ct. Rule 15.25	CASA: 705 ILCS 405/2-17.1(3), (5); Misc.: 750 ILCS 5/506(b)	CASA: 705 ILCS 405/2-17.1(8)		

STATE	DEFINITIONS	DUTIES	FEES	IMMUNITY	QUALIFICATIONS	OTHER
Indiana		CASA/GAL: I.C. 31-17-6-3 to 31-17-6-5, 31-32-3-6 & 31-32-3-7	Atty: I.C. 31-32-4-4 CASA/GAL: I.C. 31-17-6-9, 31-32-3-9, 31-40-3-1, 31-40-3-2	CASA/GAL: I.C. 31-17-6-8, 31-32-3-10	CASA/GAL: I.C. 31-17-6-2, 31-32-3-2 to 31-32-3-5, 3-2 to 31-32-3-5,	CASA/GAL: I.C. 31-32-3-8
Iowa	I.C.A. §232.2(6) (child in need of assistance);§232.2(20) (family in need of assistance); §232.2(22)(a) (GAL)	Atty. & GAL: I.C.A. §232.89(4) CASA: I.C.A. §§ 232.89(5),232.126 GAL: I.C.A. §§ 232.2(b),600A.6(2)	Atty: I.C.A. §598.12(3) GAL: I.C.A. §§ 232.71C(3), 232.89(3), 232.141(2)&(3)(c)		GAL: I.C.A. §600A(9) (in term. of parental rights)	
Kansas	K.S.A. §38-1502 (child in need ?)	GAL: KS Sup. Ct. Rules GAL Guidelines	Atty./GAL: K.S.A. §38-1505(e) GAL: §38-1122	CASA/GAL: K.S.A. §38-1505a(b)		
Kentucky	CASA: K.R.S. §620.500	Atty./GAL: JFRP Appendix CASA: K.R.S. §620.525	Atty.: §620.100(1)(a) & §645.060(3) GAL: K.R.S. §625.041(2)		CASA: K.R.S. §620.515	
Louisiana	LSA-Ch. C. Art. 606 (child in need of care)	CASA: LSA-Ch. C. Art. 424.3	Atty: LSA-R.S. 9:345(F); Gen. Admin. Rules Part G §9; LSA-Ch. C. Arts. 607(B), 1137(B)	CASA: LSA-Ch. C. Art. 424.10		
Maine	22 M.R.S.A. §4002(3) (child protection proceeding)	GAL: 19-A M.R.S.A. §1507(3)-(4);22 M.R.S.A. §§4005(1)(B)-(E); ME R GAL Rules App. A	Atty: 22 M.R.S.A. §4005(1)(F) GAL: 18-A M.R.S.A. §9-204(c)(1); 19-A M.R.S.A. §1507(7)	CASA: 4 M.R.S.A. §1506 GAL: 22 M.R.S.A. §4005 (1)(G);ME R GAL Rule III		

STATE	DEFINITIONS	DUTIES	FEES	IMMUNITY	QUALIFICATIONS	OTHER
Maryland	MD Code CJC §3-801(f) (child in need of assistance)		Atty.: MD Code CJC §3-813(f); MD Code Family Law §1-202(2)	CASA: MD Code CJC §3-830(d)		
Massachusetts			GAL: M.G.L.A. 215 §§56A, 56B, 231, 85P ½ (d)(4)			
Michigan	M.C.L.A. 712A.13a: (1)(b) - Atty.;(1)(e) – GAL; (1)(f) - Lawyer-GAL (LGAL)	LGAL: M.C.L.A. 712A.17d	GAL: MCR 3.204(D) LGAL: M.C.L.A. 700.5213(5)(b), 712A.17e(8,722.24(4)		GAL:M.C.L.A. 712A.13a(1)(e)	
Minnesota	Juv. Protection Proc. Rule 2.01(k) (juvenile protection matter); M.S.A. §260C.007 Subdiv. 6 (child in need of protection or services)	GAL: M.S.A. §§ 260C.163 Subdiv. 5(b) & 518.165 Subdiv. 2a; Juv. Protection Proc. Rules 26.04 & 38.05; GAL Guidelines[1] Rules 908.01 & 908.02	Atty.:M.S.A. §260C.212 Subdiv.1(d), 4(c)(1), & 4(c)(4); Juv. Protection Proc. Rule 25.03 GAL: M.S.A. §518.165 Subdiv. 3 & Juv. Prot. Proc. Rule 26.05		GAL: GAL Guidelines Rules 902, 910.01 to 910.03, 911	
Mississippi		GAL: Miss. Code Ann. §43-21-121(3)	Atty: Miss. Code Ann. §43-21-619(1) GAL: Miss. Code Ann. §43-21-121(6), §93-17-8(1)(b), §97-5-42(3)		GAL: Miss. Code Ann. §43-21-121(4)	

[1] 51 M.S.A., Guardian Ad Litem (General Rules of Practice for Dist. Cts.).

State	Definitions	Duties	Fees	Immunity	Qualifications	Other
Missouri		GAL: V.A.M.S. 210.160(6), 211.462(3), 452.423(2)	CASA: V.A.M.S. 210.160(5), 452.423(5) GAL: V.A.M.S. 210.160(4), 210.842, 211.462(4), 452.423(4)		GAL: V.A.M.S. 210.160(6)	
Montana		GAL: MCA 40-4-205(2), 41-3-112(2)	GAL: MCA 3-5-901(1)(e)(iv), 40-4-205(4), 40-6-119(2), 41-3-112(1)			
Nebraska		CASA: Neb. Rev. St. §43-3711	Atty.: Neb. Rev. St. §§ 42-358(1), 43-1505(2) CASA: Neb. Rev. St. §43-3711(1)	CASA: Neb. Rev. St. §43-3711	CASA: Neb. Rev. St. §§43-3708, 43-3709	
Nevada		GAL: N.R.S. 432B.500(3) (protective custody)	Atty.: N.R.S. 128.100(3) (TPR), 150.060(5) (probate), 432B.420(3) (abuse/neglect) Atty. for Indian Child: N.R.S. 128.023(2)(c) GAL: N.R.S. 126.171 (paternity), 432B.420(3) (abuse/neglect), 432B.500(2) (protective custody)		GAL: N.R.S. 432B.505	

STATE	DEFINITIONS	DUTIES	FEES	IMMUNITY	QUALIFICATIONS	OTHER
New Hampshire		GAL: GAL Guidelines 1, 3-5, & 8; GAL Practice §§ 2.3, 2.4.1(a), 2.4.2, 2.4.3, 2.4.5, & 2.5.1	GAL: N.H. Rev. Stat. §170-C:13 (TPR), §458:17-a, II-a & §458:17-b, -e (divorce), GAL Guidelines 2, 6-7, 9, & 14; GAL Practice §2.4.4		Atty. & GAL: Abuse & Neglect Cases Guideline 12; GAL Practice §2.4.1(b)	
New Jersey	N.J.S.A. 3B:12-69 (standby guardian); N.J.S.A. 9:3-38(e) (GAL-adoption); N.J.S.A. 9:6-8.21(d) (A/N-law guardian); N.J.S.A. 9:6-8.21(e) (A/N-Atty.)	Atty.: NJ R. Ch. Div. Fam. Pt. R. 5:8B (custody)	Atty.: NJ R. Ch. Div. Fam. Pt. R. 5:8A & 5:8B (custody) Atty. & GAL: N.J.S.A. 9:2-4(c) (custody) GAL: N.J.S.A. 9:17-54 (paternity)	N.J.S.A. 9:6-8.23 (amend. proposed for GAL & law-guardian)	Atty.: NJ R. Ch. Div. Fam. Pt. R. 5:8A & 5:8B (custody)	
New Mexico			GAL: N.M.S.A §40-4-8(A)		GAL: N.M.S.A §40-4-8(A)	
New York	Atty./LG: McKinney's §242		Atty./LG:McKinney's §245			
North Carolina		GAL: N.C.G.S.A. §§ 7B-601; 35A-1379	GAL: N.C.G.S.A. §7B-603	GAL:N.C.G.S.A. §7B-1204		
North Dakota			GAL: N.D.C.C. §§ 14-07.1-05.1, 14-09-06.4	GAL: N.D.C.C. §14-09-06.4	GAL: N.D.R.Ct. 8.7(a)-(b)	

STATE	DEFINITIONS	DUTIES	FEES	IMMUNITY	QUALIFICATIONS	OTHER
Ohio		GAL: R.C. §2151.281(I); Cuyahoga Cty. Common Pleas Domestic Relations (CCPDR) Rule 35(H); Summit Cty. Juv. Ct. (SCJC) Rule 22.05	Atty./GAL: Juv. R. Rule 4(G) GAL: CCCPDR Rule 35(E); SCJC Rule 22.11-22.12		GAL: R.C. §§2151.281(H), (J); CCCPDR Rule 35(B)	
Oklahoma	10 Okl. St.Ann. §7001-1.3(14) (deprived child)	Atty.: 10 Okl. St. Ann. §7003-3.7 (A)(2)(c) CASA: 10 Okl. St. Ann. §7003-3.7(C)(3) GAL: 10 Okl. St. Ann. §7003-3.7 (B)(4), 43 Okl. St. Ann. §107.3(A)(2)	Atty.: 10 Okl.St.Ann. §7003-3.7(A)(3), CASA: 10 Okl.St.Ann. §7003-3.7 (C)(4) GAL: 43 Okl. St. Ann. §107.3(A)(3)	CASA: 10 Okl. St. Ann. §7003-3.7(D)	Atty.: 10 Okl. St. Ann. §1211(F) CASA: 10 Okl.St. Ann. §1211(G)	
Oregon		CASA: O.R.S. §419A.170(2),(9)	Atty.: O.R.S. §107.425(6); CASA: O.R.S. §419A.170(1),(6)	CASA: O.R.S. §419A.170(4),(5)		
Pennsylvania	42 Pa.C.S.A. §6302 ("dependent")	GAL: 42 Pa.C.S.A. §6311(b)	Atty.: 23 Pa.C.S.A. §2313(b)		Atty.: Pa. Phila. Co. Family Div. R. 1915.11(a)(1)	

STATE	DEFINITIONS	DUTIES	FEES	IMMUNITY	QUALIFICATIONS	OTHER
Rhode Island				CASA: Gen. Laws 1956, §42-73-11		
South Carolina		GAL: Code 1976 §§ 20-7-122, 20-7-124, 20-7-1549, 20-7-1551	Atty./GAL: Rule 41, SCRFC (abuse or neglect cases) GAL: Code 1976 §20-7-1553		GAL: Code 1976 §20-7-1547	
South Dakota			Atty.: S.D.C.L. §§ 25-4-45.4, 25-4A-15, 26-7A-31 GAL: S.D.C.L. §15-6-17(c)			
Tennessee		CASA: T.C.A. §37-1-149(b)(2)	Atty.: T.C.A. §37-1-150(a)(2) GAL: T.C.A. §§37-1-150(a)(3), 36-4-132(b)	CASA/GAL: T.C.A. §37-1-149(b)(3) GAL: : T.C.A. §36-4-132(c)		

STATE	DEFINITIONS	DUTIES	FEES	IMMUNITY	QUALIFICATIONS	OTHER
Texas	V.T.C.A. Family Code §107.001	Amicus Atty. (AA): V.T.C.A. Family Code 107.005 Atty. ad Litem (AAL): V.T.C.A. Family Code 107.004, 107.008 AA & AAL: V.T.C.A. Family Code 107.003 GAL: V.T.C.A. Family Code 107.002	Atty. ad Litem: V.T.C.A. Family Code §107.015 AA/AAL/GAL: V.T.C.A. Family Code §107.023	AA/AAL/GAL: V.T.C.A. Family Code §107.009		
Utah		Atty. GAL: U.C.A. §78-7-45(3) GAL: U.C.A. §78-3a-912(1)	Atty. GAL: U.C.A.§§ 78-3a-912(6), 78-7-9(5)-(6), 78-7-45(2)	Atty. GAL: U.C.A. §§78-3a-912(7), 78-7-9(7), 78-7-45(5) GAL: U.C.A. §30-3-10.8(2)		
Vermont		GAL: Vt. R. Fam. P. Rule 7				
Virginia		CASA: Va. Code Ann. §9.1-153 GAL: Va. Code Ann. §16.1-266.1	Atty.: Va. Code Ann. §16.1-267(A)			

STATE	DEFINITIONS	DUTIES	FEES	IMMUNITY	QUALIFICATIONS	OTHER
Washington		GAL: R.C.W.A. §§ 13.34.100(5), 13.34.105(1), 26.12.175(1)(b)	Atty.: R.C.W.A. §§ 26.09.110, 26.10.070 GAL: R.C.W.A. §§ 13.34.108, 26.12.183, 26.12.175(1)(d)	GAL: R.C.W.A. §13.34.105(2)	GAL: R.C.W.A. §§13.34.102(1), 26.12.177	
West Virginia						
Wisconsin	W.S.A. 48.13 (child in need of protection or services); W.S.A. 48.23(1g) (counsel)	CASA: W.S.A. 48.236(3)-(4) GAL: W.S.A. 48.235(3)-(4) & 767.045(4)	Atty.: W.S.A. 48.23(4) GAL: W.S.A 48.235(8), 757.48(1)(b)-(3), 767.045(6)	CASA: W.S.A. 48.236(5)	CASA: W.S.A. 48.236(2) GAL: W.S.A 48.235(2), 757.48(1)(a), 767.045(3)	
Wyoming			GAL: W.S.1977 §20-7-101(a)			

Summary of Statutes

STATE	IN GENERAL	ADOPTION	CUSTODY	DEPENDENCY	DIVORCE	PATERNITY	SHELTER/ INSTITUTION	TERMINATION OF PARENTAL RIGHTS
Alabama	X			X		X	X	
Alaska		X	X	X	X			
Arizona				X	X		X	
Arkansas				X	X			
California	X		X					X
Colorado				X	X	X		
Connecticut	X			X	X			
Delaware	X		X	X				
D.C.				X	X			
Florida				X	X		X	X
Georgia	X				X			
Hawaii				X	X			
Idaho				X	X			
Illinois				X	X	X		
Indiana	X		X	X	X			X
Iowa		X (foster care)		X	X	X		X
Kansas				X		X		
Kentucky				X				X
Louisiana			X	X			X	X
Maine		X	X	X		X		X
Maryland			X	X				
Mass.		X (contact w/ birth parents)	X	X				X

STATE	IN GENERAL	ADOPTION	CUSTODY	DEPENDENCY	DIVORCE	PATERNITY	SHELTER/ INSTITUTION	TERMINATION OF PARENTAL RIGHTS
Michigan		X	X	X				
Minnesota			X	X		X		X
Mississippi		X		X		X		X
Missouri			X	X	X	X		X
Montana			X	X		X		X
Nebraska		X		X	X	X		X
Nevada				X		X		X
New Hamp.				X	X			X
New Jersey		X	X	X		X		X
New Mexico			X	X				
New York	X							
North Carolina				X				X
North Dakota			X	X	X			
Ohio				X				
Oklahoma		X	X	X				X
Oregon			X	X	X	X		
Pennsylvania				X				X
Rhode Island				X				X
South Carolina		X	X	X			X	X
South Dakota			X	X				
Tennessee				X	X			
Texas	X							X
Utah			X	X				X
Vermont		X	X					

STATE	IN GENERAL	ADOPTION	CUSTODY	DEPENDENCY	DIVORCE	PATERNITY	SHELTER/ INSTITUTION	TERMINATION OF PARENTAL RIGHTS
Virginia			X	X		X		
Washington			X	X		X		
West Virginia					X			
Wisconsin		X		X		X		X
Wyoming				X		X		X

Representation of Children in Court

STATE	ISSUE	STATUTE(S)	TITLE OF APPOINTED	MANDATORY?
Alabama	In general	Ala. Code §12-15-8(a)	GAL	discretionary
	Dependency, Abuse/Neglect	Ala. Code §26-14-11	GAL (must be atty.)	mandatory
	Dependency, multiple needs children	Ala. Code §12-15-71(h)(4)	GAL	discretionary
	Involuntary commitment	Ala. Code §12-15-90(d)(2)	Atty. or GAL	mandatory
	Legitimation	Ala. Code §26-11-2(b)	GAL	mandatory if mother objects, otherwise discretionary
	Paternity	Ala. Code §26-17-17(b)	GAL	mandatory if not represented by counsel
Alaska	Adoption	AS 25.23.125(b)	Atty. &/or GAL	discretionary
	Child Protection (Abuse/Neglect)	AS 47.17.030(e)	GAL	mandatory
	Custody	AS 47.10.010(b)	Atty.	discretionary
	Divorce/Dissolution	AS 25.24.310	Atty. &/or GAL	discretionary
Arizona	Abuse/Neglect	ARS §8-221(I)	GAL	mandatory
	Divorce/Dissolution	ARS §25-321	Atty.	discretionary
	Institutionalization	ARS §8-221(C)	Atty.	mandatory unless waived
Arkansas	Dependency	ACA §§ 9-27-316(f)* 9-27-316(g)**	*Attorney ad litem – best interest **CASA	*mandatory **discretionary
	Divorce/Dissolution	ACA §9-13-101(d)	Attorney ad litem – best interest	discretionary
	Probate	ACA §9-13-106(b)	Attorney ad litem	discretionary
California	Custody	West's Ann. Cal. Fam. Code §3150	Attorney (best interests)	discretionary
	Minors, in general	West's Ann. Cal. C.C.P. §372	GAL	discretionary
	Termination of Parental Rights	West's Ann. Cal. Fam. Code §7861	Atty.	discretionary

STATE	ISSUE	STATUTE(S)	TITLE OF APPOINTED	MANDATORY?
Colorado	Dependency/Neglect	C.R.S.A. §§ 19-1-111* 19-1-111.5**	*GAL **CASA	*mandatory **discretionary
	Divorce/Dissolution	C.R.S.A. §14-10-116	Atty. &/or Special Advocate (best interest)	discretionary
Colorado continued	Paternity	C.R.S.A. §19-4-110	GAL	discretionary
Connecticut	In general	C.G.S.A. §46b-136	Atty.	discretionary
	Abuse/Neglect	C.G.S.A. §46b-129a(2)	*Atty. **GAL	*mandatory **mandatory if conflict b/t best interests & child's wishes
	Divorce/Dissolution	C.G.S.A. §46b-54	Atty.	discretionary
Delaware	In general	13 Del. C. §701(c)	*GAL (atty. or CASA) **Atty.	*mandatory **discretionary
	Custody	13 Del. C. §721(c)	Atty.	discretionary
	Dependency (Welfare)	10 Del. C. §925 (17); Del. Fam. Ct. R. Civ. Proc. Rule 204	GAL (atty. or CASA)	discretionary
D.C.	Divorce/Dissolution	D.C. Code §§ 16-914(g), 16-918	Atty. &/or GAL	discretionary
	Neglect	D.C. Code § 16-2304(b)(5)	GAL	mandatory
Florida	Dependency	F.S.A. §39.822	GAL	mandatory
	Divorce/Dissolution	F.S.A. §61.401	Atty. &/or GAL	discretionary
	Residential Treatment	F.S.A. §39.407(5)	GAL	mandatory
	Shelter Placement	F.S.A. §39.402(8)(c)(1)	GAL	discretionary
Georgia	In General	Ga. Code Ann. §§9-11-17(c); 29-4-7	GAL	discretionary
	Grandparent Visitation	Ga. Code Ann. §19-7-3(d)(1)	GAL	discretionary
	Termination of Parental Rights	Ga. Code Ann. §15-11-98(a)	*Atty. **GAL	* mandatory ** discretionary
Hawaii	Dependency	H.R.S. §587-34	*Atty.	* discretionary

STATE	ISSUE	STATUTE(S)	TITLE OF APPOINTED	MANDATORY?
			**GAL	** mandatory
	Divorce/Dissolution	H.R.S. §571-46(8)	GAL	discretionary
Idaho	Dependency	I.C. §16-1618	*GAL **Atty.	*mandatory **discretionary
	Divorce/Dissolution	I.C. §32-704 (4)	Atty.	discretionary
Illinois	Dependency	705 ILCS 405/2-17,* 405/2-17.1**	*GAL **CASA	*discretionary **discretionary
	Divorce/Dissolution	750 ILCS 5/506	Atty. or GAL or Best Interest Representative	discretionary
Illinois continued	Paternity	750 ILCS 45/18 (a-5)	Atty. or GAL or Best Interest Representative	discretionary
Indiana	In General	I.C. 31-32-3-1,* 31-32-4-2 (b)**	*GAL &/or CASA **Atty.	*discretionary **discretionary
	Custody/Visitation	I.C. 31-17-6-1	GAL &/or CASA	discretionary
	Dependency (Children in Need of Services)	I.C. 31-34-10-3	GAL &/or CASA	depends on type of harm; see statute for details
	Divorce/Dissolution & Legal Separation	I.C. 31-15-6-1	GAL &/or CASA	discretionary
	Termination of Parental Rights	I.C. 31-35-2-7	GAL &/or CASA	mandatory if parent objects
Iowa	Abuse	I.C.A. §232.71C(3)	GAL	mandatory
	Child in Need of Assistance	I.C.A. §§232.89(2)* (5)**	*Atty. & GAL ** CASA	*mandatory **discretionary
	Divorce	I.C.A. §598.12(1)	Atty.	discretionary
	Family in Need of Assistance	I.C.A. §232.126	Atty. or GAL (GAL may be a CASA)	mandatory
	Foster Care	I.C.A. §232.179	GAL; Atty.	GAL – mandatory Atty. – discretionary
	Paternity	I.C.A. §598.21(4B)	GAL	mandatory
	Termination of Parental Rights	I.C.A. §§232.112(2), 600A.6(2)	GAL (§600A(9) - must be atty.)	mandatory
Kansas	Child in Need	K.S.A. §§	*GAL (must be	*mandatory

STATE	ISSUE	STATUTE(S)	TITLE OF APPOINTED	MANDATORY?
	(?)	38-1505(a)* & ** 38-1505a(a)***	atty.) **Atty. *** CASA (best interests)	**discretionary *** discretionary
	Paternity	K.S.A. §38-1125	GAL	mandatory
Kentucky	Abuse/Neglect	K.R.S. §620.100(1)(a)* §620.100(1)(d)**	*Atty. **CASA	*mandatory **discretionary
	Mental Health?	K.R.S. §645.060(1)	Atty.	mandatory
	Termination of Parental Rights	K.R.S. §625.041(1)	GAL	mandatory
Louisiana	Abuse	LSA-R.S. 9:345(B)	Atty.	mandatory
Louisiana continued	Child in Need of Care	LSA-Ch. C. Arts. 607(A)* 424.1(A)**	*Atty. **CASA	*mandatory **discretionary
	Custody	LSA-R.S. 9:345(A)	Atty.	discretionary
	Mental Health Institutionalization	LSA-Ch. C. Arts. 607(C), 1409(K)	Atty.	mandatory if requested
	Termination of Parental Rights - when opposed	LSA-Ch. C. Art. 1137(B)	Atty.	mandatory
	TPR – permanency planning	LSA-Ch. C. Art. 1146(C)-(D)	Atty.	mandatory if in state's custody, discretionary if not
Maine	Abuse/Neglect	22 M.R.S.A. §4005(1)(A)* §4005(1)(F)**	*GAL **Atty.	*mandatory **GAL may request atty., but unclear if ct. must appoint
	Adoption	18-A M.R.S.A. §9-304(d)	GAL	discretionary
	Custody/Divorce – when contested	19-A M.R.S.A. §1507	GAL (best interest, but also req'd to make child's wishes known – subsection (4))	discretionary
	Paternity	18-A M.R.S.A §9-201(f)	Atty.	mandatory

STATE	ISSUE	STATUTE(S)	TITLE OF APPOINTED	MANDATORY?
	Termination of Parental Rights	18-A M.R.S.A. §9-204(c)	GAL	discretionary
Maryland	Child in Need of Assistance	MD Code Cts. & Judicial Proceedings (CJC) §3-813(d)(1)* §3-813(e)**	*Atty. **CASA	*mandatory **discretionary
	Custody/Support/ Visitation – when contested	MD Code Family Law §1-202	Atty.	discretionary
Mass.	Abuse/Neglect	M.G.L.A. 119 §29	Atty.	mandatory
	Abuse – Visitation w/ Abusive Parent	M.G.L.A. 208 §31A, 209 §38, 209A §3, 209C §10	Atty. or GAL	discretionary
	Care & Protection	MA R. Juv. Ct. Order 1-93(4)	Atty.	mandatory
Mass. continued	Child Care, Custody, & Maintenance (but not in Divorce?)	M.G.L.A. 215 §§56A, 56B	GAL	discretionary
	Child Performers	M.G.L.A. 231 §85P ½ (d)(4)	GAL	discretionary
	Enforcement of Post-Adoption Contact	M.G.L.A. 210 §6D	GAL	discretionary
	Omission of Child from Will - Accidental	M.G.L.A. 192 §1C	GAL	mandatory
	Permanency Hearing	MA R. Permanency Hearings Rule 4(C)	Atty.	mandatory
	Termination of Parental Rights	MA R. Prob. Ct. Practice 10a(6)	*Atty. **GAL	*mandatory **discretionary
Michigan	Abuse/Neglect	M.C.L.A. 722.630	Lawyer-GAL[1]	mandatory
	Adoption	M.C.L.A. 710.23e (3)* & (6)**	*Atty. **GAL	*discretionary **discretionary
	Custody	M.C.L.A. 722.24(2)* & MCR 3.204(D)**	*Lawyer-GAL **GAL	*discretionary **GAL
	Guardianship	M.C.L.A.	*Lawyer-GAL	*discretionary

STATE	ISSUE	STATUTE(S)	TITLE OF APPOINTED	MANDATORY?
		700.5213 (4)* & (6)**	**GAL	**discretionary
Minnesota	Child in Need of Protection or Services[2]	M.S.A. §260C.212 Subdiv. 4(c)(4)	Atty. & GAL	mandatory
	Custody/Support/ Parenting Time	M.S.A. §518.165 Subdiv. 1 & 2	GAL	mandatory if allegations of abuse or neglect that are not being litigated in another court; otherwise discretionary
	Juvenile Protection Matters,[3] Generally	Juv. Protection Proc. Rule 25.02 Subdiv. 1(a);* Juv. Protection Proc. Rule 26.01**	*Atty. **GAL	*mandatory ** it depends; see M.S.A. §260C.163 Subdiv. 5
	Out-of-home Placement Plan	M.S.A. §260C.212 Subdiv. 1(d)	Atty. & GAL	mandatory
Minnesota continued	Paternity	M.S.A. §257.60	GAL	Ct. must appoint either guardian or GAL
	Permanent Placement – Plan	M.S.A. §260C.212 Subdiv. 4(c)(4)	Atty. & GAL	mandatory
	Permanent Placement – Change	M.S.A. §260C.212 Subdiv. 6(2)	GAL	mandatory
	Termination of Parental Rights	M.S.A. §260C.212 Subdiv. 4(c)(4)	Atty. & GAL	mandatory
Mississippi	Abandonment	Miss. Code Ann. §§93-17-8(5)	GAL	mandatory
	Abuse/Neglect	Miss. Code Ann. §43-21-121(1)(e)* §43-21-201(1) & §43-21-151(1)**	*GAL **Atty.	*mandatory; must also appoint an attorney if GAL is not a lawyer **mandatory
	Abuse – Visitation w/ Abusive Parent	Miss. Code Ann. §97-5-42(3)	GAL	mandatory
	Adoption – contested	Miss. Code Ann. §93-17-8(1)(b)	GAL (must be an attorney)	mandatory
	Paternity – Appeal	Miss. Code Ann.	GAL	discretionary?

STATE	ISSUE	STATUTE(S)	TITLE OF APPOINTED	MANDATORY?
	from Judgment	§93-9-41		
	Termination of Parental Rights	Miss. Code Ann. §93-15-107(1)	GAL	mandatory
Missouri	Abuse	V.A.M.S. 210.160	GAL	mandatory
	Abuse – Orders of Protection	V.A.M.S. 455.513	GAL or CASA	mandatory
	Custody/Support/ Visitation	V.A.M.S. 452.423(1)	GAL	discretionary
	Divorce			
	Grandparent Visitation	V.A.M.S. 452.402(3)	GAL (must be an attorney)	discretionary
	Paternity	V.A.M.S. 210.830	GAL	discretionary
	Termination of Parental Rights	V.A.M.S. 211.462(1)	GAL	mandatory
Montana	Abuse	MCA 41-3-112(1)* 41-3-1013(4)**	*GAL **CASA	*mandatory **discretionary
	Custody/Support/ Visitation	MCA 40-4-205(1)	GAL	discretionary
	Grandparent Visitation	MCA 40-9-102(4)	Atty.	discretionary
	Paternity	MCA 40-6-110	GAL	Ct. must appoint either guardian or GAL
Montana continued	Termination of Parental Rights – involuntary	MCA 41-3-607	GAL	mandatory
Nebraska	Abuse/Neglect	Neb. Rev. St. §43-3710(1)	CASA	discretionary
	Adoption – Contact with Birth Parent(s)	Neb. Rev. St. §43-163(1)	GAL	mandatory
	Divorce	Neb. Rev. St. §42-358(1)	Atty.	discretionary
	Conservator – Appointment	Neb. Rev. St. §30-2636(a)	GAL (must be an atty.)	discretionary
	Guardian - Appointment	Neb. Rev. St. §30-2611(d)	GAL	discretionary
	Indian Child – Foster Care Placement	Neb. Rev. St. §43-1505(2)	Atty. (best interests)	discretionary
	Indian Child – Term.	Neb. Rev. St.	Atty. (best	discretionary

STATE	ISSUE	STATUTE(S)	TITLE OF APPOINTED	MANDATORY?
	of Parental Rights	§43-1505(2)	interests)	
	Paternity	Neb. Rev. St. §43-104.05	GAL	mandatory
	Termination of Parental Rights	Neb. Rev. St. §42-364(7)* §43-3710(1)**	*GAL (must be an atty.) **CASA	*mandatory, when not in Juv. Ct. **discretionary
Nevada	Abuse/Neglect	N.R.S. 432B.420 (1), (3)	Atty. &/or GAL (same person)	discretionary
	Abuse/Neglect – Protective Custody Hearing	N.R.S. 432B.500(1)	GAL	mandatory
	Indian Child – Foster Care Placement	N.R.S. 62D.210(2)(b)	Atty.	discretionary
	Indian Child – Term. of Parental Rights	N.R.S. 128.023(2)(b)	Atty.	discretionary
	Paternity	N.R.S. 126.101(1)	GAL (D.A. or Div. of Welfare)	must have either guardian or GAL
	Probate	N.R.S. 136.200	Atty.	discretionary
	Termination of Parental Rights	N.R.S. 128.100(1)	Atty. &/or GAL (same person?)	discretionary
New Hampshire	Abuse/Neglect – initial action	N.H. Rev. Stat. §169-C:10, I* & II[4]**	*GAL or CASA **Atty.	*mandatory **discretionary
	Abuse/Neglect – Preliminary Hearing	N.H. Rev. Stat. §169-C:15, III	Atty.	mandatory upon finding of reas. belief
New Hamp. continued	Conservator – Appointment	N.H. Rev. Stat. §464-A:41, I	GAL	discretionary if sua sponte, mandatory if requested
	Domestic Violence	N.H. Rev. Stat. §173-B:6	GAL	discretionary
	Divorce/Legal Sep./ Annulment	N.H. Rev. Stat. §458:17-a, I	GAL (must be atty.)[5]	discretionary
	Guardian - Appointment	N.H. Rev. Stat. §464-A:41, I	GAL	discretionary if sua sponte, mandatory if requested
	Termination of Parental Rights	N.H. Rev. Stat. §170-C:8	GAL	mandatory
New Jersey	Abuse/Neglect – in general	N.J.S.A. 9:6-8.23* Atty.: NJ R. Ch.	*law guardian **CASA	*mandatory **discretionary

STATE	ISSUE	STATUTE(S)	TITLE OF APPOINTED	MANDATORY?
		Div. Fam. Pt. R. 5:8C**		
	Abuse/Neglect – runs away fr. placement	N.J.S.A. 9:6-8.68	law guardian	mandatory if child at hearing
	Adoption – child fr. approved agency	N.J.S.A. 9:3-47(b)	GAL	mandatory if adverse info vs. prospective parent (PP)
	Adoption – child not fr. approved agency	N.J.S.A. 9:3-48 (a)(4) & (d)	GAL	mandatory if child removed from PP; if not, discretionary
	Custody	N.J.S.A. 9:2-4(c)	Atty. or GAL	discretionary
	Paternity	N.J.S.A. 9:17-47	GAL (atty. or State agency)	discretionary
	Standby Guardian – Appointment	N.J.S.A. 3B:12-77	Atty. or GAL	discretionary
	Termination of Parental Rights	N.J.S.A. 30:4C-15.4(b)	law guardian	mandatory
New Mexico	Custody	N.M.S.A §40-4-8	GAL	discretionary
	Family in Need	N.M.S.A § 32A-3B-8(C)	GAL	mandatory
New York	In General	McKinney's Family Court Act §241	Atty. or law guardian	depends; see McKinney's §249(A) for specifics
North Carolina	Abuse/ Neglect	N.C.G.S.A. §7B-601	GAL	mandatory (attorney also mandatory if GAL is not one)
North Carolina continued	Dependency	N.C.G.S.A. §7B-601(A)	GAL	discretionary (attorney also mandatory if GAL is not one)
	Termination of Parental Rights	N.C.G.S.A. §7B-1108	GAL	discretionary (Mandatory if material allegations denied.)
North Dakota	Abuse (Order of Protection)	N.D.C.C. 14-07.1-05.1	GAL (must be an atty.)	discretionary
	Custody/Support/ Visitation	N.D.C.C. 14-09-06.4	GAL	discretionary

State	Issue	Statute(s)	Title of Appointed	Mandatory?
Ohio	Abuse/Neglect	R.C.§2151.281 (B)-(J)	*GAL **Atty.	*mandatory **depends (see R.C. §2151.281(H); Juv. R. Rule 4(A),(C))
Oklahoma	Abuse/Neglect	10 Okl.St.Ann. §7002-1.2(C)	GAL & atty.	mandatory
	Custody/Visitation	43 Okl.St.Ann. §107.3(A)(1)	GAL (must be attorney)	discretionary
	Adoption	10 Okl.St.Ann. §7505-1.2	Atty. & GAL	Atty. – mandatory if contested, discretionary if not; GAL – mandatory if requested, discretionary if not
	Deprived Child	10 Okl.St.Ann. §§7003-3.7(A)(2)* 7003-3.7(B)**	*Atty. **GAL (see (C) - may be a CASA)	*mandatory **discretionary
	Termination of Parental Rights	10 Okl.St.Ann. §7505-2.1(E)(5)	Atty.	mandatory
Oregon	Abuse/Neglect	O.R.S.§§ 419A.170* & 419B.195**	*CASA (best interests) **Atty.	* mandatory **see O.R.S.§§ 419B.195(1), 419B.100
	Custody, Divorce, & Paternity	O.R.S. §107.425(6)	Atty.	mandatory if requested by child(ren), discretionary if not
Penn.	Dependency	42 Pa.C.S.A. §6311	GAL	mandatory
	Termination of Parental Rights	23 Pa.C.S.A. §2313(a)	Atty. &/or GAL	Atty. - mandatory in contested actions; otherwise atty. or GAL - discretionary
Rhode Island	Abuse/Neglect	Gen. Laws 1956, §40-11-14	GAL &/or CASA	mandatory? (confusing wording)
	Termination of Parental Rights	R. Juv. P., Rule 18(c)(3)	GAL &/or CASA	mandatory
South Carolina	Abuse/Neglect	Code 1976 §20-7-110(1)	Atty. & GAL	mandatory

STATE	ISSUE	STATUTE(S)	TITLE OF APPOINTED	MANDATORY?
	Adoption	Code 1976 §20-7-1732	GAL	mandatory
	Custody/Visitation	Code 1976 §20-7-1545	GAL	discretionary
	Involuntary Commitment	Code 1976 §44-24-90	Atty.	mandatory
	Termination of Parental Rights	Code 1976 §20-7-1570(B)	GAL	mandatory; attorney also mandatory if GAL is not one in contested suits, but atty. is discretionary if uncontested
South Dakota	In General - Civil Actions	S.D.C.L. §15-6-17(c)	GAL	mandatory if no guardian or conservator
	Abuse/Neglect	S.D.C.L. §§ 26-8A-9; 26-8A-18; 26-8A-20	*Atty. **GAL or CASA (all best interests)	*mandatory; **discretionary during allegations, mandatory if adjudicated A/N & removed
	Custody/Divorce	S.D.C.L. §25-4-45.4	Atty. (best interests)	discretionary
Tennessee	Abuse/Neglect	T.C.A. §§ 37-1-149(a),* (b)(1)**	*GAL **CASA (best interests)	*mandatory **discretionary
	Divorce	T.C.A. §36-4-132	GAL	discretionary
Texas	In General	V.T.C.A. Family Code §51.11	GAL	mandatory if parent/guardian not available, discretionary otherwise (see §107.021)
	Conservator Appointment	V.T.C.A. Family Code §§107.011, 107.012	GAL & atty. ad litem (AAL)	mandatory
	Termination of Parental Rights	V.T.C.A. Family Code §§107.011, 107.012	GAL & AAL	mandatory

STATE	ISSUE	STATUTE(S)	TITLE OF APPOINTED	MANDATORY?
Utah	In General	U.C.A. §§78-3a-912(2), (3)	Attorney GAL	discretionary
	Abuse/Neglect	U.C.A. §78-3a-314(3),(5)* 78-7-9**	*GAL; **Attorney GAL	*mandatory; **discretionary
	Custody/Support/ Visitation	U.C.A.§§ 30-3-11.2* 78-7-45(1)**	*Atty.; **Attorney GAL	*discretionary; **discretionary
	Parenting Plan	U.C.A. §30-3-10.8(7)	GAL	discretionary (when parents file inconsistent plans)
	Protective Orders	U.C.A. §78-3h-102	Attorney GAL	discretionary
	Termination of Parental Rights	U.C.A. §78-3a-314(5)	Attorney GAL	mandatory
Vermont	Adoption	15A V.S.A. §3-201(2)	GAL	mandatory in contested, discretionary if uncontested
	Custody/Support	15 V.S.A. §669	GAL	discretionary
Virginia	Abuse/Neglect	Va. Code Ann. §16.1-266(A),* (D)**	*GAL (must be attorney) **Atty.	* mandatory **discretionary
	Custody	Va. Code Ann. §16.1-266(E)	Atty. or GAL	discretionary
	Guardianship	Va. Code Ann. §16.1-350(C)	GAL	mandatory if petition filed by non-parent, otherwise discretionary
	Paternity: establishing & disestablishing	Va. Code Ann. §§20-49.2, 20-49.10	GAL	mandatory
Washington	In General, Family Court	R.C.W.A. §26.12.175(1)(a)	GAL	discretionary
	Abuse/Neglect	R.C.W.A. §§ 13.34.100(1)* 13.34.100(6)** 13.34.100(8)***	*GAL ** Atty. (best interests? – see §13.34.100(7)) *** CASA	* mandatory, unless has indep. atty. or for other good cause **discretionary ***discretionary

STATE	ISSUE	STATUTE(S)	TITLE OF APPOINTED	MANDATORY?
	Custody/Support/ Visitation	R.C.W.A. §26.10.070	Atty.	discretionary
	Parenting Plan	R.C.W.A. §26.09.110	Atty.	discretionary
Washington continued	Paternity	R.C.W.A. §26.26.555	GAL	mandatory (but see R.C.W.A. §74.20.310(1))
West Virginia	Divorce	W.Va. Code §48-5-107(f)	GAL	discretionary
	Grandparent Visitation	W.Va. Code §48-10-403	GAL	discretionary
	Guardianship	W.Va. Code §§ 48-9-302(1)-(2)	*GAL **Atty.	*discretionary; **discretionary
Wisconsin	In General, Child in Need of Service or Protection	W.S.A. 48.23 (1m)(b)	Atty. or GAL (if under 12 yrs.)	discretionary, unless petition to remove child from home is contested
	In General	W.S.A. 48.236 (1)	CASA	discretionary
	Abuse/Neglect	W.S.A. 48.23 (3m)	*Atty. **Atty. or GAL (if under 12 yrs.)	* mandatory for 12+ **mandatory for <12 years
	Abortion	W.S.A. 48.23(cm)*; 48.235(d)**	*Atty. **GAL	*mandatory to waive parental consent; **discretionary
	Action by Minor Parent for Child	W.S.A. 769.302	GAL	discretionary
	Adoption - contested	W.S.A. 48.235(c)	GAL	mandatory
	Guardianship	W.S.A. 48.235(c)	GAL	mandatory
	Paternity	W.S.A. 767.475(1)	GAL	usu. discretionary; see 767.045(1)(a) or (c) for mandatory appointments
	Restraining Order	W.S.A. 813.122 (3)(b)(1)	GAL	discretionary
	Termination of Parental Rights	W.S.A. 48.235(c)	GAL	mandatory
Wyoming	In General, Child Protection	W.S.1977 §14-3-416	GAL	discretionary

STATE	ISSUE	STATUTE(S)	TITLE OF APPOINTED	MANDATORY?
	Abuse/Neglect	W.S.1977 §14-3-211	Atty. & GAL (best interests)	mandatory
	Grandparent Visitation	W.S.1977 §20-7-101(a)	GAL	discretionary
	Paternity	W.S.1977 §14-2-812	Atty. (best interests)	discretionary
	Termination of Parental Rights	W.S.1977 §14-2-312	GAL	discretionary

[0] A Lawyer-GAL represents the child's best interest, taking into account the child's wishes. *See* M.C.L.A. 712A.17d(1)(h).

[0] Includes children who have been abandoned, abused, deprived of basic living necessities, and medically neglected. *See* M.S.A. §260C.007 Subdiv. 6.

[0] Includes children in need of protection and services, foster care placement, etc. *See* Juv. Protection Proc. Rule 2.01(k).

[0] N.H. Rev. Stat. §169-C:10, II(a) was held unconstitutional by *In re Shelby R.*, NK"http://web2.westlaw.com/Find/Default.wl?DocName=804A%2E2d435&SerialNum=2002526900&FindType=a&CaseCite=NH+ST+s+169%2DC%3A10&CaseStatKey=NHSTS169%2DC%3A10&AP=&RS=WLW4.06&VR=2.0&SV=Split&MT=LawSchool&FN=_top"\t"_top"804 A.2d 435, but the case only dealt with language re: representation for parents. The proposed legislative amendments leave the representation for the child intact.

[0] GAL Guidelines 1.

APPENDIX

2

IN THE SUPERIOR COURT OF FULTON COUNTY

STATE OF GEORGIA

,	)	
	)	
Petitioner	)	
	)	CIVIL ACTION
vs.	)	
	)	FILE NO.
,	)	
	)	
Respondent.	)	

CONSENT ORDER FOR APPOINTMENT OF GUARDIAN AD LITEM

The parties having consented to the appointment of a Guardian Ad Litem concerning the issue of custody and visitation with the two (2) minor children of the parties, to wit: (hereinafter referred to as the "Children");

It is hereby CONSIDERED, ORDERED AND ADJUDGED as follows:

1.

That this Court shall appoint DAWN SMITH, ESQ., as Guardian Ad Litem for the minor children of the parties, and she shall represent the best interests of the children before this Court. The Guardian Ad Litem shall be an officer of the Court and shall assist the Court in reaching a decision as to the issues involving custody and visitation of said minor children.

2.

In order to perform her other functions, the Guardian Ad Litem shall have full right and authority to completely investigate all aspects of the case and to interview all parties and other persons with an interest in the custody, visitation and/or education of the minor children upon request by the Guardian Ad Litem with reasonable notice. In the event that a party, or other person, shall refuse to cooperate or be interviewed, the Guardian Ad Litem shall so report to the Court and shall prepare the case without the assistance of the party or witness unless the court otherwise directs.

3.

The Guardian Ad Litem shall have the right to inspect all records relating to the minor children maintained by the Clerk of this Court, the Department of Family and Children's Services, the Juvenile Court, any school, hospital, doctor or other mental health provider, and any other social or human services agency without necessity of written consent by the parents or the Court. This Order authorizes any individual or organization to release those records to the Guardian Ad Litem. The Guardian Ad Litem shall have the right to request that a party undergo psychological evaluation or any other type of psychiatric or psychological testing, or other evaluation, by an appropriate psychologist, psychiatrist medical doctor, or expert. Further, the Guardian Ad Litem shall have the authority to require either party to be randomly tested for drugs or alcohol as she deems appropriate.

4.

The Guardian Ad Litem shall have the right to examine any residence wherein any person seeking custody and/or visitation proposes to house the minor children.

5.

The Guardian Ad Litem shall not release any information obtained herein to any other person without the express permission of this Court, except to counsel for the parties.

6.

The Guardian Ad Litem shall be entitled to notice of, and shall be entitled to participate in, all hearings, trials, investigations, depositions, mediations or other proceedings concerning the children and counsel for both parties are responsible for ensuring that the Guardian Ad Litem receives this notice at the earliest possible dates. The Guardian Ad Litem shall be served with copies of all pleadings, notices, discovery, reports and any other documents filed in this action.

7.

The Guardian Ad Litem shall be notified of, and shall participate in, settlement negotiations and offers of settlement as they affect the best interests of the children.

8.

The Guardian Ad Litem's hourly rate is $325.00 per hour and the Parties shall split the costs of the initial retainer of $5,000.00 to be applied against time Dawn Smith spends. Said payments shall be made within ten (10) days of the execution of the Consent Order. Once the retainer balance has been exhausted, any additional retainer of equal amount shall be required within ten (10) days of notice of the exhaustion of same and shall be paid equally by the Parties. The Parties agree that the final apportionment of said costs will be decided by the Court.

9.

The appointment of a Guardian Ad Litem shall last until such time as the matters pertaining to custody and visitation raised in this action are settled, dismissed or otherwise adjudicated.

10.

The Guardian Ad Litem will prepare a written report that shall be submitted to the Court and to the attorneys for both parties. The report shall remain confidential and shall not be disseminated by either party or their lawyers, except as otherwise ordered by the Court.

SO ORDERED this _____ day of _____, 2011.

_____

Superior Court of Fulton County

Consented to by:

STATE OF MAINE

. DISTRICT COURT _____
Location _____
Docket No. _____

Plaintiff _____

v.

ORDER APPOINTING GUARDIAN AD LITEM (GAL)
☐Limited-Purpose ☐Standard ☐Expanded

Defendant _____

APPOINTMENT

1. Pursuant to 19-A M.R.S. §1507(1) and subject to the conditions set forth below, the Court appoints a guardian ad litem (GAL) for the following child(ren) in this matter whose name(s) and date(s) of birth are:_____
_____ .

2. ☐ The GAL appointed by the court and listed below is currently on the roster of qualified Maine GALs; **or**

   ☐ The GAL appointed by the court and listed below is a qualified attorney licensed to practice in Maine who is not currently listed on the GAL roster. The following findings establish good cause for appointing an unrostered GAL:
      ☐ the GAL has agreed to serve in a *pro bono* capacity; or

      ☐ (other)_____

   The GAL's name is: _____
   The GAL's contact information is:_____
_____

3. ☐ Neither party objects to the GAL appointment or the fee arrangements specified below; **or**

   ☐ Plaintiff/Defendant objects to appointment of a GAL but, after careful consideration, the Court concludes the following factors in 4 M.R.S. § 1555(1)(B) support the appointment: _____
_____
_____ ; **and/or**

   ☐ Plaintiff/Defendant objects to the fee arrangement below but, after careful consideration, the Court concludes the following factors in M.R.G.A.L. 4(b)(4)(C) support the fee arrangement_____
_____
_____ .

TYPE OF GAL APPOINTMENT AND GAL'S INVESTIGATIVE DUTIES
(Choose one: limited-purpose, standard or expanded)

4. ☐ **Limited-Purpose Appointment.**

A. *Duties.* . The GAL must perform the following specific duties: _____
_____
_____ .

The GAL shall appear at the ☐ interim / ☐ final hearing in this matter to testify and be available for cross-examination.

The GAL may not perform and is not expected to perform any duties beyond those specified in this order (including responding to telephone calls, emails, and other communications from the parties) unless or until a new order is entered.

THIS FORM MAY NOT BE ALTERED OR MODIFIED

B. ***Duration.*** This GAL appointment terminates at the end of the ☐ interim / ☐ final hearing.

4. ☐ Standard Appointment.

A. ***Duties.*** The GAL shall appear at the final hearing in this matter to testify and to be available for cross-examination. Before the hearing, the GAL must perform the following specific duties:

☑ Observe the child(ren) in the home or homes where the child(ren) regularly reside, and for each child over age 3, conduct a face-to-face interview with the child; and

☑ Interview each parent and any adult who resides in the home(s) where the child(ren) regularly reside.

The GAL may not perform and is not expected to perform any duties beyond those specified in this order (including responding to extra communications by the parties) unless or until a new appointment order is entered.

B. ***Duration.*** This appointment expires: ☐ on _____ (date) **or**
☐ when ordered by the court (usually after the final hearing).

4. ☐ Expanded Appointment.

A. ***Duties.*** Until this appointment expires, the GAL shall appear at all hearings in this matter to testify and to be available for cross-examination. Before the hearing, the GAL must perform the following specific duties:

☑ Observe the child(ren) in the home or homes where the child(ren) regularly reside, and for each child over the age of 3, conduct a face-to-face interview with the child; and

☑ Interview each parent and any adult who resides in the home(s) where the child(ren) regularly reside;

☐ Interview the following teachers and other people who have knowledge of the child or family: _____
_____ ;

☐ Review_____ 's ☐ mental health ☐ medical and/or ☐ educational records;

☐ Engage a qualified ☐ medical or ☐ mental health ☐ educational provider to evaluate _____
by _____ (date) with the cost not to exceed: $_____ ;

☐ By _____ (date), procure counseling for these child(ren): _____ ;

☐ Subpoena witnesses and documents and examine and cross-examine witnesses;

☐ Serve as a contact person between the parents and the child(ren) as follows _____
_____ ;

☐ Appear at ☐ Mediation (in person) and/or the ☐ Status Conference (telephonically) and/or ☐ the other court-related event(s) listed here:_____ .

☐ Other:_____
_____

The GAL may not perform and is not expected to perform any duties beyond those specified in this order (including responding to excessive communications by the parties) unless or until a new appointment order is entered.

B. ***Duration.*** This appointment expires: ☐ on _____ (date) **or**
☐ when ordered by the court (usually after the final hearing).

WRITTEN REPORT

5. (Choose one):

☐ The GAL is not required to submit a written report before testifying at the hearing (*limited appointments only*), **or**

☐ The GAL shall submit a written report to the court and to the parties 14 days before the hearing, unless the GAL has been notified that the case has settled, in which case no written report is required. If the GAL is notified by a party that the case has settled before the GAL has completed the written report, the GAL may not bill the parties for any further work on the written report.

The written report, if required, shall include the results of the GAL's investigation and the GAL's recommendations on the following issues: _____
_____
_____ :

THIS FORM MAY NOT BE ALTERED OR MODIFIED

FEE ARRANGEMENT

6. The GAL shall use the standardized billing, itemization requirements and time reporting processes established by the Family Division.

A. The total fee amount is as follows (*choose one*):

☐ The GAL will complete all the duties required in this appointment order for a flat fee of $_____.

☐ The GAL may charge a total fee of no more than $ _____ by spending no more than _____ total hours on this matter at the hourly rate of $ _____ / hr. (Additional hours and fees require prior court approval.)

B. The GAL's fee shall be paid as follows:

☐ On or before _____ (date), Plaintiff shall pay $ _____ and Defendant shall pay $ _____. These amounts are subject to re-allocation at the final hearing.

☐ In addition, the GAL shall submit an itemized bill to the parties on a ☐ monthly / ☐ bi-weekly basis.

☐ Plaintiff shall pay _____% of each bill and Defendant shall pay _____% of each bill, subject to re-allocation at the final hearing. Each party shall pay the GAL within 14 days after receiving the each bill; **or**

☐ Plaintiff shall pay $_____ per ☐ week / ☐ month toward the GAL fees and expenses and Defendant shall pay $ _____ per ☐ week / ☐ month toward the GAL fees and expenses, subject to reallocation at the final hearing.

The final fee payments shall be made within 14 days after the filing of the written report or, if no written report is required because the case has settled, within 14 days after the court has adopted the settlement. If the fee is not paid in accordance with this order, the GAL shall notify the court and the parties, and the court may vacate the appointment or take such other action it deems appropriate under the circumstances.

GENERAL PROVISIONS APPLICABLE TO ALL GAL APPOINTMENTS

7. The GAL has quasi-judicial immunity from liability resulting from actions undertaken pursuant to her/his appointment.

8. The GAL shall make the wishes of the child(ren) known to the court if the child(ren) has/have expressed them, regardless of the recommendation of the GAL.

9. Given the confidential nature of the material that may be reviewed by the GAL, all of the GAL's reports shall be confidential and sealed after the report is submitted to the court and to the parties. The reports shall not be disclosed by the parties or the GAL or further released by the Court, except as otherwise ordered by the Court.

10. The parties in this matter shall fully cooperate with the GAL's investigation, including, but not limited to, participating in interviews, making themselves and the child(ren) available to the GAL at such reasonable times and places as he or she may request for the purposes of carrying out the duties specified in this appointment order, and signing releases permitting the GAL to access all medical, mental health, or education records that the GAL has been ordered (above) to review.

11. The guardian ad litem may advocate for special procedures to protect the child witness from unnecessary psychological harm resulting from the child's testimony, with or without the consent of other parties.

12. The parties are restrained and enjoined from exercising undue influence over the child(ren) who are involved in this litigation. Undue influence includes coaching the child(ren) as to their communications or interactions with the GAL or the Court, or orchestrating the child(ren)'s actions with respect to the GAL or the court.

The Clerk is directed to incorporate this Order by reference into the docket for this case, pursuant to Rule 79(a), Maine Rules of Civil Procedure.

Date:_____   _____
                                                 Judge/ Magistrate, Maine District Court

THIS FORM MAY NOT BE ALTERED OR MODIFIED

███

IN THE CIRCUIT COURT FOR MONTGOMERY COUNTY, MARYLAND

███	*	
Plaintiff	*	
v.	*	Case No.: ███
	*	
███	*	
Defendant	*	

* * * * * * * * * * * * *

<u>ORDER APPOINTING COUNSEL FOR CHILD</u>
(305)

This matter having come before the Court, it is this ███ day of ███, 2016, by the Circuit Court for Montgomery County, Maryland

ORDERED, that Melissa A. Kucinski, Esquire, telephone number 202-713-5165, is hereby appointed as a **Best Interest Attorney (BIA)** at the hourly rate of $███ with the rights and responsibilities set forth in the Maryland Guidelines for Practice for Court-Appointed Lawyers Representing Children in Cases Involving Child Custody or Child Access (hereafter "The Guidelines") to represent ███, DOB; ███ and ███, DOB; ███. A Best Interest Attorney is a court-appointed attorney who provides independent legal services for the purpose of protecting a child's best interests, without being bound by the child's directives or objectives. The BIA shall have all the rights and responsibilities of a Child's Privilege Attorney (CPA), including but not limited to deciding whether to assert or waive the child's/children's statutory privilege, in accordance with *Nagel v. Hooks*, 296 Md. 123 (1983); and it is further

ORDERED, that the parties, counsel for the parties and all persons who are custodians of records pertinent to this Order, and all persons who otherwise have privileged or confidential information pertaining to the children shall fully cooperate with the court-appointed attorney in the performance of the duties instructed by this Court; and it is further

ORDERED, that the court-appointed attorney shall have reasonable access to the child(ren) and to all otherwise privileged or confidential information, including but not limited to any protected health information, about the child(ren), without the necessity of any further Order of Court or without the necessity of a subpoena, but upon written request by the court-appointed attorney together with a copy of this Order. The court-appointed attorney's access to privileged and confidential information shall be without the necessity of a signed release, including medical, dental, psychiatric/psychological, social services, drug and alcohol treatment, law enforcement and educational records and information; and it is further

ORDERED, that the court-appointed attorney shall be compensated as indicated:

☐ The court-appointed attorney shall provide representation on a pro-bono basis.

☐ Having met the criteria as a Court Funded Appointment, the court-appointed attorney shall be compensated by the Court at the flat rate of $1,500.00 for fees and/or expenses as a BIA and that at the conclusion of the case, the court-appointed attorney shall submit a fee petition.

☒ **Plaintiff's Payment into court-appointed attorney's trust account.** Plaintiff is hereby directed to pay the court-appointed attorney, for deposit into the court-appointed attorney's trust account, the sum of $███████ within 10 days of the date of this Order as an initial contribution towards the court-appointed attorney's fees in performance of the services identified herein and file a line indicating same.

☒ **Defendant's Payment into court-appointed attorney's trust account.** Defendant is hereby directed to pay the court-appointed attorney, for deposit into the court-appointed attorney's trust account, the sum of $███████ within 10 days of the date of this Order as an initial contribution towards the court-appointed attorney's fees in performance of the services identified herein and file a line indicating same.

☒ The court-appointed attorney shall not be required to begin work representing the child(ren) until payment is made by the parties into the court-appointed attorney's trust account, as indicated above.

☒ Final allocation of fees shall be determined by the Court at a hearing on the merits of this case or upon the Petition of the court-appointed attorney. The Court may hold the parties jointly and severally liable for all fees due to the court-appointed attorney, subject to the parties' rights to seek indemnification from each other to the extent that either party pays more than his/her allocated share; and it is further

ORDERED, that, the court-appointed attorney shall send monthly itemized statements of work completed, time spent, expenses incurred, and total fees incurred to counsel of record for each party, or if none, to each party. This provision does not apply to a pro bono or Court-funded attorney; and it is further

ORDERED, that the court appointed attorney shall be permitted to reasonably delegate tasks to appropriate personnel, including but not limited to associate attorneys, paralegals, and clerical staff, provided however that the court-appointed attorney shall supervise delegated tasks and must appear at substantive child-related court proceedings; and it is further

ORDERED, that if a party objects to an entry on a monthly itemized statement, the party shall indicate that in writing to the court-appointed attorney not later than 30 days from the date of the statement. Once the 30-day period has passed without objection, the amount billed shall be deemed fair and reasonable and court-appointed attorney is authorized to draw the amount billed from his or her trust account; and it is further

ORDERED, that the court-appointed attorney may submit a motion for interim fees for services rendered and expenses advanced, and for anticipated services or expenses that need to be incurred, which the Court shall order to be paid by a date certain, provided that the Court is satisfied as to the necessity of services rendered and expenses incurred by the court-appointed attorney, and the need for additional services and expenses to be incurred. If an opposition is filed to the request, a hearing may be scheduled at the discretion of the Court, in accordance with The Montgomery County Circuit Court Child Counsel Appointment Policies & Procedures; and it is further

ORDERED, that absent further Order of this Court, the court-appointed attorney shall not be required to participate in any appeal in this matter; and it is further

ORDERED, that either party's failure to make payment in accordance with this Order, in addition to any other consequences, including a finding of contempt of Court, shall be cause for the court-appointed attorney to request withdrawal of his/her representation, upon written Motion to the Court; and it is further

ORDERED, that although the minor child(ren) are not parties to this action, the court-appointed attorney shall be entitled to engage in discovery, including but not limited to all methods thereof authorized by the Maryland Rules, Title 2, Chapter 400, as part of the performance of the duties assigned herein, and to file motions or seek orders as appropriate in the fulfillment of the duties appointed herein; and it is further

ORDERED, that although the minor child(ren) are not parties to this action, the service and notice provisions in Title 1 of the Maryland Rule apply as though the child(ren) were parties; and it is further

ORDERED, that within ten (10) days of the date of this Order, the Plaintiff (or counsel) shall provide to the court-appointed attorney copies of all pleadings and papers filed in the above action and any correspondence between the parties or counsel for the parties. Also, each party, or their counsel, shall provide to the court-appointed attorney, within ten (10) days of the date of this Order, copies of any of the following reports pertaining to the minor child(ren) which are in the possession, custody or control of the party: medical records, school records, reports and/or evaluations pertaining to the physical, mental or emotional condition of any child, learning assessments of any kind, police reports, and reports from Departments of Social Services pertaining to any alleged abuse or neglect (including abuse or neglect in which the child(ren) were not involved); and it is further

ORDERED, that within ten (10) days of the date of this Order, each party shall provide the court-appointed attorney the names and known addresses and telephone numbers of any and all mental health providers who have evaluated or treated the child(ren) and anyone else with whom the child(ren) may have a privilege pursuant to the Statute; and it is further

ORDERED, that the court-appointed attorney shall not have any ex parte communications with the Court. In addition, the attorney/client privilege shall be respected at all times. As such, the court-appointed attorney may not speak to the parties without the prior permission of their respective attorneys, and the attorneys for the parties may not speak with the child(ren) without the prior permission of the court-appointed attorney; and it is further

ORDERED, that the court-appointed attorney shall not testify at trial nor file a written report with the Court, except that the CPA may file a document with the Court prior to the hearing or trial at which the privilege is to be asserted or waived; and it is further

ORDERED, that pursuant to The Guidelines, the court-appointed attorney shall ensure that the child(ren)'s position is made part of the record whether or not different from the position the court-appointed attorney advocates; and it is further

ORDERED, that unless otherwise specifically ordered, the court-appointed attorney's appearance shall terminate 30 days after the entry of the Order resolving the issues for which the attorney was appointed.

_____
Family Magistrate

_____
County Administrative Judge

STATE OF NEW YORK
SUPREME COURT   COUNTY OF SARATOGA

███████████

                              Plaintiff,   **ORDER APPOINTING**
                                                ATTORNEY FOR THE
                                                CHILDREN

        -against-   **Index No:** ███████
                                                RJI No: 45-1-2015██

███████████████████

                              Defendant.

      Upon proceedings at which time all parties were present, it appears that the best interests

of the minor children of the marriage, to wit: ████████████████ born November██

██and████████████████ born April████ requires the appointment of an

Attorney for the Children; it is hereby

      ORDERED, that ████████████████████████████████████

PO Box ████████████ **NY 12**██ **(telephone no: (518**██████ **)** is appointed Attorney for

the Children for ████████████ and ████████████████ to appear for

and protect the interests of said infants in this action; and it is further

      ORDERED, that the children shall be made available to speak with the Attorney for the

Children and the Attorney for the Children shall conduct a preliminary investigation to obtain

information from any appropriate source and be prepared to report to the Court; and it is further

      ORDERED, that all individuals, institutions, educational facilities, medical care

providers and others having information about such children, shall release same to the Attorney

for the Children upon presentation of a photocopy of this Order without specific authorization by

the children's parents; and it is further

      ORDERED, that ████████ and/or ████████████████ hereby directed to

provide the Attorney for the Children appointed herein with any and all required HIPPA

authorizations in order to obtain any medical, psychological and/or educational records that are

required or requested.

DATED: ██████ 2016

                              _____
                              HON. RICHARD A. KUPFERMAN
                              ACTING SUPREME COURT JUSTICE

3A

IN THE CIRCUIT COURT FOR MONTGOMERY COUNTY, MARYLAND

PARENT 1	:	
	:	
Plaintiff	:	
	:	
v.	:	**Case No. 12345FL**
	:	
PARENT 2	:	
	:	
Defendant	:	

RECOMMENDATION REGARDING WAIVER OF PRIVILEGE

Having been appointed by this Honorable Court for the sole purpose of waiving (or not) the psychiatric or psychological privilege for the minor child, A.B. (age X), pursuant to the case of *Nagle v. Hooks*, 296 Md. 123 (1983) [insert your jurisdiction's authority], the undersigned attorney states as follows:

1. A.B. is x years old. [follow your jurisdiction's privacy rules as to whether to list the child's name, birthdate, age, etc.]

2. Undersigned counsel spoke to Defendant on [date]. Undersigned counsel spoke to the minor child's therapist, Ms. Angela Brown on [date]. Undersigned counsel attempted to reach Plaintiff by telephone on [date] and on [date], but Plaintiff's voicemail

box was full. Undersigned counsel also attempted to reach Plaintiff by e-mail on [date] and [date], but as of the filing of this Recommendation has received no response.

3. Undersigned counsel reviewed the court's online docket, the pleadings in the case, and Y and Z documents.

4. Undersigned counsel has been informed that A.B. is currently in therapy with Ms. Angela Brown.

5. After due consideration of the factors in the appointment, the contacts Undersigned counsel has had with Defendant and Ms. Brown, it is the recommendation of the Undersigned counsel as follows:

RECOMMENDATION

6. As to A.B.: That the privilege of confidentiality (not) be waived as it relates to A.B. and Ms. Angela Brown and that Ms. Brown (not) be permitted to speak on matters relating to her therapeutic association with A.B. if so requested, and may (not) produce privileged documents.

Respectfully submitted,

MK FAMILY LAW

Melissa A. Kucinski, #xxxx
1750 K Street, N.W., 8th Floor
Washington, D.C. 20006
(202) 713-5165
(202) 618-9638 fax
melissa@mkfamilylawfirm.com
Child Privilege Attorney

CERTIFICATE OF SERVICE

I HEREBY CERTIFY that a copy of the foregoing Recommendation was e-mailed and mailed, postage prepaid, this _____ day of _____ 2017 to:

Parent 1
123 Avenue
Rockville, Maryland 20850
Plaintiff, Pro Se
Lawyer for Parent 2
456 Street
Rockville, Maryland 20850
Attorney for Defendant

_____

Melissa A. Kucinski

3B

[Date]

VIA ELECTRONIC MAIL/US POSTAL MAIL/FACSIMILE

Parent 1
c/o Lawyer for Parent 1
123 Street
Rockville, Maryland 20850

Parent 2
c/o Lawyer for Parent 2
456 Street
Rockville, Maryland 20850

Re: *Parent 1 v. Parent 2*
    Montgomery County Circuit Court
    Case No. 12345FL

Dear Parent 1 and Parent 2:

I have been appointed as the Best Interest Attorney [Guardian *Ad Litem*, Child Advocate, Child's Attorney, etc.] for your children, [Name] and [Name]. I will represent each as his/her attorney in your custody case in Montgomery County Circuit Court. This letter is to provide you with the general protocol I will follow in representing each child's interests. Occasionally, there may be need for me to deviate from the protocol, as the circumstances dictate.

Pursuant to the Circuit Court Order appointing me as Best Interest Attorney [Guardian *Ad Litem*, Child Advocate, Child's Attorney, etc.], both of you are to provide me with a deposit of $xxx that I will hold in my attorney escrow account. The Court Order further says I am not required to begin work on this case, as a best interest attorney [GAL, CA, CC, etc.], until I receive this retainer deposit. The Court will be sending you a copy of the order that appoints me as the children's attorney, and I attach a copy to this letter. The Court order states that Parent 1 (or his/her attorney) must provide me with a copy of all pleadings and papers in this custody case within ten (10) days, which may be done by e-mail to save time and cost, if you so desire. Both parents may also send me anything you think will help me in my review of your children's circumstances. I would like to schedule a time to meet with both of you at your earliest convenience. Pursuant to the Maryland Rules of Professional Conduct, I will not speak or meet with you alone if you have a lawyer, unless that lawyer authorizes me, in writing, to speak or meet with you alone. I ask that you, or your lawyer, contact me upon receipt of this letter. I will be flexible in meeting location. My office is in Washington, D.C., but there are numerous options where I can easily meet you in Montgomery County, including at your attorney's office, unless my office is more convenient for you.

I ask that you forward to my attention a list of witnesses, along with each witness's preferred contact information, including telephone numbers, addresses, and e-mail addresses. The witness lists should include, if applicable, your children's therapist(s), psychologist(s), psychiatrist(s), teacher(s), child care provider(s), counselor(s), doctor(s), coach(es) and any other person that you feel is relevant to each child's care and well-being. I ask that you make note, next to each witness, as to the nature of the relationship between that person and any of the children, and preferably, list the witnesses in descending order of importance so that I can best focus my time on the most relevant witnesses first. If either child has a therapeutic relationship with a mental health professional, I will need to assess whether or not it is in that child's best interest that I waive his/her privilege with that person so that others can seek information from that person.

Based on my discussions with you and review of your court pleadings in this case, I will decide in what location I should first meet the children. I will do my best to accommodate everyone's schedule, and given each child's age, I will want to minimize any disruption to his/her school day or activities. I will want to meet the children in various environments, including with both of you, accounting for any existing custody order. It is my normal protocol to visit my clients in each parent's home. Also, given the trial date in xxx, it may make sense to capitalize on any school breaks that the children have between now and then for my meetings, if doing so would not otherwise interrupt their scheduled plans. I will also want to ensure I meet with the children together and individually.

It is also important that you realize I do not share an attorney-client privilege with either of you. I do not intend to provide reports after every conversation with either child or other individual, but I will endeavor to be transparent in the children's best interests. I do [check your jurisdiction's rules] maintain a confidential relationship with each child.

I ask that both of you be mindful of your communication with the children about the pending court case, and not engage in communication that could confuse or concern him/her. (Please do not share court filings with the child, discuss the pending litigation, or ask the child questions about their preferred outcome in the court case. I, as their attorney, will discuss these matters with them.)

When you exchange documents between each other, I ask that you provide me with copies of those documents, to the extent that they relate to the custody matter. Please do not spend time or money copying financial documents, paystubs, bank account statements, etc., unless there is something of significance in those documents to my investigation. [Or, if your jurisdiction requires you to address financial issues.] You may also e-mail me [or other secure electronic means of sending/receiving documents that your office employs] any documents in lieu of providing each in paper form. If a deposition is scheduled, please contact me to clear the dates so that I may attend, if necessary. If there are communication exchanges, particularly settlement offers, please copy me on your correspondence. If there are pending court dates, please alert me immediately so I can ensure each are on my calendar.

I will await your payment of the amounts in accordance with the Court's Order, and then proceed to meet with both of you. I maintain monthly statements of all work I do on the children's behalf, and you should review the Order appointing me, as it clearly states the procedure for Best Interest Attorney's billing practices.

It is my hope that, upon reviewing all the facts and circumstances, I can aid you in resolving matters prior to your trial date. Thank you for entrusting me with this very important role. I look forward to hearing from both of you to schedule a time to discuss the children.

Very truly,

Melissa A. Kucinski

APPENDIX

3C

IN THE CIRCUIT COURT FOR MONTGOMERY COUNTY, MARYLAND

PARENT 1	:	
Plaintiff	:	
	:	
v.	:	**Case No. 12345FL**
	:	
PARENT 2	:	
	:	
Defendant	:	

MOTION FOR FEES FOR BEST INTEREST ATTORNEY

COMES NOW the minor children's Best Interest Attorney, ("BIA"), Melissa A. Kucinski, Esquire and MK Family Law, PLLC and respectfully files this Motion for Fees for Best Interest Attorney and states as follows:

1. On [date], this Honorable Court appointed undersigned counsel as the three (3) minor children's Best Interest Attorney.

2. This Court's Order Appointing Counsel for Child[ren], man-dated that Plaintiff pay into the BIA's trust fund the sum of $xxx and that Defendant pay into the BIA's trust fund the sum of $xxx, within ten (10) days of the BIA Order. The BIA Order

further stated, "Final allocation of fees shall be determined by the Court at a hearing on the merits of this case or upon the Petition of the court-appointed attorney."

3. On [date], Defendant, Parent 2, paid the court ordered retainer of $xxx into the BIA's trust account.

4. On [date], Plaintiff, Parent 1, paid the court ordered retainer of $xxx into the BIA's trust account.

5. The BIA conducted a thorough independent investigation, which included, but is not limited to, travel to ABC, Maryland, to both parents' homes, to the middle child's school, to a restaurant near the homes to meet with the two younger children, at least three separate phone calls with the oldest child's treating therapist, multiple phone calls with both counsel, review of medical records from at least six medical facilities, a formal waiver of privilege, and participation in a two and a half day trial before the Honorable Jane C. Smith.

6. The BIA issued billing statements on [date], [date], and [date].

7. The BIA applied retainer funds from escrow in accordance with her Order of Appointment.

8. As of [date], no funds remain in escrow. There is an outstanding balance of $xxx.

9. There is no remaining work to be completed on behalf of the minor children. [*Alternatively*: The BIA anticipates additional work post-trial, including a review of Judge Smith's final order, which the court has indicated it may render in approximately one month's time, and any post-order interaction with all three children to discuss the court's order with them, and answer any questions the children may have.]

10. The BIA has attached her billing statements to this Motion and asks that the billing statements be incorporated hereto and made a part hereof.

11. The BIA's billing statements reflect an outstanding balance due and owing of $xxx as of [date].

WHEREFORE, the BIA respectfully requests the following relief:

a. GRANT the BIA's Motion for Fees for Best Interest Attorney;

b. Allocate the payment of the [date] balance of fees and costs to be paid between Plaintiff and Defendant;

c. Order payment of fees to the BIA;

d. If fees are not paid in accordance with the Court's order, issue a judgment against that party who did not pay the Court ordered fees;

e. Order that the parties be held jointly and severally liable for the fees due to the BIA; and

f. For such other and further relief as this Court deems necessary and just.

Respectfully submitted,

MK FAMILY LAW

Melissa A. Kucinski, #xxxx
1750 K Street, NW, 8th Floor
Washington, DC 20006
(202) 713-5165
(202) 618-9638 fax
melissa@mkfamilylawfirm.com
Best Interest Attorney

CERTIFICATE OF SERVICE

I HEREBY CERTIFY that a copy of the foregoing Motion for Fees for Best Interest Attorney was mailed, postage prepaid, this day of _____ 2017 to:

Lawyer for Parent 1, Esquire
123 Street
Rockville, Maryland 20850
Plaintiff's Attorney
Lawyer for Parent 2, Esquire
456 Street
Rockville, Maryland 20850
Defendant's Attorney

_____

Melissa A. Kucinski

IN THE CIRCUIT COURT FOR MONTGOMERY COUNTY, MARYLAND

PARENT 1   :
                                :
    Plaintiff   :
                                :
v.   :   **Case No. 12345FL**
                                :
PARENT 2   :
                                :
    Defendant   :

ORDER

UPON CONSIDERATION of the Motion for Fees for Best Interest Attorney, any response thereto, and good cause having been shown, it is this _____ day of _____, 2017, by the Circuit Court for Montgomery County, Maryland, hereby,

ORDERED that the Motion for Fees be and hereby is GRANTED; and it is further

ORDERED that Melissa A. Kucinski, Esquire and MK Family Law, PLLC shall be paid a total of _____ dollars and _____/100 cents; and it is further

ORDERED that Plaintiff shall pay _____ dollars ($_____) toward this balance and Defendant shall pay _____ dollars ($_____) toward this balance; and it is further

ORDERED that Plaintiff and Defendant shall be held jointly and severally liable for the fees due to Melissa A. Kucinski, Esquire; and it is further

ORDERED that if either party shall not pay said court ordered amount to the Best Interest Attorney within 10 days of entry of this Order, a judgment shall be entered against the parties, as joint and severally liable, in favor of Melissa A. Kucinski, Esquire.

IT IS SO ORDERED.

_____

JUDGE, Circuit Court for Montgomery County, Maryland

THIS IS A PROPER ORDER

TO BE PASSED:

_____

Magistrate, Circuit Court for Montgomery County, Maryland

Copies to: Melissa A. Kucinski, Esq.
            Lawyer for Parent 1, Esq.
            Lawyer for Parent 2, Esq.

APPENDIX

4

American Bar Association Section of Family Law Standards of Practice for Lawyers Representing Children in Custody Cases

Approved by the American Bar Association House of Delegates
August 2003

I. INTRODUCTION

Children deserve to have custody proceedings conducted in the manner least harmful to them and most likely to provide judges with the facts needed to decide the case. By adopting these Standards, the American Bar Association sets a standard for good practice and consistency in the appointment and performance of lawyers for children in custody cases.

Unfortunately, few jurisdictions have clear standards to tell courts and lawyers when or why a lawyer for a child should be appointed, or precisely what the appointee should do. Too little has been done to make the public, litigants, domestic relations attorneys, the judiciary, or children's lawyers themselves understand children's lawyers' roles, duties and powers. Children's lawyers have had to struggle with the very real contradictions between their perceived roles as lawyer, protector, investigator, and surrogate decision maker. This confusion breeds dissatisfaction and undermines public confidence in the legal system. These Standards distinguish two distinct types of lawyers for children: (1) The Child's Attorney, who provides independent legal representation in a traditional attorney-client relationship, giving the child a strong voice in the proceedings; and (2) The Best Interests Attorney, who independently investigates, assesses and advocates the child's best interests as a lawyer. While some courts in the past have appointed a lawyer, often called a guardian ad litem, to report or testify on the child's best interests and/or related information, this is not a lawyer's role under these Standards.

These Standards seek to keep the best interests of children at the center of courts' attention, and to build public confidence in a just and fair court system that works to promote the best interests of children. These Standards promote quality control, professionalism, clarity, uniformity and predictability. They require that: (1) all participants in a case know the duties, powers and limitations of the appointed role; and (2) lawyers have sufficient training, qualifications, compensation, time, and authority to do their jobs properly with the support and cooperation of the courts and other institutions. The American Bar Association commends these Standards to all jurisdictions, and to individual lawyers, courts, and child representation programs.

II. SCOPE AND DEFINITIONS

A. Scope

These Standards apply to the appointment and performance of lawyers serving as advocates for children or their interests in any case where temporary or permanent legal custody, physical custody, parenting plans, parenting time, access, or visitation are adjudicated, including but not limited to divorce, parentage, domestic violence, contested adoptions, and contested private guardianship cases. Lawyers representing children in abuse and neglect cases should follow the ABA Standards of Practice for Representing a Child in Abuse and Neglect Cases (1996).

B. Definitions

1. "Child's Attorney": A lawyer who provides independent legal counsel for a child and who owes the same duties of undivided loyalty, confidentiality, and competent representation as are due an adult client.

2. "Best Interests Attorney": A lawyer who provides independent legal services for the purpose of protecting a child's best interests, without being bound by the child's directives or objectives.

Commentary

These Standards and these definitions apply to lawyers fitting these descriptions regardless of the different titles used in various states, and regardless of whether the lawyer is appointed by the court or retained by the child.

A lawyer should be either a Child's Attorney or a Best Interests Attorney. The duties common to both roles are found in Part III of these Standards. The unique duties of each are described separately in Parts IV and V. The essential distinction between the two lawyer roles is that the Best Interests Attorney investigates and advocates the best interests of the child as a lawyer in the litigation, while the Child's Attorney is a lawyer who represents the child as a client. Neither kind of lawyer is a witness. Form should follow function in deciding which kind of lawyer to appoint. The role and duties of the lawyer should be tailored to the reasons for the appointment and the needs of the child.

These Standards do not use the term "Guardian Ad Litem." The role of "guardian ad litem" has become too muddled through different usages in different states, with varying connotations. It is a venerable legal concept that has often been stretched beyond recognition to serve fundamentally new functions, such as parenting coordinator, referee, facilitator, arbitrator, evaluator, mediator and advocate. Asking one Guardian Ad Litem to perform several roles at once, to be all things to all people, is a messy, ineffective expedient. A court seeking expert or lay opinion testimony, written reports, or other non-traditional services should appoint an individual for that purpose, and make clear that that person is not serving as a lawyer, and is not a party. This person can be either a non-lawyer, or a lawyer who chooses to serve in a volunteer non-lawyer capacity.

III. DUTIES OF ALL LAWYERS FOR CHILDREN

In addition to their general ethical duties as lawyers, and the specific duties set out in Parts IV and V, Child's Attorneys and Best Interests Attorneys also have the duties outlined in this section.

A. Accepting Appointment

The lawyer should accept an appointment only with a full understanding of the issues and the functions to be performed. If the appointed lawyer considers parts of the appointment order confusing or incompatible with his or her ethical duties, the lawyer should (1) decline the appointment, or (2) inform the court of the conflict and ask the court to clarify or change the terms of the order, or (3) both.

B. Lawyer's Roles

A lawyer appointed as a Child's Attorney or Best Interests Attorney should not play any other role in the case, and should not testify, file a report, or make recommendations.

Commentary

Neither kind of lawyer should be a witness, which means that the lawyer should not be cross-examined, and more importantly should neither testify nor make a written or oral report or recommendation to the court, but instead should offer traditional evidence-based legal arguments such as other lawyers make. However, explaining what result a client wants, or proffering what one hopes to prove, is not testifying; those are things all lawyers do.

If these Standards are properly applied, it will not be possible for courts to make a dual appointment, but there may be cases in which such an appointment was made before these Standards were adopted. The Child's Attorney role involves a confidential relationship with privileged communications. Because the child has a right to confidentiality and advocacy of his or her position, the Child's Attorney can never abandon this role while remaining involved in the case in any way. Once a lawyer has a lawyer-client relationship with a minor, he or she cannot and should not assume any other role for the child, especially as Best Interests Attorney or as a witness who investigates and makes a recommendation.

C. Independence

The lawyer should be independent from the court and other participants in the litigation, and unprejudiced and uncompromised in his or her independent action. The lawyer has the right and the responsibility to exercise independent professional judgment in carrying out the duties assigned by the court, and to participate in the case as fully and freely as a lawyer for a party.

Commentary

The lawyer should not prejudge the case. A lawyer may receive payment from a court, a government entity, or even from a parent, relative, or other adult so long as the lawyer retains the full authority for independent action.

D. Initial Tasks

Immediately after being appointed, the lawyer should review the file. The lawyer should inform other parties or counsel of the appointment, and that as counsel of record he or she should receive copies of pleadings and discovery exchanges, and reasonable notification of hearings and of major changes of circumstances affecting the child.

E. Meeting With the Child

The lawyer should meet with the child, adapting all communications to the child's age, level of education, cognitive development, cultural background and degree of language acquisition, using an interpreter if necessary. The lawyer should inform the child about the court system, the proceedings, and the lawyer's responsibilities. The lawyer should elicit and assess the child's views.

Commentary

Establishing and maintaining a relationship with a child is the foundation of representation. Competent representation requires a child-centered approach and developmentally appropriate communication. All appointed lawyers should meet with the child and focus on the needs and circumstances of the individual child. Even nonverbal children can reveal much about their needs and interests through their behaviors and developmental levels. Meeting with the child also allows the lawyer to assess the child's circumstances, often leading to a greater understanding of the case, which may lead to creative solutions in the child's interest.

The nature of the legal proceeding or issue should be explained to the child in a developmentally appropriate manner. The lawyer must speak clearly, precisely, and in terms the child can understand. A child may not understand legal terminology. Also, because of a particular child's developmental limitations, the lawyer may not completely understand what the child says. Therefore, the lawyer must learn how to ask developmentally appropriate, non-suggestive questions and how to interpret the child's responses. The lawyer may work with social workers or other professionals to assess a child's developmental abilities and to facilitate communication.

While the lawyer should always take the child's point of view into account, caution should be used because the child's stated views and desires may vary over time or may be the result of fear, intimidation and manipulation. Lawyers may need to collaborate with other professionals to gain a full understanding of the child's needs and wishes.

F. Pretrial Responsibilities

The lawyer should:

1. Conduct thorough, continuing, and independent discovery and investigations.

2. Develop a theory and strategy of the case to implement at hearings, including presentation of factual and legal issues.

3. Stay apprised of other court proceedings affecting the child, the parties and other household members.

4. Attend meetings involving issues within the scope of the appointment.

5. Take any necessary and appropriate action to expedite the proceedings.

6. Participate in, and, when appropriate, initiate, negotiations and mediation. The lawyer should clarify, when necessary, that she or he is not acting as a mediator; and a lawyer who participates in a mediation should be bound by the confidentiality and privilege rules governing the mediation.

7. Participate in depositions, pretrial conferences, and hearings.

8. File or make petitions, motions, responses or objections when necessary.

9. Where appropriate and not prohibited by law, request authority from the court to pursue issues on behalf of the child, administratively or judicially, even if those issues do not specifically arise from the court appointment.

Commentary

The lawyer should investigate the facts of the case to get a sense of the people involved and the real issues in the case, just as any other lawyer would. This is necessary even for a Child's Attorney, whose ultimate task is to seek the client's objectives. Best Interests Attorneys have additional investigation duties described in Standard V-E.

By attending relevant meetings, the lawyer can present the child's perspective, gather information, and sometimes help negotiate a full or partial settlement. The lawyer may not need to attend if another person involved in the case, such as a social worker, can obtain information or present the child's perspective, or when the meeting will not be materially relevant to any issues in the case.

The lawyer is in a pivotal position in negotiations. The lawyer should attempt to resolve the case in the least adversarial manner possible, considering whether therapeutic intervention, parenting or co-parenting education, mediation, or other dispute resolution methods are appropriate. The lawyer may effectively assist negotiations of the parties and their lawyers by focusing on the needs of the child, including where appropriate the impact of domestic violence. Settlement frequently obtains at least short-term relief for all parties involved and is often the best way to resolve a case. The lawyer's role is to advocate the child's interests and point of view in the negotiation process. If a party is legally represented, it is unethical for a lawyer to negotiate with the party directly without the consent of the party's lawyer.

Unless state law explicitly precludes filing pleadings, the lawyer should file any appropriate pleadings on behalf of the child, including responses to the pleadings of other parties, to ensure that appropriate issues are properly before the court and expedite the court's consideration of issues important to the child's interests. Where available to litigants under state laws or court rules or by permission of the court, relief requested may include, but is not limited to: (1) A mental or physical examination of a party or the child; (2) A parenting, custody or visitation evaluation; (3) An increase, decrease, or termination of parenting time; (4) Services for the child or family; (5) Contempt for non-compliance with a court order; (6) A protective order concerning the child's privileged communications; (7) Dismissal of petitions or motions.

The child's interests may be served through proceedings not connected with the case in which the lawyer is participating. For example, issues to be addressed may include: (1) Child support; (2) Delinquency or status offender matters; (3) SSI and other public benefits access; (4) Mental health proceedings; (5) Visitation, access or parenting time with parents, siblings; or third parties, (6) Paternity; (7) Personal injury actions; (8) School/education issues, especially for a child with disabilities; (9) Guardianship; (10) Termination of parental rights; (11) Adoption; or (12) A protective order concerning the child's tangible or intangible property.

G. Hearings

The lawyer should participate actively in all hearings and conferences with the court on issues within the scope of the appointment. Specifically, the lawyer should:

1. Introduce herself or himself to the court as the Child's Attorney or Best Interests Attorney at the beginning of any hearing.

2. Make appropriate motions, including motions in limine and evidentiary objections, file briefs and preserve issues for appeal, as appropriate.

3. Present and cross-examine witnesses and offer exhibits as necessary.

4. If a child is to meet with the judge or testify, prepare the child, familiarizing the child with the places, people, procedures, and questioning that the child will be exposed to; and seek to minimize any harm to the child from the process.

5. Seek to ensure that questions to the child are phrased in a syntactically and linguistically appropriate manner and that testimony is presented in a manner that is admissible.

6. Where appropriate, introduce evidence and make arguments on the child's competency to testify, or the reliability of the child's testimony or out-of-court statements. The lawyer should be familiar with the current law and empirical knowledge about children's competency, memory, and suggestibility.

7. Make a closing argument, proposing specific findings of fact and conclusions of law.

8. Ensure that a written order is made, and that it conforms to the court's oral rulings and statutorily required findings and notices.

Commentary

Although the lawyer's position may overlap with the position of one or more parties, the lawyer should be prepared to participate fully in any proceedings and not merely defer to the other parties. The lawyer should address the child's interests, describe the issues from the child's perspective, keep the case focused on the child's needs, discuss the effect of various dispositions on the child, and, when appropriate, present creative alternative solutions to the court.

A brief formal introduction should not be omitted, because in order to make an informed decision on the merits, the court must be mindful of the lawyer's exact role, with its specific duties and constraints. Even though the appointment order states the nature of the appointment, judges should be reminded, at each hearing, which role the lawyer is playing. If there is a jury, a brief explanation of the role will be needed.

The lawyer's preparation of the child should include attention to the child's developmental needs and abilities. The lawyer should also prepare the child for the possibility that the judge may render a decision against the child's wishes, explaining that such a result would not be the child's fault.

If the child does not wish to testify or would be harmed by testifying, the lawyer should seek a stipulation of the parties not to call the child as a witness, or seek a protective order from the court. The lawyer should seek to minimize the adverse consequences by seeking any appropriate accommodations permitted by law so that the child's views are presented to the court in the manner least harmful to the child, such as having the testimony taken informally, in chambers, without the parents present. The lawyer should seek any necessary assistance from the court, including location of the testimony, determination of who will be present, and restrictions on the manner and phrasing of questions posed to the child. The child should be told beforehand whether in-chambers testimony will be shared with others, such as parents who might be excluded from chambers.

Questions to the child should be phrased consistently with the law and research regarding children's testimony, memory, and suggestibility. The information a child gives is often misleading, especially if adults have not understood how to ask children developmentally appropriate questions and how to interpret their answers properly. The lawyer must become skilled at recognizing the child's developmental limitations. It may be appropriate to present expert testimony on the issue, or have an expert present when a young child is directly involved in the litigation, to point out any developmentally inappropriate phrasing of questions.

The competency issue may arise in the unusual circumstance of the child being called as a live witness, as well as when the child's input is sought by other means such as in-chambers meetings, closed-circuit television testimony, etc.   Many jurisdictions have abolished presumptive ages of competency and replaced them with more flexible, case-by-case analyses. Competency to testify involves the abilities to perceive and relate. If necessary and appropriate, the lawyer should present expert testimony to establish competency or reliability or to rehabilitate any impeachment of the child on those bases.

    H. Appeals

        1. If appeals on behalf of the child are allowed by state law, and if it has been decided pursuant to Standard IV-D or V-G that such an appeal is necessary, the lawyer should take all steps necessary to perfect the appeal and seek appropriate temporary orders or extraordinary writs necessary to protect the interests of the child during the pendency of the appeal.

        2. The lawyer should participate in any appeal filed by another party, concerning issues relevant to the child and within the scope of the appointment, unless discharged.

        3. When the appeals court's decision is received, the lawyer should explain it to the child.

Commentary

The lawyer should take a position in any appeal filed by a party or agency. In some jurisdictions, the lawyer's appointment does not include representation on appeal, but if the child's interests are affected by the issues raised in the appeal, the lawyer should seek an appointment on appeal or seek appointment of appellate counsel.

As with other court decisions, the lawyer should explain in terms the child can understand the nature and consequences of the appeals court's decision, whether there are further appellate remedies, and what more, if anything, will be done in the trial court following the decision.

    I. Enforcement

The lawyer should monitor the implementation of the court's orders and address any non-compliance.

    J. End of Representation

When the representation ends, the lawyer should inform the child in a developmentally appropriate manner.

IV. CHILD'S ATTORNEYS

A. Ethics and Confidentiality

1. Child's Attorneys are bound by their states' ethics rules in all matters.

2. A Child's Attorney appointed to represent two or more children should remain alert to the possibility of a conflict that could require the lawyer to decline representation or withdraw from representing all of the children.

Commentary

The child is an individual with independent views. To ensure that the child's independent voice is heard, the Child's Attorney should advocate the child's articulated position, and owes traditional duties to the child as client, subject to Rules 1.2(a) and 1.14 of the Model Rules of Professional Conduct (2002).

The Model Rules of Professional Conduct (2002) (which in their amended form may not yet have been adopted in a particular state) impose a broad duty of confidentiality concerning all "information relating to the representation of a client", but they also modify the traditional exceptions to confidentiality. Under Model Rule 1.6 (2002), a lawyer may reveal information without the client's informed consent "to the extent the lawyer reasonably believes necessary ... to prevent reasonably certain death or substantial bodily harm", or "to comply with other law or a court order", or when "the disclosure is impliedly authorized in order to carry out the representation". Also, according to Model Rule 1.14(c) (2002), "the lawyer is impliedly authorized under Rule 1.6(a) to reveal information about the client, but only to the extent reasonably necessary to protect the client's interests" when acting under Rule 1.14 to protect a client with "diminished capacity" who "is at risk of substantial physical, financial or other harm."

Model Rule 1.7 (1)(1) (2002) provides that "a lawyer shall not represent a client if ... the representation of one client will be directly adverse to another client ... ." Some diversity between siblings' views and priorities does not pose a direct conflict. But when two siblings aim to achieve fundamentally incompatible outcomes in the case as a whole, they are "directly adverse." Comment [8] to Model Rule 1.7 (2002) states: "... a conflict of interest exists if there is a significant risk that a lawyer's ability to consider, recommend or carry out an appropriate course of action for the client will be materially limited ... a lawyer asked to represent several individuals ... is likely to be materially limited in the lawyer's ability to recommend or advocate all possible positions that each might take because of the lawyer's duty of loyalty to the others. ... The critical questions are the likelihood that a difference in interests will eventuate and, if it does, whether it will materially interfere with the lawyer's independent professional judgment in considering alternatives or foreclose courses of action that reasonably should be pursued on behalf of the client."

B. Informing and Counseling the Client

In a developmentally appropriate manner, the Child's Attorney should:

1. Meet with the child upon appointment, before court hearings, when apprised of emergencies or significant events affecting the child, and at other times as needed.

2. Explain to the child what is expected to happen before, during and after each hearing.

3. Advise the child and provide guidance, communicating in a way that maximizes the child's ability to direct the representation.

4. Discuss each substantive order, and its consequences, with the child.

Commentary

Meeting with the child is important before court hearings and case reviews. Such in-person meetings allow the lawyer to explain to the child what is happening, what alternatives might be available, and what will happen next.

The Child's Attorney has an obligation to explain clearly, precisely, and in terms the client can understand, the meaning and consequences of the client's choices. A child may not understand the implications of a particular course of action. The lawyer has a duty to explain in a developmentally appropriate way such information as will assist the child in having maximum input in decision-making. The lawyer should inform the child of the relevant facts and applicable laws and the ramifications of taking various positions, which may include the impact of such decisions on other family members or on future legal proceedings. The lawyer may express an opinion concerning the likelihood of the court or other parties accepting particular positions. The lawyer may inform the child of an expert's recommendations germane to the issue.

As in any other lawyer/client relationship, the lawyer may express his or her assessment of the case, and of the best position for the child to take, and the reasons underlying such recommendation, and may counsel against the pursuit of particular goals sought by the client. However, a child may agree with the lawyer for inappropriate reasons. A lawyer must remain aware of the power dynamics inherent in adult/child relationships, recognize that the child may be more susceptible to intimidation and manipulation than some adult clients, and strive to detect and neutralize those factors. The lawyer should carefully choose the best time to express his or her assessment of the case. The lawyer needs to understand what the child knows, and what factors are influencing the child's decision. The lawyer should attempt to determine from the child's opinion and reasoning what factors have been most influential or have been confusing or glided over by the child.

The lawyer for the child has dual fiduciary duties to the child which must be balanced. On the one hand, the lawyer has a duty to ensure that the client is given the information necessary to make an informed decision, including advice and guidance. On the other hand, the lawyer has a duty not to overbear the will of the client. While the lawyer may attempt to persuade the child to accept a particular position, the lawyer may not advocate a position contrary to the child's expressed position except as provided by the applicable ethical standards.

Consistent with the rules of confidentiality and with sensitivity to the child's privacy, the lawyer should consult with the child's therapist and other experts and obtain appropriate records. For example, a child's therapist may help the child to understand why an expressed position is dangerous, foolish, or not in the child's best interests. The therapist might also assist the lawyer in understanding the child's perspective, priorities, and individual needs. Similarly, significant persons in the child's life may educate the lawyer about the child's needs, priorities, and previous experiences.

As developmentally appropriate, the Child's Attorney should consult the child prior to any settlement becoming binding.

The child is entitled to understand what the court has done and what that means to the child, at least with respect to those portions of the order that directly affect the child. Children sometimes assume that orders are final and not subject to change. Therefore, the lawyer should explain whether the order may be modified at another hearing, or whether the actions of the parties may affect how the order is carried out.

C. Client Decisions

The Child's Attorney should abide by the client's decisions about the objectives of the representation with respect to each issue on which the child is competent to direct the lawyer, and does so. The Child's Attorney should pursue the child's expressed objectives, unless the child requests otherwise, and follow the child's direction, throughout the case.

Commentary

The child is entitled to determine the overall objectives to be pursued. The Child's Attorney may make certain decisions about the manner of achieving those objectives, particularly on procedural matters, as any adult's lawyer would. These Standards do not require the lawyer to consult with the child on matters which would not require consultation with an adult client, nor to discuss with the child issues for which the child's developmental limitations make it not feasible to obtain the child's direction, as with an infant or preverbal child.

1. The Child's Attorney should make a separate determination whether the child has "diminished capacity" pursuant to Model Rule 1.14 (2000) with respect to each issue in which the child is called upon to direct the representation.

Commentary

These Standards do not presume that children of certain ages are "impaired," "disabled," "incompetent," or lack capacity to determine their position in litigation. Disability is contextual, incremental, and may be intermittent. The child's ability to contribute to a determination of his or her position is functional, depending upon the particular position and the circumstances prevailing at the time the position must be determined. Therefore, a child may be able to determine some positions in the case but not others. Similarly, a child may be able to direct the lawyer with respect to a particular issue at one time but not at another.

2. If the child does not express objectives of representation, the Child's Attorney should make a good faith effort to determine the child's wishes, and advocate according to those wishes if they are expressed. If a child does not or will not express objectives regarding a particular issue or issues, the Child's Attorney should determine and advocate the child's legal interests or request the appointment of a Best Interests Attorney.

Commentary

There are circumstances in which a child is unable to express any positions, as in the case of a preverbal child. Under such circumstances, the Child's Attorney should represent the child's legal interests or request appointment of a Best Interests Attorney. "Legal interests" are distinct from "best interests" and from the child's objectives. Legal interests are interests of the child that are specifically recognized in law and that can be protected through the courts. A child's legal interests could include, for example, depending on the nature of the case, a special needs child's right to appropriate educational, medical, or mental health services; helping assure that children needing residential placement are placed in the least restrictive setting consistent with their needs; a child's child support, governmental and other financial benefits; visitation with siblings, family members, or others the child wishes to maintain contact with; and a child's due process or other procedural rights.

The child's failure to express a position is different from being unable to do so, and from directing the lawyer not to take a position on certain issues. The child may have no opinion with respect to a particular issue, or may delegate the decision-making authority. The child may not want to assume the responsibility of expressing a position because of loyalty conflicts or the desire not to hurt one of the parties. In that case, the lawyer is free to pursue the objective that appears to be in the client's legal interests based on information the lawyer has, and positions the child has already expressed. A position chosen by the lawyer should not contradict or undermine other issues about which the child has expressed a viewpoint. However, before reaching that point the lawyer should clarify with the child whether the child wants the lawyer to take a position, or to remain silent with respect to that issue, or wants the point of view expressed only if the party is out of the room. The lawyer is then bound by the child's directive.

3. If the Child's Attorney determines that pursuing the child's expressed objective would put the child at risk of substantial physical, financial or other harm, and is not merely contrary to the lawyer's opinion of the child's interests, the lawyer may request appointment of a separate Best Interests Attorney and continue to represent the child's expressed position, unless the child's position is prohibited by law or without any factual foundation. The Child's Attorney should not reveal the reason for the request for a Best Interests Attorney, which would compromise

the child's position, unless such disclosure is authorized by the ethics rule on confidentiality that is in force in the state.

Commentary

One of the most difficult ethical issues for lawyers representing children occurs when the child is able to express a position and does so, but the lawyer believes that the position chosen is wholly inappropriate or could result in serious injury to the child. This is particularly likely to happen with respect to an abused child whose home is unsafe, but who desires to remain or return home. A child may desire to live in a dangerous situation because it is all he or she knows, because of a feeling of blame or of responsibility to take care of a parent, or because of threats or other reasons to fear the parent. The child may choose to deal with a known situation rather than risk the unknown.

It should be remembered in this context that the lawyer is bound to pursue the client's objectives only through means permitted by law and ethical rules. The lawyer may be subject personally to sanctions for taking positions that are not well grounded in fact and warranted by existing law or a good faith argument for the extension, modification, or reversal of existing law.

In most cases the ethical conflict involved in asserting a position which would seriously endanger the child, especially by disclosure of privileged information, can be resolved through the lawyer's counseling function, if the lawyer has taken the time to establish rapport with the child and gain that child's trust. While the lawyer should be careful not to apply undue pressure to a child, the lawyer's advice and guidance can often persuade the child to change a dangerous or imprudent position or at least identify alternative choices in case the court denies the child's first choice.

If the child cannot be persuaded, the lawyer has a duty to safeguard the child's interests by requesting appointment of a Best Interests Attorney. As a practical matter, this may not adequately protect the child if the danger to the child was revealed only in a confidential disclosure to the lawyer, because the Best Interests Attorney may never learn of the disclosed danger.

Model Rule 1.14 (2002) provides that "when the lawyer reasonably believes that the client has diminished capacity, is at risk of substantial physical, financial or other harm unless action is taken and cannot adequately act in the client's own interest, the lawyer may take reasonably necessary protective action ... the lawyer is impliedly authorized under Rule 1.6(a) to reveal information about the client, but only to the extent reasonably necessary to protect the client's interests."

If there is a substantial danger of serious injury or death, the lawyer must take the minimum steps which would be necessary to ensure the child's safety, respecting and following the child's direction to the greatest extent possible consistent with the child's safety and ethical rules. States that do not abrogate the lawyer-client privilege or confidentiality, or mandate reporting in cases of child abuse, may permit reports notwithstanding privilege.

4. The Child's Attorney should discuss with the child whether to ask the judge to meet with the child, and whether to call the child as a witness. The decision should include consideration of the child's needs and desires to do either of these, any potential repercussions of such a decision or harm to the child from testifying or being involved in case, the necessity of the child's direct testimony, the availability of other evidence or hearsay exceptions which may substitute for direct testimony by the child, and the child's developmental ability to provide direct testimony and withstand cross-examination. Ultimately, the Child's Attorney is bound by the child's direction concerning testifying.

Commentary

Decisions about the child's testifying should be made individually, based on the circumstances. If the child has a therapist, the attorney should consult the therapist about the decision and for help in preparing the child. In the absence of compelling reasons, a child who has a strong desire to testify should be called to do so.

D. Appeals

Where appeals on behalf of the child are permitted by state law, the Child's Attorney should consider and discuss with the child, as developmentally appropriate, the possibility of an appeal. If the child, after consultation, wishes to appeal the order, and the appeal has merit, the Child's Attorney should appeal. If the Child's Attorney determines that an appeal would be frivolous or that he or she lacks the expertise necessary to handle the appeal, he or she should notify the court and seek to be discharged or replaced.

Commentary

The lawyer should explain not only any legal possibility of an appeal, but also the ramifications of filing an appeal, including delaying conclusion of the case, and what will happen pending a final decision.

E. Obligations after Initial Disposition

The Child's Attorney should perform, or when discharged, seek to ensure, continued representation of the child at all further hearings, including at administrative or judicial actions that result in changes to the child's placement or services, so long as the court maintains its jurisdiction.

Commentary

Representing a child continually presents new tasks and challenges due to the passage of time and the changing needs of the child. The bulk of the Child's Attorney's work often comes after the initial hearing. The Child's Attorney should stay in touch with the child, with the parties or their counsel, and any other caretakers, case workers, and service providers throughout the term of appointment to attempt to ensure that the child's needs are met and that the case moves quickly to an appropriate resolution.

F. End of Representation

The Child's Attorney should discuss the end of the legal representation with the child, what contacts, if any, the Child's Attorney and the child will continue to have, and how the child can obtain assistance in the future, if necessary.

V. BEST INTERESTS ATTORNEYS

A. Ethics

Best Interests Attorneys are be bound by their states' ethics rules in all matters except as dictated by the absence of a traditional attorney-client relationship with the child and the particular requirements of their appointed tasks. Even outside of an attorney-client relationship, all lawyers have certain ethical duties toward the court, parties in a case, the justice system, and the public.

Commentary

Siblings with conflicting views do not pose a conflict of interest for a Best Interests Attorney, because such a lawyer is not bound to advocate a client's objective. A Best Interests Attorney in such a case should report the relevant views of all the children in accordance with Standard V-F-3, and advocate the children's best interests in accordance with Standard V-F-1.

B. Confidentiality

A child's communications with the Best Interests Attorney are subject to state ethics rules on lawyer-client confidentiality, except that the lawyer may also use the child's confidences for the purposes of the representation without disclosing them.

Commentary

ABA Model Rule 1.6(a) bars any release of information "except for disclosures that are impliedly authorized in order to carry out the representation." Under DR 4-101(C)(2), a lawyer may reveal confidences when "required by law or court order". As for communications that are not subject to disclosure under these or other applicable ethics rules, a Best Interests Attorney may use them to further the child's best interests, without disclosing them. The distinction between use and disclosure means, for example, that if a child tells the lawyer that a parent takes drugs; the lawyer may seek and present other evidence of the drug use, but may not reveal that the initial information came from the child. For more discussion of exceptions to confidentiality, see the Commentary to Standard IV-A.

C. Limited Appointments

If the court appoints the Best Interests Attorney to handle only a specific issue, the Best Interests Attorney's tasks may be reduced as the court may direct.

D. Explaining Role to the Child

In a developmentally appropriate manner, the Best Interests Attorney should explain to the child that the Best Interests Attorney will (1) investigate and advocate the child's best interests, (2) will investigate the child's views relating to the case and will report them to the court unless the child requests that they not be reported, and (3) will use information from the child for those purposes, but (4) will not necessarily advocate what the child wants as a lawyer for a client would.

E. Investigations

The Best Interests Attorney should conduct thorough, continuing, and independent investigations, including:

1. Reviewing any court files of the child, and of siblings who are minors or are still in the home, potentially relevant court files of parties and other household members, and case-related records of any social service agency and other service providers;

2. Reviewing child's social services records, if any, mental health records (except as otherwise provided in Standard VI-A-4), drug and alcohol-related records, medical records, law enforcement records, school records, and other records relevant to the case;

3. Contacting lawyers for the parties, and nonlawyer representatives or court-appointed special advocates (CASAs);

4. Contacting and meeting with the parties, with permission of their lawyers;

5. Interviewing individuals significantly involved with the child, who may in the lawyer's discretion include, if appropriate, case workers, caretakers, neighbors, relatives, school personnel, coaches, clergy, mental health professionals, physicians, law enforcement officers, and other potential witnesses;

6. Reviewing the relevant evidence personally, rather than relying on other parties' or counsel's descriptions and characterizations of it;

7. Staying apprised of other court proceedings affecting the child, the parties and other household members.

Commentary

Relevant files to review include those concerning child protective services, developmental disabilities, juvenile delinquency, mental health, and educational agencies. These records can provide a more complete context for the current problems of the child and family. Information in the files may suggest additional professionals and lay witnesses who should be contacted.

Though courts should order automatic access to records, the lawyer may still need to use subpoenas or other discovery or motion procedures to obtain the relevant records, especially those which pertain to the parties.

Meetings with the children and all parties are among the most important elements of a competent investigation. However, there may be a few cases where a party's lawyer will not allow the Best-Interests Attorney to communicate with the party. Model Rule 4.2 prohibits such contact without consent of the party's lawyer. In some such cases, the Best-Interests Attorney may be able to obtain permission for a meeting with the party's lawyer present. When the party has no lawyer, Model Rule 4.3 allows contact but requires reasonable efforts to correct any apparent misunderstanding of the Best-Interests Attorney's role.

The parties' lawyers may have information not included in any of the available records. They can provide information on their clients' perspectives.

Volunteer CASAs can often provide a great deal of information. The CASA is typically charged with performing an independent factual investigation, getting to know the child, and reporting on the child's best interests. Where there appears to be role conflict or confusion over the involvement of both a lawyer and a CASA in the same case, there should be joint efforts to clarify and define the responsibilities of both.

F. Advocating the Child's Best Interests

    1. Any assessment of, or argument on, the child's best interests should be based on objective criteria as set forth in the law related to the purposes of the proceedings.

    2. Best Interests Attorneys should bring to the attention of the court any facts which, when considered in context, seriously call into question the advisability of any agreed settlement.

    3. At hearings on custody or parenting time, Best Interests Attorneys should present the child's expressed desires (if any) to the court, except for those that the child expressly does not want presented.

Commentary

Determining a child's best interests is a matter of gathering and weighing evidence, reaching factual conclusions and then applying legal standards to them. Factors in determining a child's interests will generally be stated in a state's statutes and case law, and Best Interests Attorneys must be familiar with them and how courts apply them. A child's desires are usually one of many factors in deciding custody and parenting time cases, and the weight given them varies with age and circumstances.

A Best Interests Attorney is functioning in a nontraditional role by determining the position to be advocated independently of the client. The Best Interests Attorney should base this determination, however, on objective criteria concerning the child's needs and interests, and not merely on the lawyer's personal values, philosophies, and experiences. A best-interests case should be based on the state's governing statutes and case law, or a good faith argument for modification of case law. The lawyer should not use any other theory, doctrine, model, technique, ideology, or personal rule of thumb without explicitly arguing for it in terms of governing law on the best interests of the child. The trier of fact needs to understand any such theory in order to make an informed decision in the case.

The lawyer must consider the child's individual needs. The child's various needs and interests may be in conflict and must be weighed against each other. The child's developmental level, including his or her sense of time, is relevant to an assessment of needs. The lawyer may seek the advice and consultation of experts and other knowledgeable people in determining and weighing such needs and interests.

As a general rule Best Interests Attorneys should encourage, not undermine, settlements. However, in exceptional cases where the Best Interests Attorney reasonably believes that the settlement would endanger the child and that the court would not approve the settlement were it aware of certain facts, the Best Interests Attorney should bring those facts to the court's attention. This should not be done by ex parte communication. The Best Interests Attorney should ordinarily discuss her or his concerns with the parties and counsel in an attempt to change the settlement, before involving the judge.

G. Appeals

Where appeals on behalf of the child are permitted by state law, the Best Interests Attorney should appeal when he or she believes that (1) the trial court's decision is significantly detrimental to the child's welfare, (2) an appeal could be successful considering the law, the standard of review, and the evidence that can be presented to the appellate court, and (3) the probability and degree of benefit to the child outweighs the probability and degree of detriment to the child from extending the litigation and expense that the parties will undergo.

VI. COURTS

A. Appointment of Lawyers

A court should appoint a lawyer as a Child's Attorney or Best Interests Attorney as soon as practicable if such an appointment is necessary in order for the court to decide the case.

1. Mandatory Appointment

A court should appoint a lawyer whenever such an appointment is mandated by state law. A court should also appoint a lawyer in accordance with the A.B.A. Standards of Practice for Representing a Child in Abuse and Neglect Cases (1996) when considering allegations of child abuse or neglect that warrant state intervention.

Commentary

Whether in a divorce, custody or child protection case, issues such as abuse, neglect or other dangers to the child create an especially compelling need for lawyers to protect the interests of children. Lawyers in these cases must take appropriate steps to ensure that harm to the child is minimized while the custody case is being litigated. Appointing a lawyer is no substitute for a child protective services investigation or other law enforcement investigation, where appropriate. The situation may call for referrals to or joinder of child protection officials, transfer of the case to the juvenile dependency court, or steps to coordinate the case with a related ongoing child protection proceeding, which may be in a different court. Any question of child maltreatment should be a critical factor in the court's resolution of custody and parenting time proceedings, and should be factually resolved before permanent custody and parenting time are addressed. A serious forensic investigation to find out what happened should come before, and not be diluted by, a more general investigation into the best interests of the child.

    2. Discretionary Appointment

In deciding whether to appoint a lawyer, the court should consider the nature and adequacy of the evidence to be presented by the parties; other available methods of obtaining information, including social service investigations, and evaluations by mental health professionals; and available resources for payment. Appointment may be most appropriate in cases involving the following factors, allegations or concerns:

a.   Consideration of extraordinary remedies such as supervised visitation, terminating or suspending parenting time, or awarding custody or visitation to a non-parent;

b.   Relocation that could substantially reduce the child's time with a parent or sibling;

c.   The child's concerns or views;

d.   Harm to the child from illegal or excessive drug or alcohol abuse by a child or a party;

e.   Disputed paternity;

f.   Past or present child abduction or risk of future abduction;

g.   Past or present family violence;

h.   Past or present mental health problems of the child or a party;

i.   Special physical, educational, or mental health needs of a child that require investigation or advocacy;

j.   A high level of acrimony;

k.   Inappropriate adult influence or manipulation;

l.   Interference with custody or parenting time;

m.   A need for more evidence relevant to the best interests of the child;

n.   A need to minimize the harm to the child from the processes of family separation and litigation; or

o.   Specific issues that would best be addressed by a lawyer appointed to address only those issues, which the court should specify in its appointment order.

Commentary

In some cases the court's capacity to decide the case properly will be jeopardized without a more child-focused framing of the issues, or without the opportunity for providing additional information concerning the child's best interests. Often, because of a lack of effective counsel for some or all parties, or insufficient investigation, courts are deprived of important information, to the detriment of the children. A lawyer building and arguing the child's case, or a case for the child's best interests, places additional perspectives, concerns, and relevant, material information before the court so it can make a more informed decision.

An important reason to appoint a lawyer is to ensure that the court is made aware of any views the child wishes to express concerning various aspects of the case, and that those views will be given the proper weight that substantive law attaches to them. This must be done in the least harmful manner — that which is least likely to make the child think that he or she is deciding the case and passing judgment on the parents. Courts and lawyers should strive to implement procedures that give children opportunities to be meaningfully heard when they have something they want to say, rather than simply giving the parents another vehicle with which to make their case.

The purpose of child representation is not only to advocate a particular outcome, but also to protect children from collateral damage from litigation. While the case is pending, conditions that deny the children a minimum level of security and stability may need to be remedied or prevented.

Appointment of a lawyer is a tool to protect the child and provide information to help assist courts in deciding a case in accordance with the child's best interests. A decision not to appoint should not be regarded as actionably denying a child's procedural or substantive rights under these Standards, except as provided by state law. Likewise, these Standards are not intended to diminish state laws or practices which afford children standing or the right to more broad representation than provided by these Standards. Similarly, these Standards do not limit any right or opportunity of a child to engage a lawyer or to initiate an action, where such actions or rights are recognized by law or practice.

3. Appointment Orders

Courts should make written appointment orders on standardized forms, in plain language understandable to non-lawyers, and send copies to the parties as well as to counsel. Orders should specify the lawyer's role as either Child's Attorney or Best Interests Attorney, and the reasons for and duration of the appointment.

Commentary

Appointment orders should articulate as precisely as possible the reasons for the appointment and the tasks to be performed. Clarity is needed to inform all parties of the role and authority of the lawyer; to help the court make an informed decision and exercise effective oversight; and to facilitate understanding, acceptance and compliance. A Model Appointment Order is at the end of these Standards.

When the lawyer is appointed for a narrow, specific purpose with reduced duties under Standard VI-A-2(o), the lawyer may need to ask the court to clarify or change the role or tasks as needed to serve the child's interests at any time during the course of the case. This should be done with notice to the parties, who should also receive copies of any new order.

4. Information Access Orders

An accompanying, separate order should authorize the lawyer's reasonable access to the child, and to all otherwise privileged or confidential information about the child, without the necessity of any further order or release, including, but not limited to, social services, drug and alcohol treatment, medical, evaluation, law enforcement, school, probate and court records, records of trusts and accounts of which the child is a beneficiary, and other records relevant to the case; except that health and mental health records that would otherwise be privileged or confidential under state or federal laws should be released to the lawyer only in accordance with those laws.

Commentary

A model Order for Access to Confidential Information appears at the end of these Standards. It is separate from the appointment order so that the facts or allegations cited as reasons for the appointment are not revealed to everyone from whom information is sought. Use of the term "privileged" in this Standard does not include the attorney-client privilege, which is not affected by it.

5. Independence

The court must assure that the lawyer is independent of the court, court services, the parties, and the state.

6. Duration of Appointments

Appointments should last, and require active representation, as long as the issues for which the lawyer was appointed are pending.

Commentary

The Child's Attorney or Best Interests Attorney may be the only source of continuity in the court system for the family, providing a stable point of contact for the child and institutional memory for the court and agencies. Courts should maintain continuity of representation whenever possible, re-appointing the lawyer when one is needed again, unless inconsistent with the child's needs. The lawyer should ordinarily accept reappointment. If replaced, the lawyer should inform and cooperate with the successor.

7. Whom to Appoint

Courts should appoint only lawyers who have agreed to serve in child custody cases in the assigned role, and have been trained as provided in Standard VI-B or are qualified by appropriate experience in custody cases.

Commentary

Courts should appoint from the ranks of qualified lawyers. Appointments should not be made without regard to prior training or practice. Competence requires relevant training and experience. Lawyers should be allowed to specify if they are only willing to serve as Child's Attorney, or only as Best Interests Attorney.

8. Privately-Retained Attorneys

An attorney privately retained by or for a child, whether paid or not, (a) is subject to these Standards, (b) should have all the rights and responsibilities of a lawyer appointed by a court pursuant to these Standards, (c) should be expressly retained as either a Child's Attorney or a Best Interests Attorney, and (d) should vigilantly guard the client-lawyer relationship from interference as provided in Model Rule 1.8(f).

B. Training

Training for lawyers representing children in custody cases should cover:

1. Relevant state and federal laws, agency regulations, court decisions and court rules;

2. The legal standards applicable in each kind of case in which the lawyer may be appointed, including child custody and visitation law;

3. Applicable representation guidelines and standards;

4. The court process and key personnel in child-related litigation, including custody evaluations and mediation;

5. Children's development, needs and abilities at different ages;

6. Communicating with children;

7. Preparing and presenting a child's viewpoints, including child testimony and alternatives to direct testimony;

8. Recognizing, evaluating and understanding evidence of child abuse and neglect;

9. Family dynamics and dysfunction, domestic violence and substance abuse;

10. The multidisciplinary input required in child-related cases, including information on local experts who can provide evaluation, consultation and testimony;

11. Available services for child welfare, family preservation, medical, mental health, educational, and special needs, including placement, evaluation/diagnostic, and treatment services, and provisions and constraints related to agency payment for services;

12. Basic information about state and federal laws and treaties on child custody jurisdiction, enforcement, and child abduction.

Commentary

Courts, bar associations, and other organizations should sponsor, fund and participate in training. They should also offer advanced and new-developments training, and provide mentors for lawyers who are new to child representation. Training in custody law is especially important because not everyone seeking to represent children will have a family law background. Lawyers must be trained to distinguish between the different kinds of cases in which they may be appointed, and the different legal standards to be applied.

Training should address the impact of spousal or domestic partner violence on custody and parenting time, and any statutes or case law regarding how allegations or findings of domestic violence should affect custody or parenting time determinations. Training should also sensitize lawyers to the dangers that domestic violence victims and their children face in attempting to flee abusive situations, and how that may affect custody awards to victims.

C. Compensation

Lawyers for children are entitled to and should receive adequate and predictable compensation that is based on legal standards generally used for determining the reasonableness of privately-retained lawyers' hourly fees in family law cases.

1. Compensation Aspects of Appointment Orders

The court should make clear to all parties, orally and in writing, how fees will be determined, including the hourly rate or other computation system used, and the fact that both in-court and out-of-court work will be paid for; and how and by whom the fees and expenses are to be paid, in what shares. If the parties are to pay for the lawyer's services, then at the time of appointment the court should order the parties to deposit specific amounts of money for fees and costs.

2. Sources of Payment

Courts should look to the following sources, in the following order, to pay for the lawyer's services: (a) The incomes and assets of the parties; (b) Targeted filing fees assessed against litigants in similar cases, and reserved in a fund for child representation; (c) Government funding; (d) Voluntary pro bono service. States and localities should provide sufficient funding to reimburse private attorneys, to contract with lawyers or firms specializing in children's law, and to support pro bono and legal aid programs. Courts should eliminate involuntary "pro bono" appointments, and should not expect all or most representation to be pro bono.

3. Timeliness of Claims and Payment

Lawyers should regularly bill for their time and receive adequate and timely compensation. Periodically and after certain events, such as hearings or orders, they should be allowed to request payment. States should set a maximum number of days for any required court review of these bills, and for any governmental payment process to be completed.

4. Costs

Attorneys should have reasonable and necessary access to, or reimbursement for, experts, investigative services, paralegals, research, and other services, such as copying medical records, long distance phone calls, service of process, and transcripts of hearings.

5. Enforcement

Courts should vigorously enforce orders for payment by all available means.

Commentary

These Standards call for paying lawyers in accordance with prevailing legal standards of reasonableness for lawyers' fees in general. Currently, state-set uniform rates tend to be lower than what competent, experienced lawyers should be paid, creating an impression that this is second-class work. In some places it has become customary for the work of child representation to be minimal and pro forma, or for it to be performed by lawyers whose services are not in much demand.

Lawyers and parties need to understand how the lawyer will be paid. The requirement to state the lawyer's hourly rate in the appointment order will help make litigants aware of the costs being incurred. It is not meant to set a uniform rate, nor to pre-empt a court's determination of the overall reasonableness of fees. The court should keep information on eligible lawyers' hourly rates and pro bono availability on file, or ascertain it when making the appointment order. Judges should not arbitrarily reduce properly requested compensation, except in accordance with legal standards of reasonableness.

Many children go unrepresented because of a lack of resources. A three-fold solution is appropriate: hold more parents responsible for the costs of representation, increase public funding, and increase the number of qualified pro bono and legal service attorneys. All of these steps will increase the professionalism of children's lawyers generally.

As much as possible, those whose decisions impose costs on others and on society should bear such costs at the time that they make the decisions, so that the decisions will be more fully informed and socially conscious. Thus direct payment of lawyer's fees by litigants is best, where possible. Nonetheless, states and localities ultimately have the obligation to protect children in their court systems whose needs cannot otherwise be met.

Courts are encouraged to seek high-quality child representation through contracting with special children's law offices, law firms, and other programs. However, the motive should not be a lower level of compensation. Courts should assure that payment is commensurate with the fees paid to equivalently experienced individual lawyers who have similar qualifications and responsibilities.

Courts and bar associations should establish or cooperate with voluntary pro bono and/or legal services programs to adequately train and support pro bono and legal services lawyers in representing children in custody cases.

In jurisdictions where more than one court system deals with child custody, the availability, continuity and payment of lawyers should not vary depending on which court is used, nor on the type of appointment.

D. Caseloads

Courts should control the size of court-appointed caseloads, so that lawyers do not have so many cases that they are unable to meet these Standards. If caseloads of individual lawyers approach or exceed acceptable limits, courts should take one or more of the following steps: (1) work with bar and children's advocacy groups to increase the availability of lawyers; (2) make formal arrangements for child representation with law firms or programs providing representation; (3) renegotiate existing court contracts for child representation; (4) alert agency administrators that their lawyers have excessive caseloads and order them to establish procedures or a plan to solve the problem; (5) alert state judicial, executive, and legislative branch leaders that excessive caseloads jeopardize the ability of lawyers to competently represent children; and (6) seek additional funding.

E. Physical accommodations

Courts should provide lawyers representing children with seating and work space comparable to that of other lawyers, sufficient to facilitate the work of in-court representation, and consistent with the dignity, importance, independence, and impartiality that they ought to have.

F. Immunity

Courts should take steps to protect all lawyers representing children from frivolous lawsuits and harassment by adult litigants. Best Interests Attorneys should have qualified, quasi-judicial immunity for civil damages when performing actions consistent with their appointed roles, except for actions that are: (1) willfully wrongful; (2) done with conscious indifference or reckless disregard to the safety of another; (3) done in bad faith or with malice; or (4) grossly negligent. Only the child should have any right of action against a Child's Attorney or Best Interests Attorney.

Commentary

Lawyers and Guardians Ad Litem for children are too often sued by custody litigants. Courts, legislatures, bar organizations and insurers should help protect all children's lawyers from frivolous lawsuits. Immunity should be extended to protect lawyers' ability to fully investigate and advocate, without harassment or intimidation. In determining immunity, the proper inquiry is into the duties at issue and not the title of the appointment. Other mechanisms still exist to prevent or address lawyer misconduct: (1) attorneys are bound by their state bars' rules of professional conduct; (2) the court oversees their conduct and can remove or admonish them for obvious misconduct; (3) the court is the ultimate custody decision-maker and should not give deference to a best-interests argument based on an inadequate or biased investigation.

APPENDIX A

IN THE _____ COURT OF _____

_____
        Petitioner,
v.   Case No. _____
_____
        Respondent.

In Re: _____, D.O.B. _____

CHILD REPRESENTATION APPOINTMENT ORDER

I. REASONS FOR APPOINTMENT

This case came on this _____, 20___, and it appearing to the Court that appointing a Child's Attorney or Best Interests Attorney is necessary to help the Court decide the case properly, because of the following factors or allegations:

A. Mandatory appointment grounds:

( ) The Court is considering child abuse or neglect allegations that warrant state intervention.
( ) Appointment is mandated by state law.

B. Discretionary grounds warranting appointment:

( ) Consideration of extraordinary remedies such as supervised visitation, terminating or suspending visitation with a parent, or awarding custody or visitation to a non-parent
( ) Relocation that could substantially reduce of the child's time with a parent or sibling
( ) The child's concerns or views
( ) Harm to the child from illegal or excessive drug or alcohol abuse by a child or a party
( ) Disputed paternity
( ) Past or present child abduction, or risk of future abduction
( ) Past or present family violence
( ) Past or present mental health problems of the child or a party
( ) Special physical, educational, or mental health needs requiring investigation or advocacy
( ) A high level of acrimony
( ) Inappropriate adult influence or manipulation
( ) Interference with custody or parenting time
( ) A need for more evidence relevant to the best interests of the child
( ) A need to minimize the harm to the child from family separation and litigation
( ) Specific issue(s) to be addressed: _____

II. NATURE OF APPOINTMENT

_____, a lawyer who has been trained in child representation in custody cases and is willing to serve in such cases in this Court, is hereby appointed as (_) Child's Attorney (_) Best Interests Attorney, for the (_) the child or children named above (_) the child(ren) _____,
to represent the child(ren) in accordance with the Standards of Practice for Lawyers Representing Children in Custody Cases, a copy of which (_) is attached (_) has been furnished to the appointee. A Child's Attorney represents the child in a normal attorney-client relationship. A Best Interests Attorney investigates and advocates the child's best interests as a lawyer. Neither kind of lawyer testifies or submits a report. Both have duties of confidentiality as lawyers, but the Best Interests Attorney may use information from the child for the purposes of the representation.

III. FEES AND COSTS

The hourly rate of the lawyer appointed is $ ____, for both in-court and out-of-court work.

(_) The parties shall be responsible for paying the fees and costs. The parties shall deposit $_____ with (_) the Court, (_) the appointed lawyer. _____ shall deposit $ _____, and _____ shall deposit $ _____. The parties' individual shares of the responsibility for the fees and costs as between the parties (_) are to be determined later (_) are as follows: _____ to pay _____ %; _____ to pay _____ %.

(_) The State shall be responsible for paying the fees and costs.

(_) The lawyer has agreed to serve without payment. However, the lawyer's expenses will be reimbursed by (_) the parties (_) the state.

IV. ACCESS TO CONFIDENTIAL INFORMATION

The lawyer appointed shall have access to confidential information about the child as provided in the Standards of Practice for Lawyers Representing Children in Custody Cases and in an Order for Access to Confidential Information that will be signed at the same time as this Order.

THE CLERK IS HEREBY ORDERED TO MAIL COPIES OF THIS ORDER TO ALL PARTIES AND COUNSEL.

DATE: _____, 20___   _____
                                                    JUDGE

APPENDIX

5

TABLE OF CASES

   i.   Van Sickle v. McGraw, 134 P. 3d 338 (2006)
   ii.   Marriage of Kleist, 538 N.W. 2d 273 (1995)
  iii.   Henggeler v. Hanson, 510 S.E. 2d 722 (1998)
  iv.   Marriage of Gambla, 853 N.E. 2d 847 (2006)
   v.   Shultz v. Elremmash, 615 So. 2d 396 (1993)
  vi.   Rico v. Rodriguez, 120 P. 3d 812 (2005)
  vii.   Nagle v. Hooks, 296 Md. 123 (1983)
 viii.   Fox v. Wills, 890 A. 2d 726 (2006)
  ix.   Karanikas v. Cartwright, 61 A. 3d 69 (2013)
   x.   *In re* Blaemire, 229 B.R. 665 (1999)
  xi.   Duguma v. Ayalew, 145 A. 3d 517 (2016)

APPENDIX

6

Websites

a. International Social Services—www.iss-usa.org
b. Hague Conference on Private International Law—www.hcch.net
c. Department of State, Office of Children's Issues—www.travel
   .state.gov
d. National Center for Missing and Exploited Children—www
   .ncmec.org
e. International Centre for Missing and Exploited Children—
   www.icmec.org
f. American Bar Association Center on Children and the Law—
   www.americanbar.org/groups/child_law.html

INDEX

Guidelines for Practice for
Court-Appointed Lawyers
Representing Children
in Cases Involving Child
Custody and Access
(Maryland), 7–8, 29–30
Gut feelings, 75

H

Hague Abduction case, 175–177
attorney's role in, 54–55
versus custody case, 54
definition of, 54
petitioner's request to return
his or her child, 175–176
representing children in, 54–55
requests for access, 177
respondent's argument against
returning his or her child,
176–177
Hague Conference on Private
International Law, 163, 170,
182, 275
Hague Convention on Child
Abduction, 54–55, 160,
175–177
Hague Convention on Parental
Responsibility and Protection
of Children, 160–162
Health Insurance Portability and
Accountability Act (HIPAA),
17–18, 78
Hearsay, 154–155
Home visits, 72–73

I

Immunity, 53–54, 268–270
In re Marriage of Nordby, 41 Wash.
App. 531, 705 P.2d 277
(1985), 9 n. 10
In re Waggener's Marriage, 13
Wash. App. 911, 917; 538
P.2d 845 (1975), 9 n. 9

Information gathering. *See also*
Investigations
from child protective or social
services, 89–91
from collaterals, 65–66
cost of, 82–83
court case search in, 94
custody evaluators and, 92–93
from experts, 88
limitations in, 91–92
from mental health professionals,
83–85
obtaining records in, 88–89
out-of-state, 93–94
from papers and documents, 78–79
from parents, 79–81
from third-party witnesses,
85–88
Initial letter to counsel/parents
(template), 233–236
Initial meeting with client, 95–100.
See also Meeting with child
client
answering children's questions in,
98–99
disclosure of court filings in,
99–100
introduction, 98
nonverbal cues in, 96–97
note-taking in, 97
In-person meeting, 125–126
Interim measures, in advocacy, 39
Intermediaries, 48
conflict coaches, 48
parenting coordinators, 48
International cases, 159–181
child abduction, 171–179
child's voice in, 159–163
cultural biases in, 179–180
direct involvement of children in,
162–163
distance access in, 185–187